PATERNOSTER BIBLICAL MONOGRAPHS

Surrendering Retribution in the Psalms
Responses to Violence in Individual Complaints

PATERNOSTER BIBLICAL MONOGRAPHS

A full listing of all title in this series
and Paternoster Theological Monographs
appears at the close of this book

PATERNOSTER BIBLICAL MONOGRAPHS

Surrendering Retribution in the Psalms
Responses to Violence in Individual Complaints

David G. Firth

Foreword by D. L. Morcom

Wipf & Stock
PUBLISHERS
Eugene, Oregon

Wipf and Stock Publishers
199 W 8th Ave, Suite 3
Eugene, OR 97401

Surrendering Retribution in the Psalms
Responses to Violence in Inidividual Complaints
By Firth, David G.
Copyright©2005 Paternoster
ISBN: 1-59752-758-0
Publication date 6/8/2006
Previously published by Paternoster, 2005

This Edition Published by Wipf and Stock Publishers
by arrangement with Paternoster

Paternoster
9 Holdom Avenue
Bletchley
Milton Keyes, MK1 1QR
Great Britain

PATERNOSTER BIBLICAL MONOGRAPHS

Series Preface

One of the major objectives of Paternoster is to serve biblical scholarship by providing a channel for the publication of theses and other monographs of high quality at affordable prices. Paternoster stands within the broad evangelical tradition of Christianity. Our authors would describe themselves as Christians who recognise the authority of the Bible, maintain the centrality of the gospel message and assent to the classical credal statements of Christian belief. There is diversity within this constituency; advances in scholarship are possible only if there is freedom for frank debate on controversial issues and for the publication of new and sometimes provocative proposals. What is offered in this series is the best of writing by committed Christians who are concerned to develop well-founded biblical scholarship in a spirit of loyalty to the historic faith.

Series Editors

I. Howard Marshall, Honorary Research Professor of New Testament, University of Aberdeen, Scotland, UK

Richard J. Bauckham, Professor of New Testament Studies and Bishop Wardlaw Professor, University of St Andrews, Scotland, UK

Craig Blomberg, Distinguished Professor of New Testament, Denver Seminary, Colorado, USA

Robert P. Gordon, Regius Professor of Hebrew, University of Cambridge, UK

Tremper Longman III, Robert H. Gundry Professor and Chair of the Department of Biblical Studies, Westmont College, Santa Barbara, California, USA

For Lynne

*who always protects,
always trusts,
always hopes,
always perseveres.*

Contents

Foreword by D. L. Morcom	xiii
Preface	xvii
Abbreviations	xix

Chapter 1
Introduction and Methodology — 1
Statement of Problem — 1
Argument — 3
The Nature of Violence — 4
   A General Definition of Violence — 4
   Categories of Violence within the Old Testament — 5
Methodology — 6
   The Approach to the Psalms — 6
   The Enemies in the Psalms — 9
   Procedure — 10

Chapter 2
Psalms of False Accusation — 17
Introduction — 17
   Overview of Research — 17
   The Place of the Canon — 18
   Method of Approach — 19
Psalm 7 — 20
   Form Critical Discussion — 20
   Structure — 22
   Nature of Violence — 23
   Response to Violence — 27
Psalm 17 — 27

Form Critical Discussion	27
Structure	30
Nature of Violence	31
Response to Violence	35
Psalm 109	36
Form Critical Discussion	36
Structure	39
Nature of Violence	39
Response to Violence	42
Psalm 139	43
Form Critical Discussion	43
Structure	45
Nature of Violence	46
Response to Violence	48
Conclusion	49

Chapter 3
Prayers for Protection — 51

Introduction	51
Overview and Critique of Research	51
Method of Approach	52
Psalm 3	54
Form Critical Discussion	54
Structure	56
Nature of Violence	57
Response to Violence	60
Psalm 27	61
Form Critical Discussion	61
Structure	65
Nature of Violence	65
Response to Violence	67
Psalm 35	68
Form Critical Discussion	68
Structure	71
Nature of Violence	72
Response to Violence	75
Psalm 55	76

Contents xi

Form Critical Discussion	76
Structure	81
Nature of Violence	82
Response to Violence	86
Psalm 56	87
Form Critical Discussion	87
Structure	89
Nature of Violence	90
Response to Violence	93
Psalm 64	94
Form Critical Discussion	94
Structure	96
Nature of Violence	97
Response to Violence	101
Psalm 143	102
Form Critical Discussion	102
Structure	104
Nature of Violence	106
Response to Violence	109
Conclusion	110

Chapter 4
Psalms of Sickness — 113

Introduction	113
Overview and Critique of Research	113
Method of Approach	114
Psalm 38	115
Form Critical Discussion	115
Structure	119
Nature of Violence	120
Response to Violence	124
Psalm 69	125
Form Critical Discussion	125
Structure	129
Nature of Violence	132
Response to Violence	137
Conclusion	138

Chapter 5
Conclusion   139
Summary of Results   139
   The Immanence of Physical Violence   140
   The Predominance of Psychological Violence
   as the Experience of the Psalmist   140
   The Rejection of the Right of Human Retribution   141
   The Limitation on the Retribution Sought   142
Implications of Results for the Study of the Psalms   142
   Form Criticism as a Guide to Function   143
   Evidence of Editorial Consistency   143
Areas for Further Research   144
   The Role of the Royal and Communal Psalms   144
   Social Context of Editors of Psalter   145
   Practical Implications of this Research   146

Bibliography   147

Author Index   153

Foreword

Like an Nguni *imbongi*, or composer and singer of praise poems, I count it an enormous privilege to provide this foreword to David Firth's book *Surrendering Retribution in the Psalms: Responses to Violence in Individual Complaints*.

Although we share Australia as our common land of birth, I first met David Firth in South Africa. I was lecturer, and later principal, of the Baptist Theological College of Southern Africa in Johannesburg during his appointment there as Old Testament lecturer in the mid 1990s, an appointment which coincided with the demise of *apartheid* and its immediate aftermath. As Firth indicates in his preface, the rampant violence in South Africa at that time posed to him the question of an appropriate personal response to violence in a particularly pointed and urgent manner. In formulating a response to this question – how to speak and act rightly in the experience of physical, psychological and structural violence – Firth has brought to bear his passionate love for the Old Testament (particularly the Psalms), his rigorous exegetical skills, and what he unabashedly refers to in his preface as the "missiological imperative that lies at the heart of [his] own study of the Old Testament." These qualities also endeared him to his students. It is a noteworthy tribute to David Firth that the majority of the students from the Baptist Theological College who had studied under him and who then went on to post-graduate study chose Old Testament as their field.

Firth shows clearly that, by their inherent nature, the individual psalms of lament offer a generous and productive source of material for formulating appropriate responses to violence. For *response* is precisely what these psalms are – response to "God's overture".[1]

Attention is often drawn to the comment of the fourth century church father Athanasius on the value of the Psalms in his *Letter to Marcellinus*:

---

[1] Bernhard W Anderson, *Out of the Depths: The Psalms Speak For Us Today*, rev ed, Philadelphia: The Westminster Press, 1983, 9.

There is also this astonishing thing in the Psalms. In the other books, those who read what the holy ones say, and what they might say concerning certain people, are relating the things that were written about those earlier people. And likewise, those who listen consider themselves to be other than those about whom the passage speaks, so that they only come to the imitation of the deeds that are told to the extent that they marvel at them and desire to emulate them. By contrast, however, he who takes up this book – the Psalter – goes through the prophecies about the Savior, as is customary with the other Scriptures, with admiration and adoration, but the other psalms he recognises as being his own words. And the one who hears is deeply moved, as though he himself were speaking, and is affected by the words of the songs, as if they were his own songs. And for the sake of clarity of expression, do not hesitate, as the blessed Apostle says, to repeat the very things they say.[2]

In essence, then, as has regularly been noted, Athanasius is drawing attention to the fact that "the Psalms have a unique place in the Bible because most of Scripture speaks to us, while the Psalms speak *for* us . . . by expressing the whole gamut of human response to God's grace and judgement and thereby teaching us how to pray."[3] As Firth demonstrates so clearly, the Psalms do provide a consistent model for prayer, and the content of such prayer, in the face of violence, is to present one's case to God and to submit to God who alone has the right of retribution. The genuine response of faith is not taking matters into our own hands, but leaving our case in God's hands.

Such a response hardly conforms to the activism that is the temptation of all who suffer violence. As I read Firth's book, I couldn't help recalling the celebrated dispute between H Richard Niebuhr and his rather more famous brother Reinhold (it was their only published disagreement). In the context of the Japanese invasion of Manchuria in 1931 and the debate that raged in the United States about an appropriate response to this unjustified act of aggression, H Richard Niebuhr wrote an article called "The Grace of Doing Nothing", which appeared in *The Christian Century* on 23 March 1932. Activists (including Reinhold Niebuhr) called for a military response on the part of the United States, arguing that life in an unideal world regrettably required unideal responses to restrain evil, and castigating H Richard for what they regarded as his ethical cop-out. "Doing nothing", as H Richard sought to explain to his detractors, was actually an act of the deepest faith – "highly impracticable", to be sure, particularly from an activist viewpoint, but non-negotiable for the believer because, as he put it, "it rests on the well-nigh

---

[2] Athanasius, "Letter to Marcellinus" 11, in Robert C Gregg (trans), *Athanasius: The Life of Antony and The Letter to Marcellinus*, New York: Paulist Press, 1980, 109; emphasis added.
[3] Anderson, *Out of the Depths*, 9; emphasis in the original.

Foreword

obsolete faith that *there is a God – a real God.*"⁴ The grace of "doing nothing" is *only* foolish "if there is no God, or if God is up in heaven and not in time itself".⁵

If that kind of faith was "well-nigh obsolete" in 1932, the position has hardly improved in the first decade of the twenty-first century. That is why David Firth's exegetical endeavours in allowing the Psalms to speak to us (and *for* us!) again about surrendering the human retributive response to violence in favour of a radical trust in God are so important.

But enough from this *imbongi*, even if the length of the praise poem is supposed to be directly proportional to the worthiness of the one being praised. I commend David Firth's work to you, because I wish you to hear his voice, and the voice of the Psalms through him, for yourself. And with him as a guide, I wish you to find in the psalms of individual complaint the language we all need to express an "impracticable" and radical faith in a sovereign God.

Rev. Dr. Donald L Morcom
Malyon College
Brisbane, Queensland, Australia

---

⁴ H Richard Niebuhr, "The Grace of Doing Nothing", *The Christian Century*, March 23, 1932, 379; emphasis added.
⁵ Niebuhr, "Grace of Doing Nothing", 380.

PREFACE

Although the thesis on which this book is based was initially submitted in 1996, the subject area it explores has remained largely uninvestigated in the intervening years. As a result, although several important commentaries on Psalms have been either completed or published in the intervening years, nothing has occurred that would lead to a change in either the main argument or the detail that supports it. Accordingly, apart from making some minor corrections highlighted by examiners, I have left the thesis essentially as it was when submitted.

I should like to record in public my thanks to my promoter, Prof W. S. Prinsloo, who was a generous, helpful and challenging supervisor. I appreciated both his scholarship and the grace with which he shared it. His tragic death in late 1997 was a significant loss for Old Testament studies in South Africa and the wider world. When I was close to completing the thesis I was considering removing the elements of it that were peculiar to the South African situation, feeling that it would have a wider readership. Prof Prinsloo convinced me, rightly I believe, that it was the very context that gave rise to the question I considered. In doing so, I am reminded of the missiological imperative that lies at the heart of my own study of the Old Testament, and my hope is that this thesis can therefore contribute to both disciplines. Also at the University of Pretoria, the theology librarian, Miss Thea Heckroodt was tireless in tracking down materials and providing general assistance in the library. She was particularly helpful in making Thorne Wittstruck's annotated bibliography on the Psalms available to me, something that saved a great deal of time. Thanks are also due to Mrs. Carla Aucamp and Mrs. Thea Otto.

I should also like to thank the faculty, staff and students of the Baptist Theological College of Southern Africa, where I was privileged to teach at the time. This project arose out of the issues being faced by some of those students in their pastoral situations. I hope that it may begin to address those problems. It was a stimulating place in which to teach and study.

The Australian Baptist Missionary Society provided a small bursary each year towards the cost of research. I am thankful for their support. The conclusions reached in this study are not necessarily those of the Society.

The move towards publication is not easy, but I should like to express my thanks to Robin Parry, Jeremy Muddit and Anthony R. Cross from Paternoster for their care at the various stages of moving this from a dissertation to a book.

Finally, I should like to express my thanks to my wife Lynne and our children Jonathan, Rhiannon and Benjamin. Lynne has been prepared to make many sacrifices to enable me to finish this study, just as she has continued to support me throughout my academic career. It is accordingly dedicated to her.

Abbreviations

BDB	F. Brown, S. R. Driver and C. A. Briggs, *Hebrew and English Lexicon of the Old Testament*
BJRL	*Bulletin of the John Rylands Library*
BZ	*Biblische Zeitschrift*
CBQ	*Catholic Biblical Quarterly*
ETL	*Ephemerides Theologicae Lovanienses*
ExpT	*The Expository Times*
GKC	*Gesenius Hebrew Grammar*, ed. E. Kautzsch, Trans. A. E. Cowley
JBL	*Journal of Biblical Literature*
JNES	*Journal of Near Eastern Studies*
JSOT	*Journal for the Study of the Old Testament*
JTS	*Journal of Theological Studies*
LXX	The Septuagint
MT	Masoretic Text
NASB	*New American Standard Bible*
NEB	*New English Bible*
NGTT	*Nederduitse Gereformeerde Teologiese Tydskrif*
NIV	*New International Version*
NRSV	*New Revised Standard Version*
REB	*Revised English Bible*
RTR	*Reformed Theological Review*
TBT	*The Bible Translator*
VT	*Vetus Testamentum*
VT Supp	*Supplements to Vetus Testamentum*
WTJ	*Westminster Theological Journal*
ZAW	*Zeitschrift für die alttestamentliche Wissenschaft*

CHAPTER 1

Introduction and Methodology

Statement of Problem

A number of recent theological studies have been concerned with the issue of violence.[1] Within the South African context, this has been prompted by the growth in violence that was associated with the final years of apartheid, and that has subsequently continued. But such reflection is not unique to South Africa. Growing social, political and economic pressures in a number of contexts have resulted in increasing levels of violence. Indeed, Ellul has claimed violence is inevitable in all societies simply because of the nature of the state.[2] The existence of such social pressures calls not only for sociological reflection but also a theological consideration of the issues involved. Both methods of reflection are necessary, and each may inform the other.

From the perspective of theology, one aim of such reflection must be to determine an appropriate response to violence through an extensive exegesis of biblical material. Such reflection can then come into dialogue with sociology and other disciplines to address the problems of violence. In terms of the biblical research carried out on the theme of violence to date, there has been a serious lacuna in the study of the book Psalms and its perspectives on violence. The major monographs on the subject of violence within the Old Testament by Lohfink[3] and Noort[4] have both concentrated on narrative texts that reflect violent actions. The research of Snyman[5] has been limited to the word חָמָס, specifically in terms of its use within prophetic pronouncements. Thus, although a body of research on violence within the Old Testament has been developing, no treatment of the topic has yet been presented that deals with the issue in the Psalter.[6] Given that there is a considerable body of psalms that

---

[1] E.g. Jacques Ellul, *Violence: Reflections from a Christian Perspective*, London: SCM Press, 1970, and W. Vorster (ed), *Views on Violence*, Pretoria: UNISA, 1985.
[2] Ellul, *Violence*, 93
[3] N. Lohfink (ed), *Gewalt und Gewaltlosigkeit im Alten Testament*, Freiburg: Herder, 1983.
[4] E. Noort, *Geweld in het Oude Testament*, Delf: Zoetermeert, 1985.
[5] S. D. Snyman, "'Violence' in Amos 3,10 and 6,3", *ETL* 71 (1995), 30-47.
[6] It is remarkable to note that the annotated bibliography by Judith E. Sanderson, "War, Peace and Justice in the Hebrew Bible: A Representative Bibliography", included in the

reflect a motif of violence, this lacuna needs to be addressed.

Since the book of Psalms has been traditionally treated as a collection of essentially disparate pieces with no particularly structured attempt having been made to bring its theology together through a redactional process, this situation comes as no surprise. The use of this approach has not necessarily meant that the editors were presumed to lack any purposes in the selection of the individual psalms that make up the book of Psalms. But it is still a prevailing assumption that there is no one overriding editorial concern in the book of Psalms.[7] In general terms, such an assumption is most probably correct. But some recent studies[8] have begun to note ways in which the shape of the Psalter may suggest the presence of some editorial purposes.[9] Admittedly, the results that have come from this are by no means conclusive, perhaps because the editors had a variety of purposes, but the probing that has begun suggests new ways of approaching the study of the Psalms. In this approach, we may be concerned to ask questions about what the editors of the canonical book of Psalms intended to convey by the particular selection of psalms that they have made available to us. In the Book of Psalms we may therefore note the contribution of both the creators of the original psalms and that of the editors.[10]

This newer approach also highlights the particular importance of the perspectives offered by Psalms on the subject of violence. The various psalms come from a range of different voices through the history of biblical Israel. Admittedly, their place within the Psalter has been determined by the criteria of orthodoxy adopted by the editors, but it is still possible to note the subtle differences that exist in varying psalms. A unity within certain editorial criteria

---

English translation of Gerhard von Rad, *Holy War in Ancient Israel*, Grand Rapids: Eerdmans, 1991, 135-166, includes no works on the Psalms. The same is true of the history of research offered by N. Lohfink, "'Gewalt' als Thema alttestamentlicher Forschung", in N. Lohfink (ed), *Gewalt und Gewaltlosigkeit*, 15-50.

[7] A social profile of the editors of the Psalter is probably achievable through the assessment of the range editorial purposes that can be discerned. But that no one grand scheme holds for the whole of the book seems borne out by the remarkably different conclusions reached by the contributors in J. Clinton McCann (ed), *The Shape and Shaping of the Psalter*, Sheffield: Sheffield Academic Press, 1993.

[8] E.g. Gerald H. Wilson, *The Editing of the Hebrew Psalter*, Chico: Scholars Press, 1985 and the various contributors to McCann, *The Shape and Shaping of the Psalter*. Note, however, the criticisms of Wilson and those influenced by him in R. D. Anderson, "The Division and Order of the Psalms", *WTJ* 56 (1994), 219-241.

[9] A helpful survey of recent publications on this trend is offered by W. S. Prinsloo, "Die Psalms as Samehangende Boek", *NGTT* 36/4 (1995), 459-469. His survey indicates the roots of this approach in the work of Gunkel and Mowinckel, whilst also highlighting the differences in current European and North American research.

[10] For one example of how this approach works, cf. Walter Brueggemann, "Bounded by Obedience and Praise: The Psalms as Canon," *JSOT* 50 (1991), 63-92.

does not mean that there is a unity in perspective on all matters.[11] But by examining the perspectives offered on violence by Psalms we are able to address a group of texts that offer the possibility of hearing a chorus on violence rather than a soloist. If, then, the exegesis reveals that the Psalms reflect a relatively unified perspective on violence then we will have grounds for presuming that such a perspective must at least be embedded deeply within the theology of the editors and thus the editorial process that produced the book of Psalms. It would, in fact, represent a didactic element within the Psalms, though whether this particular element is consciously or unconsciously didactic cannot be determined. How deeply this theology is embedded in the rest of the Old Testament would then need to be the subject of further research.

The problem before us then is to determine what perspective or perspectives are offered by the Psalms on violence. It is the aim of the present research to attempt to begin to answer that question. Since the body of material in the Psalms is vast, we shall focus on one aspect only, which is the response to violence as it is reflected in the lament psalms of the individual.

Argument

The thesis argued here is that the consistent theology of those psalms that we can identify as lament psalms of the individual that reflect a motif of violence is that they reject all forms of human violence. Within the "I" psalms only the violence that may be enacted by Yahweh is acceptable. The only apparent exception to this occurs in an area that falls outside of the range of this investigation, in the actions attributed to the king in the royal psalms. Here, however, the perspective changes so that the king is understood as the one who acts on behalf of Yahweh. As the representative of Yahweh, the king exercises his right in violence. At points, this royal violence may reflect the level of force that was required for Israel to function as a state, but must be more generally understood as an enactment of Yahweh's right to violence. Thus, only violence initiated and carried out by Yahweh, either directly or through the king as his representative, can be regarded as acceptable. From the human perspective, violence may be received, pondered and suffered, but it may not be initiated. That is a right that belongs solely to Yahweh, and is a right that is handed over in worship.

The presence of this consistent theology of worship is not to be understood as something that was necessarily original to these psalms. Most of them had an original cultic setting where the language that is used in them had a specific purpose and function. But the collection of the psalms into a canonical text has given them a new function, one that instructs those who suffer from violence as to the nature of prayer that they should employ in response. In particular, it

---

[11] Cf. J. A. Burger, "The Psalms", in J. J. Burden and W. S. Prinsloo (eds), *Dialogue With God*, Cape Town: Tafelberg, 1987, 34.

shall be argued that the instruction is not only that the right of retributive violence belongs to Yahweh alone, but also that it is limited by the *lex talionis*. That is to say, the retribution that may be sought from Yahweh does not exceed the harm that has been inflicted by the enemy, or that may be inflicted were an accusation to be proved. How Yahweh is to act is not stated, but the limitation on retributive violence is clear.

As readers of the Psalms, we are thus called to recognise that no human has the right to initiate violence. To do so is to usurp that which by right belongs only to God. In recognising this factor, we may observe that the Psalter therefore seeks to inculcate an attitude of dependence on Yahweh, though without making specific how the problems faced by petitioners will be resolved.

The Nature of Violence

A General Definition of Violence

As a preliminary point, it is necessary to describe what is meant by "violence." In discussing violence, we are not here directly concerned with the narrower question of war and peace. Although war is an obvious and extreme form of violence it is not the only way in which violence is expressed. Violence occurs whenever there is an unnecessary use of force. Such force is not only physical, but can also be applied through unjust structures within a state system or through the application of psychological pressure. Working within an historical paradigm, Whitelaw says that physiological and psychological violence

> may therefore be understood as that which causes injury to the person or property by the excessive or hurtful application of force......From the societal standpoint it may be regarded as that which tears apart or damages the created order, and which violates or inhibits the positive processes of being and becoming by which humans interact.[12]

When we work with such a definition it becomes apparent that violence can be viewed as being operative within three main categories. It may be physical, psychological or structural, or it may reflect any combination of these elements. Violence occurs whenever an unnecessary level of force is applied in any one of these areas. This is not to suggest that the Old Testament itself consciously distinguishes between these categories. Rather, the use of this sociological model enables us to analyse the material, and to note where the distinction is present, even if it is not consciously reflected. Such a distinction can, in fact, be

---

[12] D. P. Whitelaw, "Christian Responses to Violence: A Historical Survey", in W. Vorster (ed), *Views on Violence*, 24.

Introduction and Methodology

seen within the Old Testament. Commenting only on the use of חָמָס, Haag observes that violence within the Old Testament is an

> infringement on the personal rights of others, motivated by greed and hate and often making use of physical violence and brutality.[13]

Such a definition is in striking agreement with that of Whitelaw, even if the sociological terms are not used. We therefore need to define what is meant by the main categories of violence.

Categories of Violence within the Old Testament

Physical violence is thus that which occurs when unnecessary force is used against someone such that it is experienced physically. This occurs, for example, in the case of striking, kicking or trampling people.

Psychological violence occurs when unnecessary force is used against someone in a non-physical way but such that it impacts upon the well-being of that person. Such violence commonly occurs in the form of a taunt, but may be experienced through the trauma associated with a false accusation or in the experience of false friends. Especially in societies such as ancient Israel where the spoken word was considered to be powerful, such violence can be experienced psychologically, but may still manifest itself physically. Typically, the psalmists describe such violence as an assault on their נֶפֶשׁ, though the breadth with which the term is used cautions against simply assuming that the use the word necessarily implies psychological assault. Specifically, psychological violence manifests itself in a sense of dread because of the fact that the threats behind the various taunts and accusations are expected to lead to serious physical violence, and often death. There is thus a sense in which psychological violence reflects the imminence of physical violence, and it is this imminence that causes a loss to the psalmist's well-being. This is, however, still violence in its own right since a threat in itself entails something violent.

Structural, or social, violence is that which attacks the order and well-being of society as a whole. It is fundamentally experienced collectively, and as such is not widely reflected in the psalms of the individual. Such violence may occur in times of war, but in the world view of the psalms also occurs when the wicked have control of society. Again, such violence may manifest itself physically, but its roots are in social structures.

In assessing the perspectives on violence within the psalms it is necessary to note that the various categories of violence offered here are not discrete, but shade into one another. Nevertheless, in each case a primary form of violence can be noted and it is this primary form that provides the basis for the response

---

[13] H. Haag, "חמס", in G. Johannes Botterweck and Helmer Ringgren (eds), *Theological Dictionary of the Old Testament*, Grand Rapids: Eerdmans, 1980, 4:482.

to violence.

The point at which force becomes unnecessary, and thus becomes violence, is difficult to determine. Although Ellul argues that there is no distinction between force and violence,[14] his unification of the two elements seems contrived. It is, for example, generally accepted that the state has the right to use a certain amount of force, a fact implied by the presence of a police force. But where the police go beyond what is necessary to arrest someone or where the legal system functions to deny that person access to normal human rights, then the force used is unnecessary and violence has occurred. Recognising the validity of some force, we may suggest that violence occurs whenever the minimum amount of force required in a given context is exceeded. Such a definition cannot function to resolve the difficult question of how one determines what violence is in respect to force in every contemporary occurrence, but can provide us with a working definition with which to approach the psalms.

Methodology

The Approach to the Psalms

The approach being taken here is to exegetically examine the psalms so as to determine their perspective on violence as we have defined it. We cannot, however, treat the psalms as a monolith. Different psalms pre-suppose different authors and contexts for use, and even the editorial process presumes some variety in approach. It is the great contribution of Hermann Gunkel that he recognised that different psalms can be organised according to different form critical categories.[15] The differing categories would reflect the differing *Sitz im Leben* within Israel's cult, though with respect to the finished book of Psalms it may be better to say that the different categories define the function of the psalm in Israel's worship. Although Psalm study has moved a long way since Gunkel,[16] his basic insights have not been overthrown, only modified. Such a form-critical approach should guide us here since this methodology allows us access to the contexts that would have generated the various psalms.

In following this approach, it is not necessary to work with all the categories noted by Gunkel. Broadly, his categories represent the experience of three main groups - the individual within Israel, the community and the king. The exact

---

[14]Ellul, *Violence*, 84.

[15]Hermann Gunkel, *The Psalms: A Form Critical Introduction*, Philadelphia: Fortress Press, 1967.

[16]Cf. Patrick D. Miller Jr, *Interpreting the Psalms*, Philadelphia: Fortress Press, 1986, 3-17.

delineation of who the speaker is in many psalms is still a point of dispute.[17] This is particularly so when the speaker is presented as an individual, but the presence of these three groups of speakers within the psalms is not disputed. Although it is possible to examine the psalms within these three broad categories, our narrower focus means that we shall only examine the psalms of the individual. Within these three broad categories, it is not unreasonable to presume that each will have either a different perspective on violence or a different response to it, even if the variation is one that is caused only by relative social standing. Given our limitation to the psalms of the individual, however, further research is necessary in the communal and royal psalms if this assumption is to be demonstrated.

A further element in the approach taken to the Psalms needs to be noted. Since this study is concerned with the theology of the Psalms as they currently stand the exegesis will be primarily guided by the concerns of a synchronic and canonical approach. This is not to deny that certain psalms have a literary history,[18] but is an attempt to recognise that whatever pre-history a given psalm may have had, our approach to it is finally determined by its current shape.

Approaching the Psalms from the perspective of the canon also affects our understanding of their role within the cult. The cult is no longer the sole home of the Psalms. Indeed, the placement of the Psalms within the canon actually pre-supposes a new use for many of them, albeit one guided by their cultic function. This can be illustrated by means of some of the festivals proposed for Israel from the Psalms. Although a variety of different approaches have sought to determine the shape of a proposed Autumn Festival through the interpretation of certain psalms,[19] particularly in reference to the king, the actual discovery of these festivals has proved to be an elusive reality.[20] Further, the fact that the psalms were only collected after the exile means that a process of re-interpretation was beginning even in the collection of the psalms. Therefore, a psalm that may have originally functioned within the context of a festival is no longer read in that way within its canonical context. Even if a royal festival once defined the use of a particular psalm it ceased to do so in the post-exilic period since the festival ceased to exist. The shaping of the Psalter assigns it a different role. The same holds true for the festival at Dan proposed

---

[17]Cf. John H. Hayes, *An Introduction to Old Testament Study*, Nashville: Abingdon, 1979, 293 and Steven J. L. Croft, *The Identity of the Individual in the Psalms*, Sheffield: JSOT Press, 1987.

[18]As a fairly obvious example, Psalm 108 is simply a combination of Psalms 57:7-11 and 60:5-12.

[19]E.g., Sigmund Mowinckel, *The Psalms in Israel's Worship* (2 vols), Oxford: Basil Blackwell, 1962, 1:106-192, describes an annual enthronement festival; Artur Weiser, *The Psalms*, London: SCM Press, 1962, 23-52, describes an annual Covenant Festival. See also John H. Eaton, *Kingship and the Psalms*, London: SCM Press, 1976, 87-134 and Croft, *Identity*, 89-113 for refinements of these theories.

[20]Peter C. Craigie, *Psalms 1-50*, Waco: Word, 1983, 48.

by Goulder,[21] though the evidence for its existence seems slighter anyway.

The development of the book of Psalms and the editorial processes associated with that development has brought a different line to the interpretation of some of the psalms. For example, a psalm such as Psalm 5 may once have functioned as the king's confession in the Autumn festival,[22] but the editorial processes that shaped Psalms have placed the psalm in a different light. Whatever festivals or cultic formulae may be hinted at by particular psalms, all direct traces of liturgy have been removed.[23] Therefore, Psalm 5 now functions as the prayer of a private individual. Without realising it, Gunkel's belief that only a few psalms were actually royal whilst the majority were the prayers of individuals may accurately reflect the canonical function of these psalms, if not their original purpose. Our treatment of the psalms of the individual therefore needs to consider the effects of this development.

Approaching the psalms in such a way does not deny the existence of the *Gattung* of the royal psalm. The editorial process followed has not resulted in an automatic identification of the "I" in various psalms as a private individual. That many psalms refer directly to the king (eg, Psalm 2), whilst others seem to have the king as the speaker (eg, Psalm 101) would suggest that his place was an established part of the tradition that shaped the Psalter. Further, the speaker in a number of psalms is almost certainly the king, even if he is not directly identified. The process of collection has not removed the king from the psalms. It has, however, removed any direct traces of festivals that may have reflected his enthronement. Factors more germane to the post-exilic community have been determinative for the canonical shape of Psalms.[24] Such a context for the royal psalms may thus have encouraged a more messianic reading, though without thereby reducing their royal significance.[25] But in some cases this process means that a psalm that might have originally been royal is now democratised. In the canon it functions as the words of a private individual. The shaping process of the book of Psalms may accordingly shift the emphasis of certain psalms. We will argue in chapter 2 that a similar process is also reflected in the psalms of false accusation. The canonical editors have removed the material that guided their use in the cult, leading to a different function being applied to these psalms.

Although the recognition of these factors is less significant for the interpretation of the psalms of the individual and the community, they still have some effect on the task of exegesis. In particular, the role of cultic spokesman

---

[21]Michael D. Goulder, *The Psalms of the Sons of Korah*, Sheffield: JSOT Press, 1982.
[22]So Croft, *Identity*, 95f.
[23]Brevard S. Childs, *Introduction to the Old Testament as Scripture*, London: SCM Press, 1979, 515f.
[24]Cf. Gerald H. Wilson, "The Shape of the Book of Psalms", *Interpretation* 46:2 (1992), 136ff.
[25]Childs, *Introduction*, 517.

Introduction and Methodology 9

in the communal psalms is now reduced since their part is to re-produce an existing liturgical response rather than announcing a new word from Yahweh. On the other hand, psalms originally written for the individual worshipper have a slightly enhanced position since they now function within the cultic community in a clearly defined manner that may not have been so clear originally. A notable example in this case is Psalm 30. It is clearly written as the psalm of an individual who has been healed from illness, but the title of the psalm now associates it with the dedication of the temple. The words of an individual have now become the words of the community. There is therefore a certain blurring of the distinction between the psalms of the individual and the psalms of the community, though the distinction is still worth retaining. Similarly, the royal psalms now merge into the individual and communal psalms. The shaping of the Psalter has softened the edges of the form critical categories without diminishing their validity as an exegetical and heuristic tool.

The Enemies in the Psalms

In the nature of an investigation such as this it is inevitable that we shall encounter references to "the enemies" in the various psalms. The obvious reason for this is that it is most commonly the enemies who are perceived as being responsible for the violence inflicted on the psalmist. It is, further, in terms of the violence of these enemies that the psalmists pray. The one exception to this situation is in the psalms of sickness where we shall argue that both Yahweh and the enemies are seen as acting in violence against the psalmists, with the difference being that the violence of Yahweh is just whilst that of the enemies is unjust. What is consistently affirmed in the relationship between the three is that the psalmists have not acted against the enemies. Neither, however, will the psalmists act against the enemies. The purpose of their prayers is to summon Yahweh to do so.

The presence of these references to the enemies invites an investigation into their identity. Although certain "grand schemes" have been proposed to provide a consistent identification of the enemies,[26] such schemes fail to convince.[27] In

---

[26]E.g., Harris Birkeland, *Die Feinde des Individuums in der israelitischen Psalmenliteratur*, Oslo: Grøndahl and Sons, 1933, and *idem*, *The Evildoers in the Book of Psalms*, Oslo: Jacob Dybwad, 1955, who identifies all of the enemies of the individual as foreign powers.

[27]For a comprehensive critique of Birkeland, cf. S. N. Rosenbaum, *The Concept "Antagonist" in Hebrew Psalm Poetry: A Semantic Field Study*, unpublished PhD Thesis, Brandeis University, 1974. Essentially, Rosenbaum demonstrates that Birkeland's position is based on a faulty assessment of semantic data. His own methodology is based on the work of John F. A. Sawyer, *Semantics in Biblical Research: New Methods of Defining Hebrew Words for Salvation*, London: SCM Press, 1972. Cf. Croft, *Identity*, 20-48, for an attempt to more adequately identify the semantic range of the enemies.

as much as it is possible in any given psalm, the enemies can only be identified on a case by case basis. The assessment of G. W. Anderson that recognises a diversity of enemy classifications in spite of the stereotyped language is surely correct.[28] Attempts to define the *Gattung* of a psalm on the basis of the enemies are therefore faulty since this can only be done with a pre-determined definition of the enemies.

The roles played by the enemies also show some variation. Consistently, however, they are responsible for enacting violence against the psalmist, though in the case of the psalms of the individual we will note the accuracy of Tate's observation that in these cases the danger is more of a threat than an actuality.[29] Such a threat broadly coincides with what we have called psychological violence.

Procedure

Working from this perspective on the Psalms, we shall examine in successive chapters different groups of the psalms of the individual so as to determine their attitude to violence. In particular, we shall seek to determine whether or not the psalms address the physical, psychological and social categories of violence that we noted above. Further, if these categories can be noted, we need to determine what perspectives the psalms provide on them. Once this has been determined we can outline the response to violence.

An important issue to be noted at this point is the question of how one may determine which psalms need to be examined. Two areas need to be resolved - which psalms reflect a motif of violence, and which are the psalms of the individual. We need to turn to these questions.

IDENTIFICATION OF PSALMS OF VIOLENCE

It is obvious that the occurrence of words such as חָמָס or שֹׁד is not of itself a sufficient criterion to regard a psalm as reflecting the motif of violence. חָמָס occurs only 14 times in Psalms,[30] often occurring adjectivally, whilst שֹׁד occurs only once.[31] Whilst one cannot deny the significance of these terms, it is quite apparent that at some points they have become simply metaphorical rather than actual. Although metaphoric uses of חָמָס may shade into references to psychological violence, it is also apparent that at some points the term is used in such a generalised way that no specific action of violence is in view. For example, in Psalm 11:5, חָמָס has become a covering term for sin in general, so that "those who love violence" (אֹהֵב חָמָס) is simply a general term for the

---

[28]G. W. Anderson, "Enemies and Evildoers in the Psalms", *BJRL* 48 (1965), 16-29.
[29]Marvin E. Tate, *Psalms 51 -100*, Dallas: Word, 1990, 61.
[30]Psalms 7:17, 11:5, 18:49, 25:19, 27:12, 35:11, 55:10, 58:3, 72:14, 73:6, 74:20, 140:2, 5 and 12.
[31]Psalm 12:6.

Introduction and Methodology 11

godless.³²

A more productive approach is to examine the psalms in terms of verbs that describe violent action. Violence is, after all, something that is best understood from experience, and experience describes violence in terms of what was done. Verbal forms that describe striking, crushing, slaying, rising up of enemies and so on clearly describe the activity of violence. Generally, these terms reflect the dimension of violence itself rather than force as a legitimate instrument. Again, one must take care to note that these verbal terms may shift to a more metaphorical meaning. Where this has taken place, though, we shall have good grounds for believing that the violence being described is of a psychological nature. For example, in Psalm 143:3, the root דכא is used. In this instance, though, the enemies are not physically crushing the psalmist. Rather, as the subsequent verse shows, it describes the type of experience endured, even though a physical crushing has not taken place. It is, in this instance, a psychological experience. Alternatively, where the objects of these verbs are communal or plural, then there is good grounds for believing that the violence being described is essentially social or structural. To stay with the root דכא, we should note its usage in Psalm 94:5 where it refers to the actions of the wicked against the people in general. Although individual cases may reflect a situation of someone physically crushed, the use of the term here reflects a situation of social violence. The root may, however, be used with its physical sense, as for example in Psalm 89:11 where דכא is used to describe what Yahweh has done to Rahab, the sea monster. Although this reflects the myth of Yahweh's conflict with the sea, the verb is clearly used in its physical sense.

Verbal forms depicting violence may thus be considered as a consistent guide to the presence of violence as a motif within a psalm. Further, the nature of their usage can function as a guide to the type of violence being described. We shall therefore examine those psalms that contain at least two non-parallel verbal terms depicting violence within the three categories outlined above.

IDENTIFICATION OF THE PSALMS OF THE INDIVIDUAL

Are there Psalms of the Individual?

As is well known, there was a considerable difference of opinion between Gunkel and Mowinckel over the question of the psalms of the individual. Despite his form critical methodology and commitment to the cult as the source of most of the psalms, Gunkel retained the view that most of the psalms that refer to an individual are to be understood in terms of the piety of an ordinary worshipper. On the other hand, Mowinckel associated the greater bulk of the individual psalms to cultic figures. Even those psalms that he understood as being for the use of the private worshipper are treated as being for "Everyman", so that they have a generalised position within the cult instead of being

---

³²A. A. Anderson, *Psalms 1-72*, Grand Rapids: Eerdmans, 1972, 122.

reflections of individual piety.³³ With such a diversity of opinions available, and there are still scholars who adhere more or less to one side of the spectrum, it is apparent that we cannot simply presume that the presence of an "I" in a psalm points to it being reflective of ordinary Israelite faith. Indeed, if psalms in the "I" form are more representative of those members of the cult that created them than the faith and piety of the individual, then there is little point in treating the individual psalms on their own. On the other hand, if the psalms of the individual are genuine compositions reflecting the faith of the ordinary Israelite, then we will have evidence that should guide us in the basic understanding of violence within Israel as well as the purposes of the editors of Psalms.

The position is somewhat more complicated when one notes the presence of a respected minority position in contemporary psalm studies, which is to identify the individual in most cases as the king.³⁴ Although this is not an issue that we can discuss in detail, it should simply be noted at this point that the position that is taken there is that much of the argument for identifying psalms as royal is circular. Although Tournay overstates the point in claiming that Eaton's position has been refuted,³⁵ there is no doubt that we cannot assign as many psalms to the king as he supposes.³⁶ The possibility that an individual in a psalm may be the king does not require that it is so. Indeed, one would need to find a range of factors present to affirm that a psalm should be treated as royal. Further, even if it is possible to show that a psalm was originally royal, and in many cases we can only operate at the level of hypothesis, the question of the canonical shaping of the psalms generally causes us to read the psalm in an alternative direction. By failing to provide, and in some cases even removing, some sort of rubric that guides us in seeing a royal figure in many of the psalms, the canonical editing leads us to read many of the psalms with an "I" as psalms of the individual.

One exception to this that should be noted is where the individual clearly acts as a cultic spokesman. For example, in Psalm 37 it is apparent that an individual speaks throughout the psalm. But the psalm is not structured so that we see in it an individual who is able to express personal faith to God. Rather, the speaker functions as a wisdom teacher, presumably within the cult, who instructs other worshippers. Although it is a psalm in which an individual

---

³³Mowinckel, *The Psalms in Israel's Worship*, II:1.
³⁴So Eaton, *Kingship*, 27-85.
³⁵Raymond Jacques Tournay, *Seeing and Hearing God with the Psalms*, Sheffield: JSOT Press, 1991, 67, citing W. H. Bellinger Jr., *Psalmody and Prophecy*, Sheffield: JSOT Press, 1984. In a note in his second edition (Sheffield: JSOT Press, 1986, 230f), Eaton has claimed that Bellinger has not understood his position.
³⁶So Croft, *Identity*, 74-75, who is basically sympathetic to Eaton's position but is forced to note that Eaton has usually only examined one possible solution to the identity of the individual.

speaks, its apparent *Sitz im Leben* within the cult rules it out from being considered as a psalm of the individual. Rather, it functions among the psalms of the community.[37] The canonical editing has not changed this.

What we have suggested so far is that within the canonical structure of Psalms there are psalms of the individual. This does not mean that all of these psalms were originally written with this purpose in mind, though that possibility is not excluded either.[38] Whatever the literary pre-history might be, certain psalms are regarded as psalms of the individual.

But if we can identify these as individual psalms, are they expressions of individual piety or "everyman" psalms written within the context of the cult? A definitive answer to this question is not possible, and it is perhaps too sharp a distinction to express the matter in "either-or" terms. Since we lack firm knowledge of the compositional process, it is not possible to exclude either option. That the cult most probably represents the home of the psalms does not require that all psalms were specifically composed within that setting. In all probability, we have to reckon with the possibility of individual psalms reflecting both options.

Again, though, the canonical process has sought to answer this question for the practical use of the psalms, if not their composition history. The psalms of the individual have, as Mowinckel correctly observed,[39] become "everyman" psalms. But they do this only because they have become a standard vehicle for ordinary worshippers to express their faith within the cult. Indeed, since the psalms represent a history of collection,[40] and probably in this reflect a variety of compilation tendencies before the final editing, it is likely that the psalms of the individual that have been included are there precisely because they reflect the faith of the individual in Israel. They are both "everyman" psalms and psalms that express the piety of the individual. As a contemporary example of a similar process one might cite Wesley's famous hymn "And Can it Be." The words of the hymn are written as a form of spiritual autobiography, yet many contemporary singers of the hymn see their own experience mirrored in the hymn. The hymn expresses the faith of one person, but its place in the worship of the church also allows it to function as a means of expressing the faith of "everyman." In addition, its continued presence in many hymn books reflects something of the understanding of conversion that is expected amongst the

---

[37]On the probability of "I" psalms being communal rather than individual, cf. Croft, *Identity*, 151-176.

[38]Thus, Leopold Sabourin, *The Psalms: Their Origin and Meaning*, New York: Alba House, 1974, 218, believes that most of the individual laments were spoken by ordinary individuals and written up subsequently for inclusion in the cult.

[39]Mowinckel, *The Psalms in Israel's Worship*, II:1.

[40]Cf. Craigie, *Psalms 1-50*, 25-31, and Hans-Joachim Kraus, *Psalms 1-59*, Minneapolis: Augsburg, 1988, 16-21, for brief overviews of how the Psalms *might* have been collected.

editors of those hymn books. This means that the hymn is then not only read and sung as a form of "spiritual autobiography" but it also becomes a form of instruction concerning the type of conversion experience that may be expected. Something similar may be said to have taken place with the psalms of the individual. Whether or not they were written by the private individual or for "everyman," their presence in the canon means that they now function to instruct "everyman."

The Identification of Particular Psalms

Granted that there are psalms of the individual within the Psalter, how are we to identify them? This becomes an important question in light of the fact that we have already noted that the presence of an "I" in the psalm does not make it a psalm of the individual. At this point we may follow the position of Croft[41] who suggests that psalms that reflect the prayers of a private person are essentially identifiable by the absence of expressly cultic or royal features. Obviously, such an approach allows us only to discover a bare minimum of individual psalms since it is conceivable (with Gunkel) that individuals would utilise more formal elements within their prayers.[42]

The psalms so identified cannot, however, be treated in any other way than as utterances of the private person.[43] Where we may need to differ from Croft is in determining the weighting to be given to the canonical process. In addition, he pays little attention to the definition of "cultic" and "royal" features so that the shape of these concepts remains unclear. As we have already argued, many psalms that may have originally been royal have lost that distinction and have merged into the psalms of the individual. Nevertheless, Croft's overall approach is still satisfactory as a methodology provided we take this additional factor into account. On this basis, we may identify Psalms 3, 7, 17, 27, 35, 38, 55, 56, 64, 69, 109, 139 and 143 as lament psalms of the individual that reflect the motif of violence. Not all of these psalms are treated by Croft as psalms of a private person, but the process of democratisation reflected in the editorial process allows these additional psalms to be treated here.

Accordingly, we may turn to the exegesis of these psalms in the next three chapters, though it will be necessary in each case to briefly examine the reasons for treating it as a private saying. Although we may identify these as psalms of the individual, it is apparent that they reflect a diversity of *Gattungen*. We shall accordingly group them as Psalms of False Accusation (7, 17, 109, 139), Prayers for Protection (3, 27, 35, 55, 56, 64, 143) and Psalms of Sickness (38, 69). It will be noted that all three groups can be said to reflect the larger

---

[41]Croft, *Identity*, 133f.

[42]For a *possible* reconstruction of the process behind this, cf. Hans-Joachim Kraus, *The Theology of the Psalms*, Minneapolis: Fortress, 1992, 139f.

[43]Croft, *Identity*, 134, identifies Psalms 6, 13, 30, 35, 41, 54, 64, 70, 86, 88, 109, 120-123, 130, 131 and 142 as representing the private person.

Introduction and Methodology 15

Gattung of the Individual Lament, and are perhaps to be regarded as sub-groups within this larger classification. However, a finer analysis will enable us to produce a more nuanced assessment, and the division may be justified on that basis. This is especially so when we recognise the fact that these differing sub-groups may reflect different contexts in which violence was experienced. Indeed, in our exegesis we shall note that although there are common features, each group has a distinctive contribution to make to this study. Although one also finds references to violence in other *Gattungen*, such as individual thanksgivings,[44] these psalms do not record a response to violence and their place as prayers of the individual are open to question. They are therefore not treated in this study.

EXEGETICAL PROCEDURE

In examining the psalms that we are able to identify as lament psalms of the individual that reflect a motif of violence, a consistent exegetical procedure consisting of four elements will be followed. The four elements are:
  1. Form Critical Discussion
  2. Structure
  3. Nature of Violence
  4. Response to Violence

We begin the study of each psalm with an overview of its form critical discussion since this enables us to place the current research within the wider debate concerning the study of the Psalms. In particular, given the diversity of opinions available on every psalm treated, this provides an opportunity to justify the inclusion of this psalm in the present study and within the classifications listed. Because the concern here is with the function of the psalm in the finished book, form criticism is utilised more as a descriptive tool than a prescriptive one. In following this approach we are therefore more concerned with how the form of the psalm would be used by the compilers of the Psalter than with an exact determination of the *Sitz im Leben*, although this latter aspect cannot be ignored.

Once the form critical discussion is resolved, the structure of the psalm is investigated. Generally, this is the most straight-forward part of the present research. Although literary devices that mark structure are noted, the primary concern here is with the development of thought within the psalm and in particular on how this development affects our understanding of the motif of violence within the psalm.

The longest section in the exegesis is typically the investigation of the nature of violence. Here, an attempt is made to determine what types of violence are reflected in the text. The possible forms of violence are those indicated above. This investigation follows the divisions indicated in the study of the structure of the psalm. Such an investigation is a necessary element in that it outlines the

---

[44] For example, Psalm 92.

violence experienced by the psalm and the violence, if any, that is sought in retribution. An understanding of the nature of violence is necessary if we are to properly interpret the response that is offered to it in any given instance. Obviously, a comprehensive exegesis of each psalm is not offered due to our specific focus, but an attempt is made to set the material that reflects the motif of violence into the wider context of the psalm.

Finally, the response to violence is examined. Here, the results of the foregoing exegesis are brought together with a specific focus on the response to violence indicated by the psalmist and also the instructional value of this available to the final editors. This element is treated last in each case because it is the goal of the current research.

CHAPTER 2

Psalms of False Accusation

Introduction

Overview of Research

The recognition of the *Gattung* of the psalms of false accusation stems from the pioneering essay of Schmidt on the prayers of the accused.[1] Basing himself on the fact that 1 Kings 8:31-32 presumes the possibility of an institutional setting within the temple for those who are accused, Schmidt identified a group of psalms that he classified as psalms of false accusation. Although by no means following Schmidt's conclusions absolutely, his basic position has been taken up and developed by Beyerlin, who has attempted to provide a more detailed exposition of the cultic situation.[2] A somewhat different, though still institutional, interpretation of these psalms is offered by Delekat who interprets them in terms of a protection oracle given to those seeking asylum in the temple.[3]

Not all scholars have accepted an institutional interpretation of these psalms. Others[4] have interpreted the references in these psalms as being more or less metaphoric and accordingly have not sought for an institutional setting. Whilst the place of the Psalms within the cult would suggest a primarily institutional setting for these prayers, the fact that real experience often tends to provide

---

[1]Hans Schmidt, *Das Gebet der Angeklagten im Alten Testament*, Giessen: Alfred Töpelmann, 1928. The psalms proposed by Schmidt for this category are 3, 4, 5, 7, 11, 13, 17, 26, 27, 31:1-9, 55:1-19, 56, 57, 59, 94:16-23, 109, 139, 140 and 142.
[2]Walter Beyerlin, *Die Rettung der Bedrängten in den Feindpsalmen der Einzelnen auf institutionelle Zusammenhänge untersucht*, Göttingen: Vandenhoeck & Ruprecht, 1970. Beyerlin only accepts 11 psalms as fitting the *Gattung*, 3, 4, 5, 7, 11, 17, 23, 26, 27, 57 and 63. It will be noted that 23 and 58 were not included by Schmidt. K van der Toorn, "Ordeal Procedures in the Psalms and the Passover Meal", *VT* 38/4 (1988), 430, seeks to build on Beyerlin's proposal, adding 16 and 139.
[3]L. Delekat, *Asylie und Schutzorakel am Zionheiligtum: Eine Untersuchung zu den privaten Feindpsalmen*, Leiden: E. J. Brill, 1967.
[4]E.g. W. O. E. Oesterley, *The Psalms* (2 vols), London: SPCK, 1939.

language that moves into the realm of metaphor may suggest that we are actually looking for something in between the two. Accordingly, Bellinger has suggested that some of these psalms may reflect an actual institutional setting, as proposed by Schmidt and refined by Beyerlin. On the other hand, others would reflect false accusers that stand outside the legal system, as perhaps we would find in the case of malicious gossip, especially that which produces shame.[5] The difficulty which must then be faced is the resolution of the question that naturally arises-how may we distinguish between a cultic and a non-cultic psalm of someone who is falsely accused? Granted that the language of reality moves into the language of metaphor, it becomes practically impossible to determine which psalms reflect a cultic origin and which ones use the language of the cult as metaphor.

The Place of the Canon

For our purposes, it is perhaps sufficient to note that a group of psalms that reflect the prayers of the accused can be identified. Admittedly, there is not yet universal agreement on exactly which psalms would fit into this *Gattung*, though that is perhaps true of most of the *Gattungen* found in the psalms. But a *Gattung* of the psalms of the falsely accused can be identified, though we shall need to argue the case for the inclusion of each psalm in this group. We need, however, to comment on the role of the canon in the interpretation of these psalms, especially since our concern here is with the finished form of the book of Psalms and not with its pre-history. Does the canonical shape of the book of Psalms suggest a line of interpretation for these psalms?

An analogy here may be drawn with the royal psalms. Just as the shaping of the canon has removed whatever cultic rubrics may have been present from the royal psalms, so these rubrics have also been removed from the psalms of false accusation. Those responsible for the editing of the book of Psalms have selected a group of these psalms, but the very fact of selection indicates that others were excluded from the list. Not all psalms of the accused have been included in the canon, and the psalms reflecting this group have been scattered so that their exact relationship can no longer be determined. The shape of a cultic liturgy that can be derived from these psalms is therefore stunted by the editorial process. The presence of this editorial process indicates that a final shift has taken place in terms of the role played by these psalms. The shift from actual situation towards metaphor that seems to be reflected in the language here has therefore reached its conclusion in the process of the completion of the book. If this reconstruction is correct, then the purpose for which these psalms were collected is not primarily cultic. Rather, as representative prayers of the accused they serve to guide and instruct the community as to the types of prayers that can be used in a situation of false accusation. It is in terms of this

---

[5]Bellinger, *Psalmody and Prophecy*, 33.

function that we shall seek to interpret these psalms. They represent a worship based form of instruction on the way in which a person who stands falsely accused ought to respond to such a situation.

Method of Approach

Since the *Gattung* of each psalm is open to some dispute, especially from those favouring a royal interpretation of Psalms, it will be necessary in each case to justify the inclusion of these psalms within this group. Once this is done we will examine each psalm in terms of the exegetical methodology outlined in our first chapter. In general, we will argue that these psalms refuse to accept the possibility of human violence in response to what is experienced, and seek instead that Yahweh might act. In the case of these psalms, violence is predominantly experienced on the psychological level, reflecting the experience of taunting and false accusation. However, the psychological violence derives its force from the fact that physical violence is perceived as imminent. Further, the responding action of Yahweh that is requested is limited by either the *lex talionis* (Ex 21:23-25) or the law governing false accusation (Deut 19:16-19). The implicit teaching on violence provided is thus one in which the right of human retribution is denied, and the retribution sought from Yahweh must not therefore exceed either the harm that has been inflicted or the potential harm were the charge to be proved.

It shall be argued that the actions of the enemies are consistently contested only through a prayer to Yahweh as the one who is summoned to act. As noted, it will be found that the request for vengeance in the prayer is controlled by two options. One is the *lex talionis*, so that the punishment sought against the enemy is only that which they have inflicted on the psalmist. The alternative, though related, approach is to request that the penalty that would have been applied to the psalmist had the accusation been proved is now to be applied to the enemy instead. Although such a direct prayer is absent from Psalm 7, it is implicit in the summons to Yahweh to arise in the case, and is then expressed through the wisdom world view of verses 13-17. We will seek to show that in no case does the psalmist seek to initiate human violence in response to the violence suffered. Indeed, each of these psalms refuses to allow the individual the right to perpetrate violence in response to violence. Instead, that right is given only to Yahweh.

It will be seen that these psalms therefore function in the context of the finished book to give the individual a voice in dealing with enemies who raise false accusations, and in particular to provide a mechanism for the mainly psychological violence that is associated with such a scenario.

Psalm 7

Form Critical Discussion

The form critical discussion of this psalm has not satisfactorily resolved the question of its type, leading some to question its original unity.[6] Certainly, verses 7-12 have a more general character, though the presence of similar references to enemies in the plural as well as to a (seemingly) particular enemy in other psalms in this group cautions against treating these verses as a gloss. Ridderbos also notes some important internal connections between these verses and the opening section of the psalm,[7] so we may agree with Kraus that the psalm is a closely knit unit, a position we shall argue in more detail in "Structure" (below).[8]

Eaton notes in the same verses language which he believes to have been characteristically royal. In particular, he points to the summons given to God to arise in judgment over the nations (verse 7ff) and thus places this psalm in the group that he classifies as being "clearly royal."[9] Croft goes further in this suggestion, claiming that the psalm reflects the king's account to Yahweh of his stewardship for the previous year.[10] Even if this is so, and it can only be a hypothesis, there is no clear evidence in the structuring of the book of Psalms that we are to read this psalm as royal.[11] Further, the references in verses 7ff can be understood in other ways without any specific reference to the king. If, as we shall argue, they refer to God's presence in the heavenly court where the plea of innocence is to be heard, then a situation of false accusation makes more sense than a royal setting. In the absence of any specifically royal markers, the final structuring of the book causes us to read it as the words of an

---

[6]E.g. C. A. and E. G. Briggs, *A Critical and Exegetical Commentary on the Book of Psalms*, 2 vols, Edinburgh: T & T Clark, 1906 and 1907, 1:52ff.

[7]Nic H. Ridderbos, *Die Psalmen. Stilistiche Verfahren und Aufbau mit besonderer Berücksichtigung von Ps 1-41*, Berlin: Walter de Gruyter, 1972, 132.

[8]Kraus, *Psalms 1-59*, 168.

[9]Eaton, *Kingship*, 30ff. An alternative royal approach is suggested, though not argued, by Tremper Longman III and Daniel G. Reid, *God is a Warrior*, Grand Rapids: Zondervan, 1995, 44. They claim that the psalm is a king's prayer before a battle. Their case seems to be based on the summons to Yahweh to "rise up" (verse 7), though specifics are lacking. In the examination of the nature of violence we shall argue an alternative understanding of this phrase which therefore undercuts their position.

[10]Croft, *Identity*, 47.

[11]This is so even if the otherwise obscure reference to "Cush the Benjamite" in the title gives some credence to the title portraying an actual historical setting for the psalm since the language is then no longer cultic. Rather, it would indicate that David is viewed as the archetypal individual whose experience of persecution is the model for others.

individual.[12]

A somewhat broader classification is proposed by Mowinckel, who includes Psalm 7 in his group of "protective psalms."[13] Although we shall note in the next chapter a number of psalms that can be included in such a classification, it remains on the whole an ill-defined group. To a certain extent, the psalms that we place there are included in that classification because of a lack of evidence that will place them in a more concrete *Sitz im Leben*. A situation of false accusation would, however, admirably fit a context in which protection is sought. Although we may agree with Mowinckel in broad terms, a finer analysis is to be sought.

As noted above, all of the major proponents of an institutional grouping of psalms dealing with false accusation include this psalm in their list.[14] A number of features would suggest that the psalm arose in such a setting.

1. The initial plea for Yahweh's deliverance (verses 2-3) presumes that the psalmist is under attack, and that asylum is sought with Yahweh.[15] The temple would provide a logical site for this.

2. The opening line of verse 4, יְהוָה אֱלֹהַי אִם־עָשִׂיתִי זֹאת, presumes that some accusation has been made, a denial of which then follows in the form of some negative confessions (cf. Job 31).[16]

3. The words שָׁפְטֵנִי יְהוָה כְּצִדְקִי, indicate a call for Yahweh to assess the case of the psalmist. This would also suggest that the summons to Yahweh to arise in verse 7 has no necessary royal setting, since it is a call for a legal decision.

4. A response based on the *lex talionis* seems to be presumed by the wisdom world view in verses 15ff. This may suggest that such a decision will reflect the legal outcome of the case.

Taken together, these factors would seem to suggest that a context of false accusation lies behind the psalm.[17] But whether the psalm now functions institutionally is another matter. As we have already noted, the book of Psalms contains no set rubric for these psalms. Although an institutional setting is the probable point of origin for a psalm such as this, we do not have any way of knowing how the institution would have functioned. In addition, there is some variety in their expression, so that there is no one model of the prayer of the falsely accused. But in its role in the finished book, the psalm provides a

---

[12]Mowinckel, *The Psalms in Israel's Worship*, 1:203 includes the psalm amongst a group that have an individual speaking on behalf of the community. Such an interpretation seems impossible when we note the presence of a specific enemy.
[13]Mowinckel, *The Psalms in Israel's Worship*, 1:220
[14]To this group we may also add Bellinger, *Psalmody and Prophecy*, 50ff.
[15]With Delekat, *Asylie*, 62.
[16]Sabourin, *The Psalms*, 221.
[17]Cf. Beyerlin, *Die Rettung*, 96f, who places special emphasis on verses 4-6 to establish an institutional setting.

pattern of prayer that can be used by the falsely accused individual.

Structure

Some of the elements of the structure of the psalm have been mentioned above. We need, however, to raise the question of the place of verses 7-12, since their place in the text is open to some question. Beyond that, we simply need to deal with those elements of the structure of the psalm that call for some further clarification. Analysis of the structure will, however, bear out the conclusions reached above on the psalm's *Gattung*.

The main objection to the unity of the psalm is that raised by Briggs[18] who suggests that verses 7-12 and 18 were added to the psalm to provide general references suitable for congregational use. Since verse 18 has little impact on our discussion, we can set the issue of its coherence within the psalm to one side and concentrate on verses 7-12.[19] In particular, Briggs points to the wider outlook of verses 7-12 as indicating a separate origin from the rest of the psalm. In Briggs' terms, this is therefore a gloss to be treated separately from the main psalm. We cannot deny that this material may have had a separate origin from the rest of the psalm. Nevertheless, we must first be concerned to examine its relationship to the rest of the psalm. If it is coherent, we shall be able to treat the psalm as a whole.

These objections fail, however, to note the presence of judicial language throughout verses 7-12. Although the plea that Yahweh arise (verse 7) has a military background, the fact that the verse ends with the plea that he decree justice indicates a close link with what has gone before. The presence of judicial language through the whole of this section, with the conclusion that "God is a righteous judge" (verse 12) strongly suggests that these verses are an integral part of the psalm. It is possible that they represent traditional material that has been worked into the psalm, but if this is so it has been integrated into the psalm's larger movement.

Accepting, then, the coherence of the psalm, we need only to outline its contents. Apart from the title (verse 1) and the closing declaration of praise (verse 18), the psalm contains four main sections, each of which reflects the experience of violence in some form.

1. Verses 2-3 represent an initial plea by the psalmist, reflecting the psalmist's need of a refuge with Yahweh.

2. Verses 4-6 are a declaration of innocence, expressed in the form of a self curse should certain charges be proved.

---

[18]Briggs, *Psalms* 1:52ff.

[19]We should note, however, that the declaration of praise in verse 18 neatly balances the plea for sanctuary in verse 2. In addition, Yahweh is to be praised כְּצִדְקוֹ, itself possibly a judicial term. These factors strongly point to the integrity of verse 18. Cf. C. S. Rodd, *Psalms 1-72*, London: Epworth Press, 1963, 18.

3. Verses 7-12 are an expression of Yahweh's authority with a summons to him to act as judge, and with a particular emphasis in verse 9 on the need for the psalmist to be judged.
4. Verses 13-17 are a statement of the assured end of the wicked, reflecting something of a wisdom world view.

The development that this demonstrates fits in well with our proposed *Gattung* for this psalm.

Within these elements, we shall suggest that it is possible to see psychological, physical and social violence, though the latter two are more implicit than explicit. Strikingly absent in this case is a prayer that calls upon Yahweh to act against the enemy concerned in terms of either the accusation being returned as upon a false accuser or a petition for the *lex talionis*. In this case, however, the latter is simply presumed.

Nature of Violence

The psalm commences with a plea to Yahweh for deliverance from generalised enemies. The language here is formularised, with similar expressions of individual trust occurring frequently within the psalms. Although the prayer in verse 2b is for deliverance from all the pursuers of the psalmist, the switch to the masculine singular יִטְרֹף, likening an accuser to a ravening lion, suggests that there may be a particular enemy that is in mind.[20] This would also seem to be borne out by the use of the masculine singular form in verse 6.[21] Such an individual cannot, however, be understood outside of the group context, so that although there is a dominant individual responsible for the accusation there is a group that supports it. If such an individual can be identified, then he is to be regarded as a ringleader among a larger group of enemies.

Although the image of the lion seeking to devour the psalmist's נֶפֶשׁ may suggest that physical violence is in view, it is more likely that it is psychological violence that is reflected. This is not immediately apparent, since the image of a lion seeking someone's life seems intensely physical. However, the very context of false accusation is in itself an intensely distressing thing, as the rest of the psalm bears out. The main reason for understanding this as psychological violence is that at this stage an actual physical assault remains potential, not actual.[22] There is an actual pursuit by the enemies, but direct physical violence is dependant upon their charge being proved, something that requires Yahweh's non-action. The charge, with its resultant threat, is clearly

---

[20]Contra Mitchell Dahood, *Psalms I: 1-50*, Garden City: Doubleday, 1965, 41, who sees the switch as simply characteristic of impassioned language.

[21]Admittedly, the singular could be collective, but in the context of a false accusation impassioned language directed against a ringleader seems probable.

[22]Note that verse 3 commences with פֶּן, which in this context stresses a potential outcome.

viewed as violence in and of itself given the use of the lion simile.

That the violence referred to here is primarily psychological becomes apparent when we note the declaration of innocence in verses 4-6.[23]

> Yahweh my God, if I have done this,[24]
> if there is guilt on my palms,
> if I have wronged my friend and spared my enemy without cause,[25]
> then let an enemy pursue and overtake me,
> and let him trample my life to the earth,
> and let my glory sleep in the dust.

A declaration of innocence such as this presumes that the claim has been made that the psalmist is guilty of the actions described in it. The declaration aims to refute this claim, but in so doing provides a context for interpreting the simile of the lion. It most probably means that a particular enemy has made these sorts of claims against the psalmist, claims that attack the poet's very being, but which have not yet brought about physical violence. Thus the psalmist suffers from psychological violence, something that flows from the possibility of physical violence if the accusations are proved. That this is a possible outcome is apparent from the self-cursing formula[26] of verse 6 which seems to suggest a death penalty being applied if the charges are proved true. The claims of the enemy are, of course, rejected, but the possibility of any action being taken is placed in the hands of Yahweh. This is true even though the prayer requests that the enemy actually carry out the sentence if the charge is proved since it presumes that the enemy may act as Yahweh's agent.

That Yahweh alone has the right to act in physical violence is apparent in verses 7-12. The prayer for Yahweh to arise and act on behalf of the psalmist is common in the psalms, but it here stresses the fact that he alone has the right to act with physical violence. In addressing Yahweh in this way, the psalmist treats Yahweh as both an enthroned king and a judge. The opening words of verse 7, קוּמָה יְהוָה may reflect the words of Numbers 10:35-36,[27] suggesting

---

[23]Cf. Christian Macholz, "Bemerkungen zu Ps 7:4-6", *ZAW* 91 (1979), 127-129 on the grammatical issues posed by these verses.

[24]Since the זֹאת stands without antecedent, it must refer to an earlier part of the proceedings. Cf. Robert L. Hubbard, "Dynamistic and Legal Processes in Psalm 7", *ZAW* 94 (1982), 269.

[25]On this translation, cf. Robert G. Bratcher, "A Translator's Note on Psalm 7:4b", *TBT* 23 (1972), 241f and David Thomas, "A Further Note on Psalm 7:4", *TBT* 25 (1974), 247f. The emendations suggested by Jeffrey H. Tigay, "Psalm 7:5 and Ancient Near Eastern Treaties", *JBL* 89 (1970), 181ff and Jacob Leveen, "The Textual Problems of Psalm VII", *VT* 16 (1966), 440 are unnecessary.

[26]Cf. F. L. Hossfeld and E. Zenger, *Die Psalmen I: Psalm 1-50*, Würzburg: Echter Verlag, 1993, 75.

[27]Kraus, *Psalms 1-59*, 171.

that Yahweh is addressed as a warrior king, summoning him to rise in judgment. Although this can be regarded as probable, the important point to be noted is that the psalm calls upon Yahweh alone to act. Thus, the psalmist desires that the evil of the wicked be brought to an end by Yahweh (verse 10). The use of the verb כָּלְיוֹת here would suggest that this may be by means of physical destruction. Since however the reference has been generalised to cover all the wicked, there may be a hint of violence addressing the social structure as well, though this point is not to be pressed. The observation of verse 11 that God is a shield for the psalmist may also provide a pointer towards the final declaration of the psalm. It is not only that the actions of the wicked inevitably rebound upon them[28] but also that Yahweh, as the righteous judge (verse 12), protects the innocent.

The statement on the end of the wicked (verses 13-17) provides the major exegetical crux of the psalm. In particular, who is the subject of the verb יָשׁוּב in verse 13? The answer to this question largely determines the meaning given to these verses.

An initial reading of the passage may suggest that the subject is God, since he was the subject of verse 12, and there is no direct grammatical marker to indicate a change of subject.[29] Even if we follow the logic of this reading through, however, it is not free from exegetical difficulties. The most pressing of these is that in verse 14 we clearly have a reference to the enemy and not God, so the problem of the change of subject without a clear marker remains. Even among those who wish to read the text with God as the subject there is sometimes the suggestion that we need to emend the text to properly substantiate it.[30] This is not a universal approach, but it does reflect the difficulties involved in defending this reading. The text can, however, be understood as it stands, though the difficulties that it poses should still be recognised.[31] It should be noted that verses 7-12 take the form of a doxology, which may suggest that traditional material is being used here. Although the doxology seems integrated into the psalm,[32] it is still essentially a digression that moves away from the central issue that is at stake. If so, then we should

---

[28] At least in the limited perspective of this part of the wisdom world view.
[29] So e.g. NIV, Craigie, *Psalms 1-50*, 102, Dahood, *Psalms 1-50*, 46, Willem A. van Gemeren, "Psalms", in F. E. Gaebelein (ed), *The Expositor's Bible Commentary*, vol 5, Grand Rapids: Zondervan, 1991, 104f.
[30] Leveen, "Textual Problems in Psalm VII", 442. Leveen's proposal involves the restoration of a line from the LXX which is absent from the MT. However, given the difficulties posed by the MT, it is equally possible that the LXX reading is an attempted correction of an awkward text. This becomes more apparent when we recognise that Leveen is still compelled to make further emendations without manuscript support to justify his change.
[31] Cf. A. A. McIntosh, "A Consideration of Psalm vii. 12f.", *JTS* 33 (1982), 481ff, for an overview of the problems that the text has caused in the history of interpretation.
[32] Against Briggs, *Psalms*, 53f.

look back to the subject of verse 6, which was the enemy, with the expectation that this should still be the subject of verse 13. God as the subject of the verb seems less probable, though it has a surface attraction.

Positive evidence that points to the enemy as being the subject of the verb may also be noted. First, weight must be given to the fact that the expression אִם־לֹא[33] is normally used to introduce an oath or make a solemn declaration.[34] Since an oath seems improbable here, we should understand this as introducing a new section within the psalm, the formula indicating the certainty of what is to follow. Further, the copula is used to join verse 13 to verses 14ff, which seems to refer to the enemy. In spite of the awkward nature of the link, we should consider the reference here to be to the psalmist's enemy.[35]

Even with this element resolved, the interpretation of verse 13 is far from clear. In particular, we need to determine the meaning of יָשׁוּב. If we are correct in interpreting אִם־לֹא as a statement of certainty, then it is improbable that שׁוּב here means "repent". Far more likely is the suggestion that it has the meaning "again."[36] We should therefore translate "Surely again he sharpens his sword." Since this is a reference back to the previous activities of the enemy, we should also understand this as referring to psychological violence. The military metaphors that are developed here are then a means of expressing the effect of a verbal attack on the psalmist expressed in the accusation.

The irony of the situation is pointed out in verses 14-17. All that the enemy does is actually pointed back at himself, so that the violence he sought to initiate on the psalmist is actually something that he experiences. Those who perpetrate violence are thought of as being the ones who finally suffer it. Since the violence inflicted upon the psalmist is primarily understood in psychological terms the experience of the enemy is also to be understood in this way. Although it is expressed in terms of a wisdom world view, it represents a view of the *lex talionis* in action. How it can be known that this is what will happen to the enemy is not stated.[37] But that this principle of retribution is active is regarded as apparent.

In summary, we may note that the psalm primarily reflects a context of psychological violence. The false accusations that have been made have within them the threat of a further assault on the psalmist, and possibly the death penalty. Such an accusation obviously causes a state of dread within the

---

[33]It is notable that both Leveen, "Textual Problem in Psalm VII", 442 and McIntosh, "Psalm vii. 12f", 488 find it necessary to delete the אִם to defend their reading of God as the subject of the verb.
[34]GKC, §149.
[35]So also Anderson, *Psalms 1-72*, 98, Bellinger, *Psalmody and Prophecy*, 52 and 108, Kraus, *Psalms 1-59*, 174f.
[36]GKC, §120d.
[37]Unless we follow Bellinger, *Psalmody and Prophecy*, 52f, and see this as evidence of a "certainty of hearing."

psalmist, which is in itself an expression of psychological violence. Within the wisdom world view of the psalm, it is assumed that once the matter is committed to Yahweh then there is an inevitable cause and effect brought into play so that the violence initiated against the psalmist is actually experienced by the enemy.

Response to Violence

The psalmist's cause must therefore be committed to God. Those who depend on God cannot follow in the path of violence that has been established by the enemy. What is notable in this psalm is that once the call for judgment has been made (verse 9), there is no further prayer for action against the enemy. The matter is regarded as being in Yahweh's hands, and the *lex talionis* will therefore be operative as an expression of his justice. How the principle of retribution within a wisdom world view and the direct request for Yahweh's action relate is never made clear. They are, however, assumed to complement one another in some way.

In the absence of a clearly defined cultic setting, the psalm also functions within the instruction offered by the Psalter as a model of how one might respond to false accusation and the psychological distress that is associated with that. The form of an original cultic setting cannot be determined with any clarity now, though that one did exist must at least be held to be probable. In its absence, however, the psalm's response to the experience of false accusation now speaks beyond the setting of the cultus, encouraging a belief in Yahweh's justice and not personal retaliation as the means of dealing with this sort of situation. Such a belief is clearly modelled by the wisdom instruction at the end of the psalm with its stress on a principle of retribution. The presence of this principle is essential to the instructional value of the psalm, since it seeks to assure the faithful that there will be a positive outcome once the event is committed to Yahweh, even though it leaves open the means by which this outcome might be reached. Trust in the justice of Yahweh and of creation is thus summoned as the means of dealing with the pain caused by a false accusation.

Psalm 17

Form Critical Discussion

There are many similarities between this psalm and Psalm 7. Although it is plainly an individual prayer that seeks protection from Yahweh, it is unclear who the speaker is. Eaton has argued that the description of the enemies and prayer relating to them suggests that the speaker is the king. In particular, he points to the reference in verse 11 to the enemies as having surrounded the psalmist, something he understands as a reference to an invasion.³⁸ In many ways, this is an attractive suggestion, though there is nothing concretely present in the psalm that requires the speaker to be a king unless we assume that references to enemies and military language can only refer to an invasion.³⁹ Yet the first part of verse 11 refers to the enemies as having tracked down the psalmist. This is hardly suggestive of an invasion, even if there is a subsequent reference to being surrounded. It seems more likely, therefore, that military language is being used metaphorically, and that it cannot therefore be used to support a royal reading.

A more subtle argument in favour of a royal interpretation is offered by Croft who argues that the references to enemies are to be understood in terms of a ritual battle that is part of the annual royal liturgy.⁴⁰ But the rendering of the psalm within the canon has again meant that the language has been democratised,⁴¹ a factor especially important when we realise that the Psalms have not been transmitted with any cultic guidelines. In any case, the reference to a single enemy within the larger group of enemies in verse 12 could suggest that it is a particular individual who is the focus of the psalmist's concerns. This makes it unlikely that the enemies here are national figures, whether real or ritual, which in turn militates against a royal interpretation. Again, the function of the psalm in the finished book leads us to read it as the words of a private individual.

Granted that this psalm is presented to us as the words of an ordinary Israelite, can we positively identify it with the Psalms of False Accusation? Two key elements point strongly in that direction.⁴²

1. The initial request to Yahweh (verses 1-2) to hear a righteous cause (צֶדֶק)⁴³ coupled with a request that a judgement (מִשְׁפָּט) be issued suggests a request for a judicial decision. Such a request presumes that an accusation has been made, whilst the fact that the psalmist claims innocence suggests that the accusation is understood to be false.

2. Verses 3-5 represent a claim of innocence against accusations that

---

³⁸Eaton, *Kingship*, 33f. So also Aubrey R. Johnson, *The Cultic Prophet and Israel's Psalmody*, Cardiff: University of Wales Press, 1979, 244.
³⁹Johnson, *The Cultic Prophet in Israel's Psalmody*, 249, differs from Eaton in that he is prepared to accept the possibility that the references to enemies are to be understood in terms of internal intrigues.
⁴⁰Croft, *Identity*, 91.
⁴¹Cf. Craigie, *Psalms 1-50*, 161.
⁴²Cf. J. Lindblom, "Bemerkungen zu den Psalmen I.", *ZAW* 59 (1942-43), 7ff.
⁴³The MT here is difficult. The LXX adds μου, which suggests a reading of צִדְקִי. Such a textual corruption is easily understood, and should probably be adopted. The meaning must, however, be understood from the parallelism. This suggests that it is a righteous cause and hence a plea for justice that Yahweh is summoned to hear. Cf. Jacob Leveen, "The Textual Problems of Psalm XVII", *VT* 11 (1961), 48 and Robert Alden, *Psalms: Songs of Devotion*, Chicago: Moody, 1974, 43.

have apparently been made, a declaration that is supported by the additional claim that Yahweh has tested the psalmist in some way.[44] We should note that the claims here are more general,[45] but they are still clearly parallel in form to the similar claim in Psalm 7:4-6. Although Croft argues that the general nature of these claims makes the psalm unsuitable for this classification,[46] the fact that the whole claim is prefaced by a confession of Yahweh's searching of the psalmist indicates that these may be understood as representative confessions. In any case, if the Psalms have moved from the specific instance, reflecting a private individual's situation, into the general experience of the cult, then we would expect such a generalisation.

While this evidence suggests that the psalm is to be understood as a prayer of one falsely accused, we still need to determine whether or not it represents a clearly cultic institution. Although formulating it quite differently, both Beyerlin and Delekat[47] presume that the psalm reflects an institutional setting, with Beyerlin pointing to the very close parallels that exist between this psalm and others of the group. He points out that

> "In all that, the text of the seventeenth psalm so completely corresponds to an institutional divine judgement procedure consisting of various acts, that its classification within such a procedure appears highly probable."[48]

Such an observation needs to be given full weight. But von Rad also points to a stage that he believes is reflected in this psalm where such language was divorced from the procedure of the sanctuary and passed into the general language of prayer.[49] It is not, however, necessary to make such a sharp distinction as this. As Kraus points out,[50] such differences in perception may reflect the different approach taken to the psalms. In all probability, Beyerlin is

---

[44]Cf. Fredrik Lindström, *Suffering and Sin: Interpretations of Illness in the Individual Complaint Psalms*, Stockholm: Almqvist & Wiskell, 1994, 420.

[45]Unless we follow Dahood, *Psalms 1-50*, 94 in believing that the psalmist has been accused of idolatry. This does, however, require the text to be revocalised. Although this has some versional support it is made less likely by the fact that there is nothing else in the psalm that would support such an interpretation. Cf. Anderson, *Psalms*, 149.

[46]Croft, *Identity*, 91.

[47]Beyerlin, *Die Rettung*, 105ff, and Delekat, *Asylie*, 224.

[48]Beyerlin, *Die Rettung*, 107 (my translation). The German reads, "In alledem entspricht der Text des 17. Psalms so volkommen einem nach verschiedenen Akten gegliederten institutionellen Gottesgerichtsverfahren, daß seine Zuordnung zu einem solchen Verfahren recht wahrscheinlich erscheint."

[49]Gerhard von Rad, *Old Testament Theology*, (2 vols), London: SCM Press, 1975, 1:402.

[50]Kraus, *Psalms 1-59*, 246.

correct in suggesting that the initial purpose of the psalm was tied to the cultus. But in the absence of any clear guidance on how such a procedure would function von Rad may be closer to the purpose assigned to the psalm by the final editors. That is to say, although the psalm's origin is probably to be tied to the cult and the role of the sanctuary in the judgment of accusations, its place in the canon reflects a shift towards the general language of prayer. The editorial process has moved the psalm out of the cult and into a more general setting where it may continue to instruct the faithful in prayer.

Structure

The language of the psalm is slightly more stereotyped than Psalm 7, perhaps reflecting its point of origin, though it also uses the simile of the lion attacking the psalmist. All the elements of the psalm reflecting motifs of violence are found in the supplication (verses 6-12) and the prayer for vengeance (verses 13-14). However, the surrounding context provides important information on the ways in which the violence is to be understood. Although the language may suggest that physical violence is intended, we shall again note that the focus of the psalm is on the psychological assault of the enemy on the psalmist. This is, of course, consistent with the nature of the psalm as one reflecting false accusation. Although physical violence could be experienced as a result of the accusation being proved, the violence as it is presently experienced is understood in primarily psychological terms.

For our purposes, we can investigate the psalm's structure in fairly broad terms. We may outline it as follows:

1. An initial appeal in verses 1-2 that establish the context of the psalm with an appeal that Yahweh hear the cry of the psalmist.

2. This is followed in verses 3-5 by a negative confession, which functions as a declaration of innocence.

3. Verses 6-12 are then a supplication that seeks Yahweh's protection from the enemies, with particular reference in verse 12 to a central individual. This supplication is based on the declaration of innocence in the previous section of the psalm.

4. Finally, verses 13-15 are a prayer for vindication, a vindication that will demonstrate Yahweh's decision in the case.

In terms of the language that describes violence, our principle concern will be with the third and fourth sections of the psalm. Apart from one reference in verse 4 to "the ways of the violent", there are no references to any direct actions of violence in the opening sections of the poem. We shall, however, briefly examine these portions of the psalm since they establish a context for reading the direct references to violence.

Nature of Violence

The opening six verses of the psalm provide little in the way of reference to violence. These verses do, however, provide the evidence necessary to determine its context within this psalm. As we noted above, the plea of the first two verses indicates that the setting of the psalm is one of a legal appeal, with Yahweh specifically seen as the judge.[51] This is especially clear in verse 2:-

> May my vindication come forth from you,
> may your eyes see what is right.

It is apparent from such language that Yahweh is therefore approached as the judge, the one who is able to make a decision in the case. Such a decision necessarily includes both the right to decide guilt or innocence and to apply the punishment that is appropriate. It therefore not only involves, as Kraus observes, the petitioner's surrender to the decision of Yahweh in terms of guilt or innocence,[52] but also a recognition of the fact that the decision necessarily includes a determination of punishment. This fact is made explicit in Deuteronomy 17:8-13, which not only includes reference to the fact that certain cases would be decided in the sanctuary, but also that one was to act in accordance with the decision reached there (Deut 17:10-11). In context, this includes both a declaration of guilt or innocence, and the punishment.[53] Since the judge in the court case is given this right of punishment, a right that can include such violent decisions as the death penalty, it is apparent that from the outset the psalm operates with the perspective that the right of violence is surrendered to Yahweh along with the right to decide guilt and innocence.

The negative confession of verses 3-5 strengthens this perspective. Although verses 3 and 5 are quite general in character, there is a specific note at the end of verse 4, where the psalmist affirms that "I have kept myself from the ways of the violent (פָּרִיץ)." The term פָּרִיץ typically refers to such violent actions as robbery and murder, so that van Gemeren is able to characterise it as the ancient equivalent of gangsterism.[54] The psalmist thus denies any association with the violent, and particularly the unlawfully violent, but also characterises human violence as that which is typical only of the wicked. Those who act by the word of Yahweh's lips (verse 4) do not therefore act in such violence. The opening appeal and the negative confession thus serve together to indicate that

---

[51] Hossfeld and Zenger, *Die Psalmen*, 116.
[52] Kraus, *Psalms 1-59*, 246f.
[53] Cf. Peter C. Craigie, *The Book of Deuteronomy*, Grand Rapids: Eerdmans, 1976, 252. Although the dates of both Deuteronomy and this psalm are by no means settled in reference to one another, J. Gordon McConville, *Grace in the End: A Study in Deuteronomic Theology*, Carlisle: Paternoster, 1993, 45-64, has shown that there is good reason for believing that at least the traditions recorded in Deuteronomy are quite early.
[54] van Gemeren, "Psalms", 162.

the psalmist has already rejected personal retributive violence, with the matter being submitted to Yahweh as judge.

Our principal concern with this psalm begins at verse 7. The summons to Yahweh immediately prior to this point (verse 6) reminds us that the description of the enemies is in the context of prayer. The enemies themselves seem to be introduced in verse 7b, though it must be admitted that the text here, along with the rest of the psalm, is difficult. Here, they are described as מִתְקוֹמְמִים, presumably with the sense of "rebels"[55] against the power and order of Yahweh.[56] It is from these people that the psalmist seeks protection.

The same group is referred to again in verse 9, where they are pictured as surrounding the psalmist, an action against the poet's נֶפֶשׁ. Although the language here draws on military metaphors, especially from the siege, it becomes clear in verse 10 that the violence that they enact against the psalmist is primarily psychological in character. This is typical of the psalms that describe an attack on the נֶפֶשׁ,[57] as we see here that the actions of the enemies are essentially related to verbal assaults on the psalmist and a lack of compassion. Most probably, this relates to the false accusation raised against the psalmist. This would seem to be especially clear from the declaration of innocence present in verses 1-5.

In making their accusation, they have inflicted a psychological assault on the psalmist because of their combination of a closed heart and arrogant speech (verse 10). These references are indicative of the threat that they pose to the psalmist, though the fact that their speech remains a threat rather than direct action is what indicates that the violence at this point is at the psychological level. Obviously, a situation of accusation presumes a possibly violent outcome, and the imminence of such a possibility is clearly a factor that contributes to the psychological distress. The language here has therefore clearly shifted from the metaphor of a military conflict over to the actual situation being faced.

Within this flow of thought verse 11 poses some particular difficulties, especially since we have here plural suffixes rather than singular ones. This makes the psalm seem more like a communal lament than an individual one. Commentators are generally agreed that some emendation to the text is necessary,[58] though it may be that the MT can be retained if we accept that the psalmist refuses to be placed out of a wider community.[59] On balance, the

---

[55] So Kraus, *Psalms 1-59*, 249.
[56] That this is rebellion בְּיָמִינְךָ may be a vestige of royal language. For a rather different interpretation, cf. Craigie, *Psalms 1-50*, 160 and Dahood, *Psalms 1-50*, 96, both of whom make use of Ugaritic parallels.
[57] Though the presence of the word is in no way decisive for the interpretation of the violence.
[58] Cf. van Gemeren, "Psalms", 165.
[59] So Derek Kidner, *Psalms* (2 vols), Leicester: IVP, 1973, 88f.

standard emendations (as represented by NIV[60]) are more probable, though no certainty can be attached to them. But on either reading of the text, the violence described is a continuation of the previous verse, which means that it reflects psychological violence and is therefore not a reflection of a military assault on the land.[61] If the initial setting of the psalm was in the temple, then the "tracking down" mentioned in verse 11 could refer to the enemies waiting outside for an ordeal to be completed. But the shift from the cult to the canon relativises such a situation so that it is now to be understood in more general terms of enemies whose verbal assaults continue in spite of the supplicant's plea to God. In particular, it refers to the action of seeking someone with the specific aim of making an accusation.

Such a context therefore suggests that the switch to the singular in verse 12 with the simile of the lion[62] is not to be understood collectively or distributively, but rather as a deliberate move that aims to highlight the actions of the ringleader within the enemies.[63] There are thus a group of enemies, portrayed as being led by a ferocious individual, whose false accusations are a psychological assault on the psalmist. The imagery of the lion ready to pounce may also suggest that the enemy leader is still seeking an opportunity to make further accusations against the psalmist, or even that the enemy hopes to be the one to carry out the decision of the divine court against the poet. Although it may thus suggest the imminence of physical violence, such violence has therefore not yet taken place. It does, however, clearly create a sense of dread in the psalmist, a sense that is typical of psychological distress. The picture of violence against the psalmist is thus one of psychological assault as a result of a false accusation that is possibly linked to a continuing stream of false accusations.

Where this psalm is notably different from Psalm 7 is in its understanding of the future of the wicked enemies. In the wisdom world view of Psalm 7 the assumed position is that the perpetrators of violence will eventually suffer that which they attempted to bring about themselves. Here, though, the psalmist specifically entreats Yahweh to act. Verse 13 thus summons Yahweh to rise as judge, the one with the right to apply the penalty of the court:

> Arise, O Yahweh. Confront him, throw him down.
> Rescue me from the wicked with your sword.

This seems to be in balance to the call for justice that was called forth in verse 2. Within this context, the violence called for in retribution is controlled by the

---

[60] NIV most probably assumes לִנְטוֹתִי for לִנְטוֹת. Cf. van Gemeren, "Psalms", 165.

[61] As argued by Eaton, *Kingship*, 33, and tentatively Johnson, *The Cultic Prophet and Israel's Psalmody*, 248f.

[62] Here using both אַרְיֵה and כְּפִיר to enforce the image.

[63] Oesterley, *Psalms*, 1:161.

lex talionis (Ex 21:23f). Evidence of this is seen in the fact that the נֶפֶשׁ of the psalmist was under attack in the form of psychological violence, as is evidenced by verse 10. Now, it is only the נֶפֶשׁ of the psalmist that is to be delivered, though this requires that the ringleader[64] (note again the singular form) suffer a similar fate to that of the psalmist, though now from the hand of Yahweh. That this is to be done with the sword of Yahweh is probably to be understood as a comparable form of psychological torment, so that the military metaphors utilised in verses 9 and 11 are matched here.

Verse 14, however, provides numerous problems in interpretation, and the text is probably corrupt. The range of options available is somewhat bewildering,[65] reflecting the extent of the difficulties. It is, indeed, unclear as to whether we are to take the verse as a reference to the enemies[66] or as a description of the saints.[67] Although a reading that relates this verse to the hope of the righteous requires remarkably small changes to the text, there does not seem to be any contextual reason for moving in that direction. Indeed, the contrast supposed by verse 15 would lose its force if we read the verse in this way. If, however, the shift takes place half way through verse 14 (at צְפִינְךָ) we may have a situation where verse 14a represents a prayer for Yahweh to act against the enemy, whilst verse 14b describes the situation of the righteous in general terms before moving to the specific situation of the psalmist in verse 15. This is analogous to the development in verses 11-12 where the movement was from the enemies in general to the ringleader.[68] Such a break may also help us understand the relationship of the two halves of the verse.

Even acknowledging this possibility, verse 14a is still exceedingly difficult. Dahood vocalises the consonants מִמְתִים as מְמִיתָם, reading it as a hiphil participle with imperative force.[69] Although this is a plausible reading of the consonants, it seems to bring in a degree of literal reference to the expressions of the psalmist that are not supported by the context. It is probably better to assume that "Deliver me" (פַּלְּטָה נַפְשִׁי) is carried over by ellipsis from the previous line.[70] If this is so, then there is no direct action summoned against the enemies beyond that of the metaphors in verse 13. The summons to bring the wicked down is therefore a call to bring them into the same situation of suffering as that faced by the psalmist. Only violence that is equivalent to that inflicted is called for in application of the *lex talionis*.

The summons to Yahweh, calling on his action, also provides a context for understanding the verses 14b-15. Yahweh has been summoned to act, and there

---

[64]Cf. J. P. M. van der Ploeg, *Psalmen I*, J. J. Romen & Zonen, Roermond, 1973, 114.
[65]Cf. the variations listed in BHS.
[66]With most commentators.
[67]Leveen, "Textual Problems of Psalm XVII", 52.
[68]Craigie, *Psalms 1-50*, 164.
[69]Dahood, *Psalms 1-50*, 98f. Cf. Anderson, *Psalms*, 151 and Craigie, *Psalms 1-50*, 161.
[70]Cf. NIV.

is therefore no role for the psalmist in response to the enemies. That role is given to Yahweh. In such a setting, the petitioner may enjoy the presence of Yahweh.[71]

In summary, we can note that the psalm develops a pattern of psychological violence against the psalmist. We have suggested that this is indicated by the fact that physical violence is imminent because of the false accusation, but also because at this stage the psalmist reflects a condition of dread caused by the speech of the enemies. These are typical of psychological oppression, though as always the imminent threat of physical violence is an important factor. Similarly, we noted that in summoning Yahweh to act against the enemy, and in particular a ringleader, that what was sought was that they too should suffer violence that should be directly equivalent to that which had been inflicted on the psalmist.

Response to Violence

Psalm 17 stands with Psalm 7 in its understanding of violence. Again, the psalmist is experiencing psychological violence that is caused by false accusations that are being vigorously pursued. And as before, the psalmist does not choose to enact retributive violence personally-which is something that only Yahweh can do. In particular, the use of legal language in the way in which Yahweh is addressed points to the fact that the right of retributive violence belongs with him alone. Even so, the pattern of the *lex talionis* that is followed in the prayer to Yahweh serves to provide a limit on retributive violence.

As with Psalm 7, we also have a psalm here that has made a shift in meaning from the cult to the canon. An initially cultic setting may suppose that some of the psalm's elements are to be understood as reflecting the liturgy of the falsely accused. This may be particularly evident in the reference to Yahweh's presence (verse 15), but also in the night probe described in verse 3. But the placement of this psalm in the finished book has meant that what was originally a plea within a cultic and forensic context now addresses a wider range of settings in life. The psalm provides instruction on how to deal with this form of violence, such that petitioners must commit their cause to Yahweh since, as the true judge, the right of retribution belongs to him alone. This forms a major part of the instruction value of the psalm, since it provides a basis for understanding why human retributive violence is rejected. Further, since false accusation entails the experience of psychological harm and pain, the violence which can be summoned in retribution cannot go beyond this boundary.

---

[71]Dahood, *Psalms I*, 99, interprets this as a reference to the beatific vision. Mark S. Smith, "Seeing God' in the Psalms: The Background to the Beatific Vision in the Hebrew Bible", *CBQ* 50 (1988), 181, develops a far more plausible case for this simply being an experience of God's presence.

The psalm's conclusion also contributes to this instruction pattern. Since the psalmist is finally able to enjoy Yahweh's presence because the matter has been committed to him, the faithful are instructed that once the accusation has been appropriately submitted to Yahweh then they too may enjoy his presence. It is, indeed, the logical outcome of the submission to Yahweh as judge with which the psalm commences.

Psalm 109

Form Critical Discussion

Although Eaton has tentatively suggested that this psalm may be royal,[72] he has gained little support for such a position. The wider consensus is that the psalm is to be understood as the words of a private individual who has been falsely accused.[73] The exact nature of the accusation is unclear, though that is typical of such psalms. The accusations must, however, be particularly serious, and probably reflect a capital crime.[74] Several features point to the psalm as originating in a context of false accusation.

1. The opening summons (verses 1-2), invites God to speak in a context of accusations being made.

2. The enemies are described as "accusers" (variants on the root שׂטן) in verses 4, 20 and 29. The word שׂטן is best understood as a technical term describing a legal adversary.

3. The prayer for Yahweh's action in verses 6-7 invokes a legal judgment on the central adversary requesting an adversary (שׂטן) for him and that he be judged and found guilty (בְּהִשָּׁפְטוֹ יֵצֵא רָשָׁע).

These factors certainly point to the psalm as having originated in the context of false accusation. What is not clear, however, is whether or not we are to regard the psalm as having a cultic origin. A cultic origin is denied by Croft, though only on the grounds that an institution of psalms of false accusation remains undemonstrated.[75] Since he does not treat the psalm, Beyerlin also appears to deny a cultic origin. Delekat, on the other hand, treats the psalm as originating within the cult,[76] though his own re-construction is not particularly

---

[72]Eaton, *Kingship*, 81, treats it in his less clear cases.
[73]Croft, *Identity*, 143f, Mowinckel, *Psalms in Israel's Worship*, 1:219, regards the psalm as being a communal psalm in the "I" form, but does not expound it.
[74]With Mitchell Dahood, *Psalms III: 101-150*, Garden City: Doubleday, 1970, 99. Delekat, *Asylie*, 120ff, associates the psalm with the suspicion of theft, though there is no unambiguous evidence to support this suggestion.
[75]Croft, *Identity*, 140ff.
[76]Delekat, *Asylie*, 120ff.

convincing.[77]

However, the probability of a cultic origin for the psalm cannot be determined only on the basis of references within the psalm itself. Texts such as Deut 17:8-13 and 19:15-21 certainly assume that difficult cases will be presented to the levitical priests, who act as judges in the central sanctuary. Such texts clearly permit the possibility of a cultic origin. On the other hand, Deuteronomy also recognises the existence of local courts (Deut 16:18-20), so the presence of legal terminology alone is not sufficient to prove that the psalm originated in the cult. Cultic origin cannot be definitely proved, though that is perhaps a result of the canonical process as much as anything else. In spite of this, a cultic origin is to be tentatively proposed on the grounds (argued under "Nature of Violence") that the imprecation of verses 6-19 seems to be based on Deut 19:16-19, or at least the traditions that lay behind that text. Since the text in Deuteronomy is set in the context of the central sanctuary, it is likely that the language of the psalm reflects a similar context.[78]

The major issue in the overall interpretation of the psalm that concerns us here is the treatment of verses 6-19. A traditional reading of the psalm has seen this as the psalmist's imprecation against the enemy. Read in this way, these verses are a statement of what the psalmist desires Yahweh to do to the adversary. Alternatively, these verses have been treated as a quote from the enemies describing their desired end for the psalmist.[79] A further option, though not one that has gained much modern support, is the suggestion of Briggs, who interprets verses 6-15 as a Maccabean insertion to an existing poem, complaining that "there is little real poetry in this piece."[80] Since an assessment of the quality of the poetry of this section is a highly subjective issue,[81] we can only assess this position in terms of the more objective evidence of the text. Since the issues relating to a later insertion are effectively the same as the assumption that verses 6-19 represent a quote from the enemies, there is no need to treat Briggs' suggestion separately. The position taken here, that verses 6-19 are a coherent part of the psalmist's prayer, should be clear from what has

---

[77]The same can be said for the suggestion of Dahood, *Psalms III*, 99, that it was composed by the psalmist during a trial over which a "knavish judge" presided.

[78]Sabourin, *The Psalms*, 257, suggests that the psalm reflects a trial by ordeal, which must therefore be cultic, but does not indicate why. There is certainly nothing in the psalm that specifically indicates an ordeal.

[79]So Leslie C. Allen, *Psalms 101-150*, Waco: Word, 1983, 72f, Hans-Joachim Kraus, *Psalms 60-150*, Augsburg: Minneapolis, 1989, 338 and Weiser, *Psalms*, 691 who represent a formidable trio in support of such a position. More recently, this position has been adopted by T. H. Booij, *Psalmen III*, Nijkerk: G. F. Callenbach, 1994, 292, though without developing the argument. All seem, however, to be dependant upon the case argued by H. L. Creager, "Note on Psalm 109", *JNES* 6 (1947), 121-123.

[80]Briggs, *Psalms*, 2:364ff.

[81]And note the critique of Briggs by Dahood, *Psalms III*, 99, who regards the poetry of these verses as being of a particularly high quality.

already been said, though it needs to be justified.

It is difficult to see how the main alternative view, that these verses comprise the psalmist's quotation of the words of the adversaries, could be proposed solely on the basis of the text.[82] There is nothing that directly suggests that a quote has been introduced,[83] unless we take the change to the singular from the plural as indicating this. Although this is possible, and quotes introduced in poetic texts are seldom clearly marked, it is much more probable that the change to the singular indicates that the psalmist is now specifically concerned with a ringleader, with one who stands at the centre of the accusations that are made.[84] Such an interpretation would seem to be confirmed by verse 20 which then generalises the desired maledictions on the rest of the psalmist's opponents.

This interpretation of verse 20 has been challenged by Creager, who notes the unusual use of פְּעֻלַּת and argues that it means "work." He accordingly suggests that we should translate verse 20a as "This is the work of my adversaries."[85] The problem that this raises is that this outcome is said to be מֵאֵת יְהוָה. Creager is sensitive to the problem, but is forced to emend the text. The textual evidence offered, however, is not persuasive. Against this view, we may note that the meaning "reward" is well established for the word (cf. Is. 49:4),[86] though the ironic sense that it is given here is unique. Given that the word only occurs 14 times in the Old Testament we are hardly in a position to determine its full semantic range, but an ironic use of a word within an established semantic field seems probable. A traditional translation of the verse as "This is the reward of my accusers from Yahweh" is therefore still to be preferred. We may thus treat this psalm within this group,[87] and regard verses 6-19 as a prayer of imprecation uttered against the accusers.

---

[82]Eaton, *Kingship*, 81, thus comments that "there is no justification whatever for avoiding the natural direct meaning, however it may jar one's pious senses." Allen, *Psalms 101-150*, 73, rightly regards this as an argument that is simply a slur on those holding an opposing view. The basic problem, however, remains.

[83]However, NRSV has added the words "They say" at the start of the verse to indicate a quote. This move is criticised by J. Clinton McCann, *A Theological Introduction to the Book of Psalms: The Psalms as Torah*, Nashville: Abingdon, 1993, 113.

[84]So A. F. Kirkpatrick, *The Book of Psalms*, Cambridge: Cambridge University Press, 1902, 654f. Edward J. Kissane, *The Book of Psalms* (2 vols), Dublin: Browne & Nolan, 1954, 181, is dismissive of such a suggestion, but does not indicate his basis for doing so.

[85]Creager, "Note on Psalm 109", 122.

[86]BDB offers "reward" as the translation at four points.

[87]As noted, Briggs, *Psalms* 2:364ff suggests that the psalm is a composite, with v6-15 being a Maccabean addition. Even if this is true, and it is doubtful, the canonical structure of the psalm forces us to read it as a unity.

Structure

We have already dealt with most of the central issues related to the structure of the psalm, even if only implicitly. It remains for us here to outline with more clarity the major sections of the psalm.

The poem consists of three main sections that we can outline as follows:[88]

1. Verses 1-5 contain the appeal to God for assistance against the slanders raised against the psalmist.

2. Verses 6-20 then contain the imprecations of the psalmist against the accusers, imprecations that move from the specific instance of a ringleader to a generalised statement on all the adversaries in verse 20. A complex question that needs to be considered here is the inter-relationship between the violence that the psalmist wishes to see inflicted on the adversaries and that which they have inflicted on the poet.

3. The psalm is concluded in verses 21-31 by a prayer for deliverance.[89]

Nature of Violence

Because of the extent of the differences apparent in the three main sections of the psalm, it will be necessary to examine the nature of violence reflected in each separately.

The primary violence experienced by the psalmist in the first section can currently be seen as operating on the psychological level. This seems to be as a result of the false accusations made by the enemies. Although we once again have military metaphors utilised in terms of the enemies having surrounded (סְבָבוּנִי) and waged war (יִלָּחֲמוּנִי) against the psalmist, it is clear that these terms function only to describe the nature of the verbal assaults rather than an actual military conflict. The "military assault" in verse 3 is obviously a verbal attack on the psalmist's character.

In the context of a setting a false accusation, and especially one where the accusation may relate to a capital crime, it is easy to understand the use of the language of warfare. Further, if the accusation relates to a capital crime then

---

[88] A somewhat different three part analysis is offered by G. A. F. Knight, *The Psalms*, 2 vols, Edinburgh: St. Andrews Press, 1982, 1983, 2:177, who sees verses 1-15, 16-19 and 21-31 as comprising the main units of the psalm. Although verse 15 clearly marks the end of a sub-section in the block from 6-20, the change of person at verse 6 surely indicates a major shift in the structure of the psalm. Minor variations, such as that represented by Booij, *Psalmen III*, 228f, who sees the second section running only to verse 19 do not significantly affect the interpretation of the psalm.

[89] On the similarities in structure between this psalm and Psalm 7, cf. Kissane, *Psalms*, 181. Such a structural similarity could be taken as further evidence of a cultic origin for the psalm, given the way in which forms of expression tend to be standardised. At best, however, it can only be a supporting argument.

physical violence is obviously imminent since the psalmist's life is threatened by the actions of the accusers. Psychological violence is thus inflicted in two main ways, though they are obviously related to one another. First, the vigour of the language no doubt suggests that deep hurts have been inflicted, but they are hurts that arise from the barrage of slanderous accusations that have been made. Direct physical violence is not recorded here. Secondly, the imminence of physical violence also creates a situation of psychological distress.[90]

More complex questions relate to the violence reflected in verses 6-20. What we shall argue is that the violence that is described here is physical violence, but that it is physical violence that is an application of the law of false accusation. That is to say, what is sought from Yahweh is that the punishment that would have been applied to the psalmist in the event of the accusations being proved be applied to the accusers, and especially the ringleader. This individual is singled out as the initiator of the accusations. Such an interpretation explains the use of the singular form in that the ringleader was the initiator of the accusation, and thus the one bound by the law, as well as the strength of the imprecations. In addition, it provides an obvious reason for the expansion of the curse to cover all the psalmist's enemies in verse 20.

It is in light of the situation outlined in verses 1-5 that the psalmist prays for a court case in which the ringleader will be confronted by an evil man (רָשָׁע), with an accuser (שָׂטָן)[91] at his right hand. The situation that is sought reflects an exact reversal of the current situation, where the psalmist feels accused by the wicked. The psalmist is, however, already convinced of the guilt of the ringleader, so that verses 7-19 are actually a declaration of the desired sentence. Such a conviction of guilt on the part of the accuser would stem, of course, from the psalmist's conviction of personal innocence from the charges that have been laid. The imprecations that are sought are extensive, and would entail considerable psychological and physical violence against the accuser and his family. Verse 20 follows as a summary that seeks to apply this judgment on all the enemies, not just the ringleader.

That physical violence is sought against the central figure in the accusations is particularly apparent from verses 8-9. Verse 7 assumes that a decision of guilty will be reached as a result of the prosecution process, and verses 8-9 then ask:-

> May his days be few,
> may another be appointed in his place,
> may his children be fatherless

---

[90]Walter Brueggemann, *The Message of the Psalms*, Minneapolis: Augsburg, 1984, 83, therefore suggests that the "song of hate" in verses 6-20 come from "someone who has suffered deep hurt and humiliation."

[91]Dahood, *Psalms III*, renders the verse, "Appoint the Evil One against him, and let Satan stand at his right hand." This probably reads more into the psalm than is intended.

and his wife a widow.

It is clear that these verses ask that the death penalty be applied to the enemy, though the piling up of references to it also serves to indicate the vigour of the psalmist's wish. This is obviously the most extreme form of physical violence, but equally it is that which was sought by the enemies with respect to the psalmist. Physical violence is not only sought against the enemy, but also against his descendants, as is evident from verse 13:-

> May his posterity be cut off,
> may their names be blotted out from the next generation.

Equally, the imprecation seeks psychological violence against both the enemy and his descendants, even if the goal of this is seen in their death. In particular, we find in verse 12 a request for no one to show pity or kindness (חֶסֶד, מֹשֵׁךְ) to them, expressions that seek to match the experiences that the enemy has inflicted on the psalmist.

It is most probable that the judgement that is called for is an expression of the fact that the law required that a false witness suffer the fate that would have befallen the person accused had they been found guilty (Deut 19:16-21).[92] In support of this, we may point to the case of Naboth, whose property was taken from his family when he was convicted of a capital crime (1 Kings 21). The effect of this on the family would be disastrous. The plea in verse 8 presumably asks for Yahweh to apply the death penalty, whilst what follows in verses 9-11 would describe the situation of a family placed in such a situation.[93] The use of court language in verses 6 -7 would certainly support this interpretation, especially in its plea for the enemy's guilt to be revealed. If this interpretation is correct, then the prayer is an expression, albeit an extended one, of the *lex talionis*. Although physical violence is summoned in response to psychological violence, the prayer is finally one that calls forth Yahweh's justice, and in particular that Yahweh might judge the ringleader for his false accusations against the psalmist. In spite of the apparent anger that is present, there is still a clearly defined limit to the violence that can be sought.[94]

Direct references to violence in verses 21-31 are lacking, though the prayer

---

[92] So J. W. Rogerson and J. W. McKay, *Psalms 101-150*, Cambridge: Cambridge University Press, 1977, 59ff. The position taken here is based on their arguments.

[93] This is so irrespective of the difficulties of verse 10; cf. A. Guillaume, "A Note on Psalm CIX. 10", *JTS* 14 (1963), 92-93.

[94] An alternative interpretation is offered by David P. Wright, "Ritual Analogy in Psalm 109", *JBL* 113/3 (1994), 385-404 Wright interprets the curses as being a part of a ritual procedure that enabled the psalmist to rhetorically reshape the world in spite of the present injustice. There may well be some value in Wright's insights, but in light of the apparently clear background in Israel's legal tradition, this interpretation can only occupy a secondary position.

continually alludes to the results of the psychological distress that the accusations have brought to the psalmist. Verse 22b, for example, affirms, that "my heart is pierced within", whilst in verse 25 the psalmist is described, with respect to the accusers, as "an object of scorn." There is no direct reference to violence, but its effects are clearly seen.

Similarly, the prayer for Yahweh's vindication of the psalmist to be apparent to all (verses 26-29) assumes that the imprecations sought in verses 6-20 are to be applied. Verse 27 asks:-

> Let them know that this is your hand,
> that you, O Yahweh, have done it.

There is thus a continuation of the wishes of the second section, albeit expressed in a more moderate manner. Nevertheless, this is a further indication of the fact that the violence in retribution is something that is wholly submitted to Yahweh for action. The psalmist does not seek justification for personal retribution.

Response to Violence

There is thus an effective acknowledgment on the part of the psalmist of the desire for vengeance, but at the same time there is a refusal to act in personal vengeance. As an expression of covenant faithfulness, that desire for vengeance is handed over to Yahweh since the right to vengeance is exclusively his.[95] That this is so is apparent from the fact that the imprecation is directed to Yahweh, and also in the further prayer that it should be apparent to all that the retributive action comes from Yahweh alone.

In addition, we once again have a situation where the retributive violence that is sought is limited by the law of retribution. As extreme as the imprecations may be, and there is perhaps an extent to which the psalmist gloats over them, they are not a request for unlimited violence. The violence that can be sought in retribution is limited by Israel's legal traditions. The psalm, for all its anger, clearly indicates the limit, even if that limit is quite extreme. The sort of retributive violence indicated by Lamech's Song of the Sword (Gen 4:23-24) is not permitted in this context.

As indicated above, the canonical place of the psalm makes it unclear if we are to read it as having originated in the cultus. If, however, we are correct in asserting that the cult was the place of origin for this psalm then the pattern offered by this psalm is similar to that of the others in this group. Overt cultic markers are no longer present, but in its present form the psalm instructs the innocent as to the limits of retributive violence and the fact that such retribution belongs to Yahweh alone.

---

[95]Cf. Bruegggemann, *Message of the Psalms*, 85ff.

Psalm 139

Form Critical Discussion

Although neither Eaton nor Johnson have included this psalm in their royal collections, such an identification is argued by Dannell, who argues that the psalm was probably used by the king as a declaration of innocence in the New Year festival.[96] Dannell reaches this conclusion on the basis of certain cultic terms that he isolates in the psalm, especially the references to Yahweh searching (√בחן) the psalmist. The most likely setting for this, he suggests, is the king's declaration of innocence in the New Year's festival. He is followed in this interpretation by Croft, who adds the more specific element of the psalm being a part of the king's declaration of innocence before the ritual battle in the Autumn Festival.[97]

The grounds for such an interpretation seem slight,[98] since there is nothing in the psalm that is expressly royal.[99] Croft's own stated methodology for identifying the individual requires that there should be expressly royal motifs in the psalm for a royal identification to be made. In the absence of any of these, a royal identification is to be doubted. Further, the evidence for the proposed New Year Festival is by no means clear. Although a number of scholars have been persuaded of its existence, the argument for a royal identification for this psalm within such a festival seems dangerously circular. The posited festival provides the *Sitz im Leben* for the psalm, which in turn supports the existence of the festival. In any case, by the time of the final editors of the Psalter were active such a festival could only have been a vague historical memory, and it is by no means clear that they have assigned it a royal status. Accordingly, it seems better to take the view that we have here the words of an individual Israelite, a view that fits the evidence provided by the absence of clearly royal features.[100]

Although the royal interpretation has not been widely favoured, there has been considerable discussion on the *Gattung* of the psalm.[101] As is well known,

---

[96]G. A. Dannell, *Psalm 139*, Uppsala: Almqvist Wiksells Boktryckeri, 1951, 32ff.
[97]Croft, *Identity*, 96.
[98]This is especially clear when Dannell, *Psalm 139*, 30, is forced to admit that his proposed incubation rite in v18 can be presupposed, though with nothing to expressly indicate its presence. This leads to circular reasoning.
[99]Kraus, *Psalms 60-150*, 512, claims that such an interpretation cannot arise from the text, but only through an exegesis governed by the Uppsala School.
[100]W. Stewart McCullough and William R. Taylor, "Psalms", in G. A. Buttrick (ed), *The Interpreter's Bible* vol 4, Nashville: Abingdon, 1955, 712, thus head the psalm as a "Prayer of a Devout Soul".
[101]Note the extensive list of suggestions in German scholarship noted by Helen Schüngel-Straumann, "Zur Gattung und Theologie des 139. Psalms", *BZ* 17 (1973), 39-

Gunkel felt that the psalm was a creation hymn, though one that burst the bounds of the group.[102] Von Rad describes this psalm as a "didactic instrument for dealing with attacks on the faith."[103] Durham, although not using a form-critical label, regards the psalm as a confession of the presence of God.[104] Whilst all these elements are undoubtedly integrated into the psalm, they are not necessarily reflective of the purpose of the psalm. A stronger case can be made for what now appears to be an emerging consensus that the psalm is to be included with the prayers of the accused.[105] A finer analysis than that is probably not possible. The following should be noted in favour of such an assessment:

1. The declaration of God's omniscience in verses 1-6 is specifically centred on Yahweh's personal knowledge of the psalmist. Omniscience as such is not the issue: it is that the psalmist is intimately known by Yahweh.

2. The declaration of omnipresence in verses 7-12 is again specifically related to the fact that there is no place where the psalmist can be separated from God.

3. The awareness of God's role in the creation of the individual (verses 13-16) is again tied to personal, intimate knowledge, including an awareness of the whole of the psalmist's life.

4. The psalmist is personally identified with God's thoughts, and implicitly with God's purposes in verses 17-18. Taken as a whole, the build up to verse 18 is a doxology of God's awareness of the psalmist, a doxology that finds its application in what follows.

5. Verses 19-22, it shall be argued, take the form of a self-curse. If the psalmist is guilty, then the elements of the curse would have to be personally applied.

6. The final petition in verses 23-24 are a summons, calling God to search and judge the psalmist. Such a summons is typical of the prayers of the accused.[106] This petition thus links back to verses 1-18. Since God has already searched the psalmist, then this is to be understood as a judicial statement that is called forth.

Taken as a whole, these elements suggest that doxological material in verses

---

41. Her own assessment is that this is a didactic psalm from the cult. S. Wagner, "Zur Theologie des Psalms CXXXIX", *Congress Volume Göttingen 1977*, VT Supp. 29, Leiden: E. J. Brill, 1978, 358, notes 6 main suggestions, but with a further 6 sub-groups under the classification of the prayers of the accused.

[102] Cited by Kraus, *Psalms 60-150*, 511.

[103] Gerhard von Rad, *Wisdom in Israel*, Nashville: Abingdon, 1972, 49.

[104] John I. Durham, "Psalms", in C. J. Allen (ed), *The Broadman Bible Commentary* vol 4, Nashville: Broadman, 1971, 445.

[105] Cf. Claus Westermann, *The Living Psalms*, Edinburgh: T & T Clark, 1989, 267.

[106] A fact that is curiously brought out by the analysis of Dannell, *Psalm 139*, 23ff, though he does not develop the insight, preferring to utilise it in his royal reconstruction.

Psalms of False Accusation

1-18 are a preparation for God's judgment of the psalmist, a judgment that is expressed in vigorous terms, presumably because the accusation that has been made is a capital offence. The psalm is thus an appeal to the omniscient God to demonstrate that the psalmist is innocent of a charge that has been made.

Finally, we must ask whether or not there is evidence that the psalm originated in the cult. Certainty here is less than possible, but a cultic point of origin is certainly probable. Three elements point towards a cultic origin for the psalm.

1. The consistent use of creation theology points to a strong contact with the priestly tradition in the Old Testament.

2. The summons to God to a specific time of searching, when he is in fact always searching the psalmist, points to a time in the temple when this would take place, possibly through some form of ordeal.

3. Finally, the possibility (noted below) that the charge against the psalmist might be idolatry, which is a fundamentally cultic crime, suggests a point of origin within the cultus as the logical place to seek a declaration of innocence of the charge.

These factors cannot prove a cultic origin for the psalm, but they are certainly suggestive of it.

Structure

It is sometimes suggested that Psalm 139 is actually a composite work in which verses 19-22 are an interpolation that break the flow of thought which otherwise moves easily between verses 18 and 23.[107] Certainly the tone of these verses is markedly different from the rest of the psalm. However, the essential unity of the psalm has been demonstrated,[108] and the sharp change at v19 is better understood as being the point to which the previous verses have been building.

As we have indicated above, the gentler material found in verses 1-18 is an essential foundation for verses 19ff. When understood in this way, the psalm is an appeal to the omniscient God to demonstrate that the psalmist is not guilty of some charge. It is probable that the charge against the psalmist is one of idolatry, a charge that simply involves a change in the pointing, reading עָצָב (idolatry) for עֹצֶב (pain) in verse 24.[109] Although there is no direct reference

---

[107] E.g. McCullough and Taylor, "Psalms", 713. A more radical analysis is proposed by Briggs, *Psalms*, 2:491, who finds three basic psalms, with extensive glosses.

[108] Cf. Leslie C. Allen, "Faith on Trial: An Analysis of Psalm 139", *Vox Evangelica* 10 (1977), 5-7.

[109] Following Dahood, *Psalms III*, 299. We should, however, note the observation of Allen, *Psalms 101-150*, 260, that the reference may be no more than a declaration of loyalty, in which case a specific charge is still not indicated. On balance, though, it would seem odd to introduce such a reference unless it was raised in the accusation.

to idolatry in the earlier section of the psalm, idolatry was a capital offence (eg, Deut 13), which would help to explain the psalmist's plea that the wicked be slain. In addition, the traditional reading is awkward, requiring a sense not apparent in the noun's other two uses. This is, admittedly, slight evidence, but an accusation of idolatry would certainly provide greater justification for the psalmist's plea in verse 19.

In terms of the psalm's unity, we may further note that there are a number of inclusions utilised. These all point to the original unity of the psalm.[110] Thus, verses 23-24 form an inclusion with verse 1. At the same time, there is a tight inner structure to verses 19-24, with אם occurring in verse 19 and verse 24, adding a small inclusion to the division.[111] These patterns attest to the unity of both the psalm as a whole and of verses 19-24. Although there is a deep caesura between verses 1-18 and 19-24, the unity of the whole psalm remains, with verses 1-18 providing a doxological theology that is specifically applied to the accusations that have been made.[112] Given the fact that it is only in verses 19-24 that the explicit references to violence occur, our primary concern is with this section of the psalm. It cannot, however, be interpreted in isolation from verses 1-18, and we will briefly need to examine the context that they provide.

Nature of Violence

If we are correct in assuming that Psalm 139 is a psalm of someone falsely accused, then we should not be surprised that its approach to violence is essentially the same as that found in the other psalms within this group.

The situation of false accusation, and especially one related to a capital offence, naturally opens the possibility of psychological violence being suffered as a result of the accusation. This would seem to be borne out by the psalm itself, though it offers fewer clues than the other psalms that we have examined. In fact, verses 1-18 provide little evidence for the form of violence suffered. There may, however, be a hint in the doxological form, and especially in its references to Yahweh's knowledge of the psalmist.

In a context in which the psalmist has suffered in some way from the violence associated with a false accusation, the problem is presented to Yahweh so that the psalmist might be vindicated.[113] That the violence experienced so far

---

[110]Dannell, *Psalm 139*, 22, says that the "psalm is woven from the top throughout, without seams."

[111]Jan Holman, "The Structure of Psalm CXXXIX", *VT* 21 (1971), 307.

[112]Allen, "Faith on Trial", 22, appropriately cites Gunkel's dictum, "nicht abstrakt-philosophisch, sondern konkret-religiös."

[113]Edward J. Young, *Psalm 139: A Study in the Omniscience of God*, Edinburgh: Banner of Truth, 1965, 94f, offers the suggestion that the language of the prayer simply reflects David's recognition of the fact that the enemies of God cannot be allowed to succeed. In doing so, however, he is unable to offer a *Sitz im Leben* for the psalm.

is primarily psychological may perhaps be seen in the conclusion of the doxological material. Here it is stressed that Yahweh knows the psalmist's thoughts, the one thing that the wicked do not know. Indeed, in verses 17-18 the psalmist claims:-

> How precious[114] are your thoughts to me,
> how vast is their sum,
> if I were to count them they would be more than the sand,
> yet I am still with you.

The point of such a claim, and especially in the face of claims to the contrary, is that the psalmist is submitting all thoughts to God for evaluation. The claim of the enemies, of course, must be that this is not true; otherwise there would be no point in making the protest. The psalmist's own claim may therefore point to psychological distress as having been suffered as a result of the accusations that have been made. Indeed, the intimate awareness that God is said to display of the psalmist throughout the psalm could all be related to the psychological distress that has been suffered as a result of the claims of the enemies. Such an interpretation is by no means certain, however, and needs to be confirmed by the more explicit material in verses 19-24, though even there the references are allusive.

Arising out of the doxological material, we should note that when the language of violence is used in verses 19-22, it is presented in the form of a prayer. Admittedly, it asks for physical violence against the wicked (רָשָׁע), but does so only on the basis that the psalmist may be included among those slain if the charge is proved to be true. This is clear from the fact that the wicked are not explicitly identified, and if the charge that has been made was true then the psalmist would be among those slain. The psalmist is effectively placed under a self-curse. The validity of this curse is rooted in the fact that Yahweh is intimately aware of all that the psalmist does and thinks. It is the ultimate application of the intimate knowledge to which the opening verses of the psalm testify.[115]

Since the psalmist allows for the possibility of being included among the wicked when the whole point of the psalm is to prove that the opposite is true, we have some evidence that may point to the violence that has been suffered. The enemies have not made a direct physical assault, but they have impugned the psalmist's character. This would represent a form of psychological violence in that it would exclude the psalmist from normal fellowship. In addition, the

---

[114]The sense of יָקְרוּ is by no means clear. If an Aramaic sense is followed (cf. Dan 2:11), then we would render the line "How difficult are your thoughts for me." The balance of usage in the Old Testament, not withstanding the number of Aramaisms in the psalm, tips the balance in favour of the more traditional rendering.

[115]Cf. Allen, *Psalms 101-150*, 257f.

fact that the wicked to whom the psalmist refers must be those who have committed a capital crime of some sort suggests that the accusation against the psalmist is also of a capital crime. This is so whether or not we can establish that the crime is one of idolatry. The imminent possibility of a death sentence suggests the presence of psychological violence, though it is not developed by the psalm as such.

Further, according to verse 21, the wicked of whom the psalm speaks seem to have acted in terms of physical violence against Yahweh, perhaps in terms of their actions against the righteous. This is clear from the fact that the psalmist speaks of those who "rise up" against Yahweh, an action that implies an assault of some sort, though the details remain unclear. The prayer seeks to demonstrate that the psalmist is aligned to Yahweh, as is clear in verse 20, so that in verse 22 the enemies of Yahweh are the enemies of the psalmist. It would seem, therefore, that the assault on Yahweh is seen in an attack, perhaps by false accusation, on the innocent psalmist. It is against these people that the psalmist summons Yahweh to act. Violence is permitted, but only against the enemies of Yahweh, and the right to such violence does not belong to the psalmist but to Yahweh. The psychological and physical violence of the wicked is rejected as an unacceptable option. Only Yahweh has the right to act in violence on behalf of the individual. In seeking this decision, the prayer effectively asks that Yahweh apply to the enemies what they have done to the psalmist.

Although, as we have noted, the evidence for the nature of violence in this psalm is not always as clear as in the other instances, this would still seem to be an application of the *lex talionis*, though it would show some modification from the law dealing with false accusation that we noted was also active in Psalm 109. To slay the wicked is no more than to carry out the punishment that they themselves apparently sought, though it continues to place the psalmist in some danger. Under those circumstances, it is only appropriate that the psalmist asks to be searched by Yahweh.[116] It is both a declaration of innocence, and an inauguration of action against the wicked.

Response to Violence

The response that we find to violence in this psalm is thus entirely consistent with that which we found in the other psalms within this group. Although the accusers here remain ill-defined, and as a result the nature of all the violence cannot be determined with accuracy, it is clear that the psalmist regards Yahweh's decision in the matter as the crucial one.

The assaults that have been made on the psalmist would appear to have resulted in considerable psychological distress. Although the psalmist then prays for physical violence in response to the wicked, its form as a self-curse

---

[116]Cf. Oesterley, *Psalms*, 557.

means that the violence that Yahweh is summoned to enact has the psalmist's own life as the first point of reference. These are not words of hatred and blind violence-they are an application of covenant loyalty that seeks vindication from God. Unlike the other psalms in this group, the psalmist does not make a declaration of innocence. Instead, a declaration of innocence from God is what is sought.

Psalm 139 thus seeks to provide a reference point for those accused. Although its original setting within the cult may have required some form of ordeal as the means of God searching the psalmist, its place within the canon offers the psalm instead as a means of instruction-those who are accused and suffer psychological assault as a result may not seek to justify themselves through personal retribution. Rather, they are summoned to seek the intervention of Yahweh as the only true judge, an intervention that requires them to submit to him first. Where violence is necessary in response, the right to that violence is his alone. To seek personal retribution is not acceptable.

Further, although the possible response here is extreme, it is still a response based on the law on false accusation. The psalmist has been charged with a capital offence, and the punishment that may be meted out by Yahweh is determined by this. Thus, in terms of its function within the book, the psalm seeks to offer instruction that not only affirms that the right of response to violence belongs to Yahweh alone, but also that there is a limit to the violence that can be sought in response. Again, unlimited violence in retribution is shown to be unacceptable for the faithful.

Conclusion

The evidence that we have examined indicates that there was a consistent response to violence in the Psalms of False Accusation. In each case, the violence that was experienced by the psalmist was predominantly psychological, being related to the verbal assaults that were made on them and the accusation itself. Since the nature of an accusation means that physical violence is an imminent possibility we are also reminded that the accusation itself is a form of psychological violence.

The pattern is developed further in each case in that the psalmist summoned Yahweh as the judge to decide the case and, effectively, to carry out a sentence on the party who actually was guilty. In the cultic setting in which these psalms probably originated this decision making process was most likely related to an ordeal of some sort. But the canonical use of the psalms has moved them from that context. These psalms no longer live only in the world of the cult-their place in the book of Psalms means that they are now available to be utilised by worshippers in a variety of contexts. Instead, they now function as models of prayer for the accused, prayers that summon Yahweh to act. As models of prayer they are no longer directly concerned with the cultic environment that gave them birth, though the influence of that environment can still be felt.

Such a shift indicates that in the placement of these psalms in the Psalter there was a definite editorial intention at work. There is an instructional value now assigned to them, an instruction that suggests that those who suffer the psychological assault of a false accusation are summoned to call on the decision of Yahweh. Admittedly, this means that there is no longer a definite means by which the decision of Yahweh can be determined, but is consistent with the wider world view of the Old Testament that sees Yahweh as the lord of all history. This also means that a new value is given to the prayer elements that ask for action against the enemies. In the judicial cultic setting, prayers that were limited by the *lex talionis* or the law of false accusation had a purpose in law. They were uttered in legal context that gave them a specific meaning. The shift that has taken place means that these prayers now model a limit on retributive violence, a limit that is given over solely to Yahweh.

The instruction that is thereby offered does not indicate the means by which the worshipper will know the decision of Yahweh. Once these prayers are removed from any ordeal procedure in the temple it is difficult to know how the decision could be communicated in any clear way. However, these psalms do not seek to answer that question, even as they did not directly answer the question when they were used in the temple. What they seek to do instead is to inculcate an attitude among the worshipping community, an attitude that declines to respond personally to various forms of accusation and the violence that accompanies it. What is encouraged instead is submission to Yahweh. How the problems are to be resolved is unclear. But the only right granted is submission to the divine response.

The consistent pattern that we have indicated as being active here thus indicates that the formation of the book of Psalms has followed a specific outline in respect to this area of violence. It is a pattern that now instructs those who are faithful but accused to commit their case and their right to Yahweh as the sole judge. Further, it models a response to violence that denies any human the right to return violence for violence, but stresses instead that the right to violence is something that belongs to Yahweh alone.

Chapter 3

Prayers for Protection

Introduction

Overview and Critique of Research

The *Gattung* of the "protective psalm" was initially proposed by Mowinckel, though building to some extent on the work of his pupil Birkeland.[1] Mowinckel saw these psalms as those that reflect an imminent danger into which Yahweh is summoned to act by providing protection. Accordingly, they reflect a situation where violence is threatened, but no act of physical violence has yet taken place. We shall modify this position by noting that the threat of imminent physical violence represents in itself a form of psychological violence. In addition, he felt that the "tone of the protective psalms is brighter than that of the psalms of lamentation."[2] As a result, these psalms often include an expression of confidence. They are, however, to be distinguished from the Songs of Trust since the motif of confidence in the Songs of Trust is expressed in the form of a hymn-like eulogy, whereas in these psalms it is related to the particular need.

It must be admitted that Mowinckel regarded the protective psalms as being among the national psalms of lamentation, including those of the "I" form. However, it is difficult to see how the reader is to identify the "I" of many of these psalms as representing the nation in some way. In part, Mowinckel's approach seems to have been shaped by Birkeland's suggestion that the enemies of the individual were always foreign nations.[3] If we follow that line of interpretation then the references to enemies in these prayers must make them national psalms. However, once we recognise the diversity of options

---

[1] Mowinckel, *The Psalms in Israel's Worship*, 1:219ff. Cf. Patrick D. Miller, *They Cried to the Lord: The Form and Theology of Biblical Prayer*, Minneapolis: Fortress, 1994, 105f.
[2] Mowinckel, *The Psalms in Israel's Worship*, 1:220.
[3] Birkeland, *Die Feinde* and *idem*, *Evildoers*.

available for the identification of the enemies,[4] then the need to identify the prayers for protection as necessarily being national prayers falls away. The enemies may be foreign powers, and under such circumstances we could consider the "I" to be the king or some other national figure. But making a decision as to the identity of the enemies, or at least the broad classification to which they belong, must be done on a case by case basis. In general terms, though, we should work on the principle that where there is nothing in the psalm that specifically indicates foreign powers, then it is best to assume that such an identification is not to be made. That is to say, one would need to find explicit evidence that the enemies are foreign powers before the "I" could be identified as a national figure.[5] Of course, it is possible that in the literary history of any particular psalm the enemies may have been foreign powers, but the absence of specific markers that indicate this means that in their canonical role the identification of these enemies is broadened. Granted that the matter will need to be assessed on a case by case basis, the probability remains open that the "I" in some of the prayers for protection is a private individual.

Some scholars regard certain of the psalms that are to be treated here as reflecting the prayers of the accused. Taking Psalm 3 as an example, we may note that Beyerlin,[6] Delekat,[7] and Kraus[8] all regard the psalm as a part of the liturgy associated with the prayers of the accused. It must be admitted that such an association within the cultic history of the Psalter is possible, though probably finally not provable. However, the absence of any explicit formula that identifies these psalms with such a setting means that the canonical context does not assign such a role to them. All that is apparent to the reader of the book of Psalms is that in these particular psalms an individual makes a request for protection from the attack of enemies. If these psalms ever were associated with the prayers of the accused, the final editors have fashioned the book of Psalms such that no clear connections remain.

Method of Approach

The group of psalms that can be classified as prayers for protection are somewhat looser than those examined in the previous chapter. The characteristic mark of these prayers is that they suppose either a situation of violence that is currently being enacted, or, more commonly, one where direct violence is threatened. Although these psalms typically conclude with an

---

[4]Cf. Anderson, "Enemies and Evildoers in Psalms" and Croft, *Identity*, 47.
[5]Against Birkeland, *Evildoers*, 31ff, who argues that because the enemies in some psalms can be positively identified with Gentile powers, those not explicitly identified as such within a given psalm must still be interpreted along those lines.
[6]Beyerlin, *Die Rettung*, 75ff.
[7]Delekat, *Asylie*, 51ff.
[8]Kraus, *Psalms 1-59*, 137f.

expectation of deliverance, they are unlike the Songs of Trust in that such an affirmation of certain deliverance is not central. Rather, what is central is the plea that is made for deliverance, a plea that is often rooted in previous experience. It is this previous experience that provides the basis for the affirmation of trust. The prayers for protection and the Songs of Trust are, however, closely related to one another with the essential difference being that one reflects an existing confidence in deliverance from Yahweh, whilst the other intercedes to request it. In a sense, therefore, the prayers for protection stand midway between the laments, as classically understood, and the Songs of Trust.

We should note that in examining these psalms we will often have to deal with the psalmist's perception of reality, especially in terms of the actions of the enemies. There is no necessary reason that requires that we affirm that the psalmists' perceptions must be correct. On the other hand they may well be quite correct – but the nature of the psalms means that we have no means of knowing how accurately they portray the enemies, and especially their motives.

Fortunately, our concern is with the responses to violence, which means that we are concerned with how the psalmist responds to the perceived actions of the enemies. We cannot determine the accuracy of the psalmists' perceptions, but neither could the final editors of the Psalter. In collecting these psalms, they assumed (either explicitly or implicitly) that the responses to violence that are expressed were appropriate. Therefore, our treatment of these psalms will examine the canonical function of these responses and what is therefore modelled and taught by these psalms as they now stand. The actual accuracy of the psalmists' perceptions does not markedly affect this process, but the consistency of the response may well be indicative of the instruction of the Psalter.

In seeking to identify these prayers for protection, we will therefore need to seek psalms that fulfil the following criteria:

1. The psalm must present a situation of either current or potential violence in which the psalmist is the victim.

2. The psalmist in this context needs to be recognisable as an individual and not a national figure.

3. The situation of violence and not the announcement of trust needs to be the central theme of the psalm.

On this basis, we shall argue that it is possible to identify Psalms 3, 27, 35, 55, 56, 64 and 143 as individual prayers for protection.[9]

---

[9] Although the unity of Psalm 27 is often disputed, and a good case can be made for seeing verses 1-6 and 7-14 as originally discrete units, the canonical context has provided us with only one psalm. In terms of our concerns at this point we can regard this as a single psalm, though some justification will be given for this position in the treatment of the psalm.

Psalm 3

Form Critical Discussion

In terms of the discussion above, a strong case can be made for identifying this psalm as a prayer for protection. In particular, the following should be noted:

1. The situation presupposed by verse 2 with its reference to numerous foes rising up against the psalmist suggests that there is a current need in which Yahweh's protection is sought from unnamed foes. A situation of oppression is clearly supposed, in which Yahweh needs to act and provide protection from the enemies.

2. The summons קוּמָה יְהוָה הוֹשִׁיעֵנִי אֱלֹהַי (verse 8) is the point at which Yahweh's protection is specifically sought. This arises naturally out of the situation described in the opening verses.

3. Although there are also expressions of confidence included in verses 4-5 and verse 9, they are expressions that are related to the plea for help, so that the prayer for protection and not the expression of confidence is the dominant motif in the psalm. Nevertheless, the presence of such expressions of confidence as these indicates that the prayers for protection and Songs of Trust shade into one another.

This evidence clearly suggests that it is appropriate to include this psalm among the prayers for protection. However, this leaves open the question of whether this is a national or individual prayer for protection, and we must therefore consider this matter.

Form critical research has not yet resolved the identity of the speaker here with any precision. Eaton regards this as a clearly royal psalm, citing the various military references within the psalm as proof of this position.[10] Such an identification is followed by Croft who is prepared to go more confidently in the direction established by Eaton and interpret the psalm as a prayer for protection in battle that is uttered by the king.[11] Weiser also follows a royal interpretation, but places the psalm in the royal ritual of the cult as a part of the expression of Yahweh's warfare against the foes of the nation.[12]

Whilst support for a royal interpretation is widespread, such a conclusion is by no means unanimous, nor is it required by the text of the psalm as we have it before us. In particular, the royal interpretation seems to depend upon a neglect of the place of metaphor within the psalms. Birkeland's assertion that the context of the psalm is one of war[13] accordingly needs to be examined since it

---

[10]Eaton, *Kingship*, 27ff.
[11]Croft, *Identity*, 114. Cf. Craigie, *Psalms 1-50*, 71ff, who defines it as a "royal protective psalm."
[12]Weiser, *The Psalms*, 117.
[13]Birkeland, *Evildoers*, 32.

provides the strongest support for a royal interpretation. If the references to war are metaphoric, then the basis for a royal interpretation will be greatly eroded.

Craigie neatly summarises the seven key points in support of a royal interpretation, all of which depend upon the military language being taken at face value. He notes:

i) The reference to "foes" (3:2) and "enemies" (3:8).
ii) The references to victory (3:3, 8).
iii) God is described as a shield (3:4).
iv) "People" (3:7) may be employed with the nuance "army".
v) The people are "deployed" against the psalmist (3:7).
vi) The expression "Rise up, O Lord" (3:8) is parallel to the words spoken on the departure of the ark for war (Num 10:35).
vii) "Victory belongs to the Lord" (3:9) sounds like a battle cry.[14]

These factors lead Craigie to accept the royal interpretation of the psalm. Apart from these elements, Eaton adds the additional point of the title, which clearly suggests a royal association for the psalm, though he does acknowledge that the title has been added later.[15] However, Eaton's point is not persuasive since the title represents a scribal midrash more than an authentic record of David's experience.[16] The title is therefore representative of a scribal re-reading of the psalm in which David becomes the model of experience, the means of orienting readers in the application of the psalm to their own context.[17]

Without attempting to refute Craigie's linguistic elements point by point, it is important that we pause to note the function of the language in the psalm. The fullest exploration of this question is that of Kim.[18] In his exegesis of the psalm, Kim notes the presence of a large number of terms that clearly reflect a military background. He notes further, however, that these terms are all drawn from Israel's holy war tradition, and that stereotyped language is therefore used in describing the enemies. Such language has no necessary foundation in an actual military conflict.[19] Although Kim concludes that the belief that the psalm finally reflects in Yahweh's saving power stems from the holy war tradition, it still does not make this a psalm that has its *Sitz im Leben* in an actual military conflict. If Kim's analysis is correct, then the stereotyped nature of the language of the psalm more probably points to a situation of an individual experiencing conflict with enemies.[20] It would represent a case where an

---

[14] Craigie, *Psalms 1-50*, 71.
[15] Eaton, *Kingship*, 29.
[16] Contra, Kidner, *Psalms*, 53f.
[17] Cf. Tournay, *Seeing and Hearing*, 192.
[18] Ee Kon Kim, *A Study of the Rapid Change of Mood in the Lament Psalms, With a Special Inquiry Into the Impetus for its Expression*, unpublished PhD Thesis, Union Theological Seminary, 1984, 187-208.
[19] Von Rad, *Holy War in Ancient Israel*, 131, points out that the holy war tradition continues into the Psalms long after the last holy war had been fought.
[20] So also W. S. Prinsloo, *Die Psalms Leef!*, Pretoria: NGKB, 1991, 1f.

individual in a situation of conflict draws on language that has now become standard to present the situation to Yahweh. Such a conflict could take a number of forms, but the presence of language that so clearly reflects on the holy war tradition, especially where that tradition provides a governing metaphor makes a royal interpretation improbable. Rather, it is evidence of a democratisation of language. Commenting specifically on Craigie's arguments, though with broader implications for the royal line of interpretation generally, Prinsloo thus observes that,

> This attempt by Craigie is a classic example of where the Gattung is not determined on the basis of the content of the text, but on the basis of a hypothetically reconstructed Sitz im Leben.[21]

Since there is nothing in the psalm that is specifically royal, we may treat this psalm as one that reflects the words of an individual, and, as we shall argue below, one that reflects the currently experienced violence primarily, though not exclusively, on the psychological level. This is reflective of the physical threat posed by the enemies. A *Sitz im Leben* beyond this point is impossible to determine. There are any number of situations in which an individual might complain to God, but the stereotyping of the language makes an actual determination impossible. However, the absence of either an affirmation of innocence or a plea for justice makes it unlikely that the final editors have included this as a psalm of the accused. As with the royal interpretation, one can only make that connection on the basis of a hypothetically reconstructed *Sitz im Leben*, and not on the basis of the text as it stands.

Structure

Although the term סֶלָה does not always provide a clear division marker within a psalm, it certainly seems to fulfil that function here, at least where the delineation of the first two and final divisions of the psalm are concerned. The divisions of the psalm would, however, be apparent even without this marker. Setting aside the superscription, the following evidence points to the structure of the psalm:

1. The form of address to Yahweh in verses 2-3, coupled with the repeated use of words based on the root רבב clearly marks this off as a separate section within the psalm indicating the present distress of the psalmist.[22]

---

[21]Prinsloo, *Die Psalms Leef!*, 8 (my translation). The Afrikaans reads, "Hierdie poging van Craigie is 'n klassieke voorbeeld van waar die *Gattung* nie bepaal word op grond van wat in die teks staan nie, maar op grond van 'n hipoteties gerekonstrueerde *Sitz im Leben*."

[22]John S. Kselman, "Psalm 3: A Structural and Literary Study", *CBQ* 49 (1987), 573f argues that the presence of rhyming features and a common syntactic structure means

Prayers for Protection 57

2. At verse 4 we read וְאַתָּה יְהוָה מָגֵן בַּעֲדִי. The change to a direct second person address here, coupled with statements that point to Yahweh's protective power through to verse 5 (eg, Yahweh as the one who answers the cry of the psalmist), indicates the basis of hope that the psalmist expresses. Although this hope has not yet reached its fulfilment, that hope is Yahweh alone. The change to first person statements in verses 6-7 ("I lie down and sleep....I will not fear") suggests a further expression of hope based in experience.[23] Since verses 4 and 7 are basically in parallel to one another, we should see the second section of the psalm as continuing from verse 4 through to verse 7. The importance of this becomes clearer when we recognise that the psalm refers to the presence of some "ten thousand"[24] (again from the root רבב) enemies who have set themselves against the psalmist.

3. From this context of known and experienced protection, we naturally shift into the prayer for protection in verses 8-9. This is marked initially by the shift to imperative verbs in verse 8 (קוּמָה יְהוָה), a shift which is in turn balanced by the declaration of hope in verse 9,[25] "Salvation comes from Yahweh!"

The structure of the psalm suggests the nature of the movement of thought within it.[26] We therefore need to examine the psalm in its major parts.

Nature of Violence

The presence of extensive holy war language means that the psalm is full of

---

that the first section should cover verses 2-4 (cf. Hossfeld and Zenger, *Die Psalmen*, 55, and Kissane, *Psalms* 1:11 for similar structures). However, the argument seems to place style before substance, and since the opening ו of verse 4 seems to be adversative, it is best to see a change at the end of verse 3.

[23]The common suggestion that we find here a reference to a period of incubation (e.g. Kraus, *Psalms 1-59*, 140) makes little sense if this is a psalm of a private individual who prays for protection from enemies. In the context of statements of hope in the previous verses, the use of the perfect שָׁכַבְתִּי is perhaps to be understood as referring to what has characteristically taken place in the past - the psalmist has always slept and woken because of Yahweh's sustaining power, or simply to a good rest the previous evening, unless we take these as euphemisms for Sheol. What is stressed is the continuing nature of Yahweh's sustaining of the psalmist - note the shift to the imperfect of סמך. It is thus the element of hope that remains central. Cf. Lindström, *Suffering and Sin*, 400.

[24]The number itself is pure hyperbole, generated to some extent by the desire to play with the root רבב.

[25]Van der Ploeg, *Psalmen I*, 47, regards verse 9 as a gloss. Although this is possible, the structural analysis of Prinsloo, *Die Psalms Leef!*, 1, indicates that it has an important functional role within the finished psalm.

[26]This structure is supported by Prinsloo, *Die Psalms Leef!*, 1 and N. A. van Uchelen, *Psalmen I*, Nijkerk: G. F. Callenbach N. V., 1971, 23.

references to violence of varying sorts. It is not surprising therefore that the title of the psalm links it to David's experience in fleeing from Absalom. Although this reflects a military situation, the title clearly portrays the psalm as one reflecting an *individual* conflict rather than a military one.[27] This suggests that those responsible for the titles of the psalms saw this psalm as reflecting a situation of conflict between individuals in which violence is expressed. Accordingly, we need to resolve the question of the nature of violence that is described. An exegesis that closely follows the structure of the psalm should make this process clearer as the divisions of the psalm will enable us to clarify its purpose.

The initial description of distress in verses 2-3 is quite general in nature. The psalmist simply refers to a multitude of undefined enemies, noting their claim that God will not provide deliverance. Although expressions such as the use of the root קום (verse 2) in the sense of rising against another would often suggest the presence of physical violence, as occurs for example in Psalm 18:40, it is also commonly used of psychological violence, such as we find in Psalm 54:5. What is probably decisive in favour of a psychological reading of the violence that is experienced is the fact that the enemies address the נֶפֶשׁ of the psalmist. As we have argued, in contexts of violence this commonly reflects some form of psychological assault on the psalmist. Against this, we should also note the semantic breadth with which the word נֶפֶשׁ is employed within the psalms. The sense attributed to נֶפֶשׁ in psalms dealing with violence tends towards a psychological sense, but is not in itself determinative. It can only be determined on a case by case basis. However, the context provided by verse 3 would also support this interpretation. The claim that the enemies deny the presence of salvation from God[28] would suggest a psychological assault, perhaps in terms of a denial of the validity of the psalmist's faith. Although a strictly military reading of these opening verses is possible, the balance of evidence would suggest that it is more probably to be understood as describing some form of psychological assault upon the faith of the psalmist. Actual physical violence remains a very real possibility, but it does not appear as if it has actually been experienced yet. It is, however, regarded as imminent, and since the charge of the enemies is "God will not save him" (verse 3) the implication would be that physical violence is highly likely. The threat itself has violent overtones, but at this stage remains in the psychological realm because of its potential nature. Nevertheless, such an interpretation is not absolutely clear, reflecting the rather generalised nature of the language used. A military reading, though, seems unlikely.

If this interpretation of the opening verses is generally correct, then the use

---

[27] In spite of the attempts of Kidner, *Psalms* 1:53ff and J. Ridderbos, *De Psalmen I*, Kampen: Kok, 1955, 29f, there is little to commend the view that the title reflects the actual *Sitz im Leben* of the psalm.

[28] A point which is refuted within the structure of the psalm in the closing declaration.

Prayers for Protection 59

of the term "shield" in verse 4 (מָגֵן, cf. Psalm 18:3) need not be understood in a military sense. Rather, it is an expression of trust, an expression that utilises the figure of a shield to describe Yahweh. That a military reading of verse 4 is not necessary would seem to be substantiated by the second half of verse 4 and the whole of verse 5:

> ....my glory who lifts my head.
> I cry aloud to Yahweh,
> and he answers me from his holy hill.

In the expression of confidence that we find here all military language is dropped, and a more general series of metaphors are applied instead. Military language only returns at verse 7 with the reference to the ten thousand who surround the psalmist. Even here, though, there are important factors which suggest a non-military reading of the psalm, although the metaphor itself is a military one. The most important of these is the fact that in this case the psalmist is clearly speaking of a hypothetical situation, the hyperbolic number of 10 000 simply reflecting the play on the root רבב from verses 2-3.[29] In addition, the balance between verses 4 and 7 should be noted.[30] Since verse 4 uses a military metaphor for protection, we should not be surprised to note that it recurs here. All of it, however, is simply employed to point to Yahweh's protective power.

The only real evidence of the situation of the psalm is provided by verse 8. The summons to Yahweh to arise is obviously taken from the holy war tradition. Although we have suggested that the psalm does not represent an actual military situation, the use of the imperative at this point suggests that the oppression of the enemies is considered to be imminent, though it leaves open the possibility of the form of a more direct assault. Protection is currently required, but the language of the psalm leaves open the possibility that there will be a further assault for which extra protection will be required. Although it is possible to treat the two perfects in verse 8b, שִׁבַּרְתָּ and הִכִּיתָ, as indicating either a past experience of deliverance or as representative of what Yahweh typically does,[31] and thus providing grounds for confidence, such an interpretation seems improbable. The present situation is clearly one in which protection is sought, and the grammatical structure requires that we translate the two perfects as imperatives.[32] Deliverance must be sought from Yahweh, and the right to violence in response is limited to him. Since the request is that

---

[29] Kim, *Rapid Change*, 191f points out that improbable numbers in battle are a part of the Holy War tradition.

[30] The relationship between these verses is clearly indicated by the structural analysis of Prinsloo, *Die Psalms Leef!*, 1.

[31] So Oesterley, *Psalms*, 128.

[32] Cf. van Gemeren, "Psalms", 78.

the enemies should be struck on the mouth (verse 8), it seems likely that the prayer for Yahweh's action is governed by the *lex talionis*. The pain inflicted by the enemies comes from what they say (verse 3), and the prayer for Yahweh to strike them on the mouth is thus intended to respond precisely to the assault.[33]

This is summed up by the declaration of verse 9, with its affirmation of the underlying truth that supports the prayer for protection - deliverance is something that only Yahweh can bring.[34] This thought then leads into the closing prayer which asks that the people of Yahweh would know this blessing.

In summary, we can affirm that the references to violence in the psalm reflect violence at the psychological level. Physical violence is both threatened and perceived as highly imminent. It is the extent of this threat that generates psychological violence against the psalmist. This pattern was established through the use of language that uses physical violence as a governing metaphor precisely because such a threat is in itself violence. In addition, the psalm sought retributive violence from Yahweh against the enemies, but the extent of this violence is limited by the extent of the actions, both actual and threatened, by the enemies.

Response to Violence

If the above exegesis is sustained, then it is readily apparent that the psalmist does not seek Yahweh's approval for any form of direct retribution on the enemies that is carried out personally. Rather, there is a need to submit oneself to Yahweh and to seek his protection. Submission of one's cause to Yahweh is, indeed, the dominant feature of the psalm's response to violence. Past experience may have suggested that this is an appropriate approach, and when the need for protection arises this is the approach that is once again followed. Personal violence in retribution is ruled out as unacceptable in the context of faith in Yahweh. Although the reference to ten thousand is hyperbolic, it is clearly intended to indicate the extent of the threat, a threat with which it is believed Yahweh is able to deal.

Instead of personal retribution, the psalm models what the editors of the Psalms must have considered to be a suitable prayer in the context of personal oppression. The psalm suggests that the appropriate response is one of trust in Yahweh, trust that is expressed in a prayer for his protection and action against

---

[33] It is therefore probable that if we have an image of Yahweh as a warrior here (so Marc Brettler, "Images of Yahweh the Warrior in the Psalms", *Semeia* 61 (1993), 141f), then the actions described are also metaphorical.

[34] As the MT of verse 9 stands it is an affirmation of the fact that deliverance belongs to Yahweh. Anderson, *Psalms*, 75, follows Kissane, *Psalms*, 11, in suggesting that we should read יהוה לי for ליהוה on the basis that it improves the parallelism. However, the improvement is at best slight.

Prayers for Protection 61

the enemies, no matter how many they may be. In praying for this protection, both the individual and the community are instructed that whatever retribution is sought, it must be related to the context of oppression-one does not seek a greater level of retributive violence than has either been personally suffered or is currently threatened. Not only must retribution only be sought from Yahweh, it must be retribution that is appropriate to the context.

Psalm 27

Form Critical Discussion

Perhaps more than elsewhere, the form critical discussion of this psalm has been less than satisfactory. In particular, the focus upon the apparently disparate concerns in verses 1-6 and 7-14 has yielded generally unhelpful results. From the time of Gunkel on it has been customary to divide the text into two separate psalms, treating verses 1-6 as a psalm of confidence and verses 7-14 as an individual lament.[35] Although there are substantial differences between the two sections of the psalm, we need to note that they are not enough to justify such an absolute separation. Craigie[36] points to the use of a number of key root repetitions in both halves of the psalm, notably ישע (verses 1 and 9), צר (verses 2 and 12), לב (verses 3, 8 and 14), קום (verses 3 and 12), בקש (verses 4 and 8) and חיים (verses 4 and 13). This use of key terms, plus an essentially common 3+2 meter in both sections, suggests that the psalm was always intended to be a unity. In addition, the presence of repeating literary patterns in both halves of the psalm (see below) also suggests its unity.[37] An appropriate reading of the psalm needs to seek to understand the ways in which the two halves function in relation to one another.[38]

On the other hand, we cannot ignore the very real points of difference between the two halves of the psalm. Even on the basis of a very superficial reading it is apparent that verses 1-6 and verses 7-14 also show marked points of dissimilarity. On the most basic level we only have to note the strong element of trust in verses 1-6 and place it in contrast to the petition of verses 7-

---

[35]Cf. Anderson, *Psalms*, 219. R. Kittel, *Die Psalmen übersetz und erklärt*, Leipzig: Deichert-Scholl, 1922, 105ff merely assumes the division, whilst van der Ploeg, *Psalmen I*, 180, observes that "The psalm clearly consists of two completely different parts" (my translation). The Dutch reads "De Psalm bestaat duidelijk uit twee geheel verschillende delen: A, vs 1-6; B vs 7-14."
[36]Craigie, *Psalms 1-50*, 231.
[37]Cf. N. H. Ridderbos, *Die Psalmen*, 210ff and J. Ridderbos, *De Psalmen I*, 230ff.
[38]Note also the unifying structural elements highlighted by the textual analysis of J. H. Coetzee, *Die Spanning tussen God se "verborge wees" en Sy "ingrype om te red." 'n Eksegetiese Ondersoek na 'n Aantal Klaagpsalms.* unpublished DD thesis, University of Pretoria, 1986, 106ff.

14.³⁹ In addition, verses 1-6 are about Yahweh whilst verses 7-14 are (in part at least) addressed to Yahweh.⁴⁰ Lindström also points to the different strophic arrangements in the two halves of the psalm. He observes that although both are two stanza poems with three strophes each, the extent of the strophes and the length of the cola vary considerably.⁴¹ Such differences certainly give credence to the suggestion of two originally separate units.

The above discussion indicates that our assessment of the poem needs to take both the unity and the diversity of the psalm seriously. On the one hand, the finished psalm shows some signs of unity, evident in meter and a shared vocabulary. On the other, there are important structural and form critical differences that cannot be ignored. A solution to this problem may, however, be tentatively offered. The points of contact between the two halves of the psalm suggest that the two halves never circulated as two units that were separate from one another. Yet they are clearly discrete units. It is possible, therefore, that the poet responsible for verses 7-14 has taken an existing Song of Trust (verses 1-6), and consciously used it as a means of expressing trust in God prior to the presentation of the prayer for protection. The rather generalised statements of trust in verses 1-6 would provide a suitable basis for then approaching Yahweh with a prayer for protection.⁴² Although verses 1-6 may therefore have originally circulated as an independent psalm and verses 7-14 are clearly a discrete unit, verses 7-14 have probably never existed apart from verses 1-6. If this analysis is correct, we must therefore interpret the psalm as a whole. Further, this analysis also suggests that the *Sitz im Leben* of the finished psalm is to be found in verses 7-14 and not verses 1-6.⁴³

The key questions then become a determination of the type of the psalm and the identity of the speaker. Again, there is a diversity of options available. Eaton again takes the military language of the opening verses literally and declares that the speaker is the king. In addition, he points to the first person designations of Yahweh such as "Yahweh is my light" (יהוה אוֹרִי, verse 1) as being typical of "royal style."⁴⁴ This latter point needs to be treated with caution, since the whole question of "royal style" often seems to reflect a circular argument in Eaton's work. Eaton also places the psalm within his

---

³⁹Oesterley, *Psalms*, 196, somewhat unfairly regards verses 7ff as a "pathetic outpouring" in contrast to verses 1-6.
⁴⁰van Uchelen, *Psalmen I*, 183, points out that third person references to Yahweh do occur in both halves of the psalm.
⁴¹Lindström, *Suffering and Sin*, 153.
⁴²The opposite alternative, that verses 1-6 have been added to an existing psalm of verses 7-14 seems less probable. It is the specific situation of verses 7-14 that motivates the prayer, suggesting that this is where the point of adaptation arose.
⁴³On this line of argument, cf. Lindström, *Suffering and Sin*, 153.
⁴⁴Eaton, *Kingship*, 39. Alternatively, Tournay, *Seeing and Hearing*, 124, sees the expression as evidence of a ritual theophany.

reconstruction of the royal rites,[45] in which approach he is followed by both Craigie and Croft, though it is notable that they each offer a different reconstruction of the ritual.[46]

The principle argument in favour of a royal interpretation of the psalm is the presence of extensive military language. The question is then whether we are to read such language literally or metaphorically. Obviously, a metaphoric reading would substantially weaken the case for a royal interpretation. In this respect, it is noteworthy that the expressly military language is limited to the opening 6 verses. From verse 7 onwards all such language is dropped. In addition, the presence of balanced אם clauses in verse 3 strongly suggests that the situation being envisaged is to be viewed as entirely hypothetical:[47]

> If an army besieges me,
> my heart will not fear.
> If war breaks out against me,
> in this I will trust.

It is therefore unlikely that an actual military situation is envisaged here.[48] It is more probable that an extreme military situation is used as a metaphor to describe the certainty of Yahweh's protection of the psalmist. In addition, we should note that the references to false witnesses in verse 12 cannot be easily reconciled to a royal reading of the completed psalm. It is more probable therefore that this is a psalm of an individual where royal elements have been used, but in a metaphoric way. Again, this reflects the democratisation of such language.

This then raises the question of the specific *Gattung* of the psalm. Granted that it is a psalm of an individual, does the content point towards this also being a prayer for protection? Here the structural division of the psalm is helpful, and the following points should be noted:

1. Just as the prayer for protection preceded the statement of assurance in Psalm 3, so this psalm also has a statement of confidence followed by the prayer for protection. Verses 1-6 are thus to be understood as an expression of confidence in Yahweh as the one who will protect the psalmist.

2. An extreme, though probably hypothetical, situation is envisaged. From this situation, an expression of confidence is given in verse 5 with an expansion in verse 6, the first two lines of which balance the reference

---

[45] Eaton, *Kingship*, 186.
[46] Craigie, *Psalms 1-50*, 231, Croft, *Identity*, 101ff.
[47] So also Coetzee, *Die Spanning*, 107 and 123f. Cf. Miller, *They Cried to the Lord*, 230.
[48] This would also hold true if a ritual battle in an annual ceremony is in view.

to enemies in verse 2,[49] while the next two lines with their focus on the worship of Yahweh balance the statement of assurance in verse 1. A similar balance is seen between the opening and closing sections of verses 7-14. The appeal in verse 7 is balanced by the affirmation of hope in verse 14,[50] while the hope of seeing Yahweh in verse 8 is balanced by the expression of hope in verse 13.

3. Although these statements of confidence might suggest that the psalm should be viewed as a Song of Confidence,[51] the fact that the final address to the psalmist in verse 14 encourages an attitude of waiting for Yahweh's deliverance in light of a situation that has clearly not been resolved suggests rather that the psalm is to be understood as a prayer for protection. This would also seem to be the most logical interpretation of the plea for Yahweh's assistance in verses 7-9, a plea that comes out of the actual *Sitz im Leben* of the psalm.

Taken together, these elements suggest that we can treat this psalm as a prayer for protection. There is, admittedly, an extensive expression of confidence within the psalm but the presence of an unresolved situation of oppression in verses 10-12 along with the closing admonition all suggest that this is the appropriate context in which to interpret the psalm.

The determination of the *Sitz im Leben* of the psalm is equally awkward. The references to false witnesses who are seemingly equated with the psalmist's foes in verse 12 has suggested to Kraus that the psalm represents a liturgy for the falsely accused in Jerusalem.[52] Oddly enough the references to dwelling in the temple have suggested to others that the psalm is one that is spoken by those away from Jerusalem.[53] Associated with the reference to accusers is the fear of being separated from a relationship with Yahweh (verse 9). These elements are taken to support the conclusion that the psalm's *Sitz im Leben* is in the liturgy of the accused. Although this is an attractive suggestion, the context of the enemies is first raised in verse 11 and the actions of the false witnesses are pictured as part of the wider range of activities associated with the enemies. Most importantly, the psalm includes neither a plea of innocence nor a prayer for Yahweh to test the psalmist. Although false accusation is therefore one of

---

[49] Although verse 2 uses both צר and איב and verse 6 only איב, the parallel is clear since the two terms are necessary for the meter in verse 2.

[50] Kraus, *Psalms 1-59*, 337, suggests that verse 14 may represent an oracle of hope given to the psalmist, since the suffix on לבך suggests someone addressing the psalmist. If so, the oracle has been well integrated into the final text of the psalm.

[51] So, tentatively, Brueggemann, *Message*, 152f.

[52] Kraus, *Psalms 1-59*, 333, cf. Beyerlin, *Die Rettung*, 122ff and Delekat, *Asylie*, 103ff and 197ff. Delekat assigns different functions to each the psalm's halves, thus ignoring the canonical shape of the psalm.

[53] Louis Dorn, *The Beatific Vision in Certain Psalms: An Investigation of Mitchell Dahood's Hypothesis*, unpublished ThD Thesis, Lutheran School of Theology, Chicago, 1980, 235.

Prayers for Protection 65

the things from which the psalmist seeks protection, we cannot limit the *Sitz im Leben* solely to the situation of false accusation. A wider context of oppression is envisaged, though the general nature of the terminology makes it impossible to be specific.

Structure

The discussion so far has already indicated the major divisions of the psalm. As indicated, the line of interpretation being followed here is that verses 1-6 probably circulated independently at one stage, and verses 7-14 were subsequently added. This then suggests a simple structure for the whole psalm as follows:

1. A declaration of confidence (verses 1-6), containing three strophes of two verses each.

2. A plea for Yahweh's protection from the activities of enemies (verses 7-14),[54] also containing three strophes of two verses each.[55]

Nature of Violence

The motif of violence occurs in both halves of the psalm. Because of the current shape of the psalm, it will be necessary to consider the form of its presentation in each half of the prayer before attempting to bring the strands together.

An initial reading of the references in verses 2-3 may suggest that a military attack is being described and that the violence described is therefore physical. However, the essentially hypothetical[56] nature of the description means that we need to understand this reference in light of the actual situation that is described in verses 7-14.[57] The situation here is complicated by the absence of any firm guidance as to the *Sitz im Leben*. In a sense, however, this opens up the range of possible situations of violence. The situation reflected in verses 2-3, with its references to enemies advancing and armies rising against the psalmist, is descriptive of the full range of forms of violence without actually being finally linked to any one of them. As an expression of full and profound trust, it looks

---

[54]Van Gemeren, "Psalms", 243, sees a chiastic structure in which verses 1-3 and 13-14 are in balance, as are verses 4-6 and 7-12. However, the balance between the middle components seems strained.

[55]The differences in the strophic arrangements are apparent in the analysis of Coetzee, *Die Spanning*, 106.

[56]As noted above, the fact that both lines in verse three begin with אם strongly suggests that there is not an actual situation of enemies being faced.

[57]It is conceivable that when verses 1-6 stood alone that an actual military situation was understood, though this is not a necessary interpretation. As noted above, Tournay, *Seeing and Hearing*, 124ff, has equally plausibly shown that a ritual context could be understood.

to Yahweh as the one who protects from all situations of oppression and violence, whether they be psychological, physical or social.

The portrayal of Yahweh in this context is important for the interpretation of the whole psalm. The description of Yahweh in verse 1 by the psalmist as אוֹרִי וְיִשְׁעִי are essentially an affirmation of the same point-Yahweh is the one who gives victory in times of assault.[58] The position that the psalmist must adopt in this is purely defensive, trusting in Yahweh, who is the מָעוֹז of the psalmist's life (verse 1). The same point is made in verses 5-6 which affirm that Yahweh protects the righteous,[59] protection that is achieved solely through what is done by Yahweh and not the righteous themselves. The confidence expressed in verses 1-6 thus addresses the possibility of all forms of violence, affirming that the fear of any form of violence is unnecessary because of the protection offered by Yahweh.[60]

These affirmations of confidence are then taken up in verses 7-14, verses which provide the actual setting of the finished psalm. That this is so is apparent from the fact that we now encounter a description of an actual situation of distress, especially in verse 12 where the psalmist uses the phrase כִּי קָמוּ־בִי in describing the activities of the enemies describes what has already taken place. In light of the general statements of confidence in verses 1-6, the psalmist now approaches Yahweh seeking that the protection described there be applied to the present situation.

A number of factors point to the violence described here as being something that is currently experienced psychologically rather than physically. In particular, we need to note that physical violence is imminent, but its threat is in itself an expression of violence. Since false accusations are a part of the actions of the enemies it remains possible that the outcome of the present distress will be physical violence of some form, and this may well contribute to the distress. However, the following factors suggest that physical violence remains potential rather than actual, and that the violence that is currently being experienced is primarily psychological:

1. In verse 9 the psalmist appeals to Yahweh not to turn away from him.[61] This is suggestive of psychological distress, because it is assumed that should Yahweh do so then physical violence would follow. It is the potential for physical violence that distresses the psalmist.

2. The appeal in verse 12 that he should not be handed over to his oppressors indicates that actual physical suffering has not yet taken place. Again, it points to the imminent possibility of such a result.

3. Although the false witnesses are pictured as breathing out violence

---

[58]Van Gemeren, "Psalms", 243.
[59]Although the psalmist is not directly characterised as righteous, the contrast with the רשׁע suggests that this is to be understood.
[60]Cf. Brueggemann, *Message of the Psalms*, 153.
[61]The masculine suffix in verse 14 indicates that the psalmist is a man.

(חָמָס) they have not yet triumphed. They are a threat rather than someone who is currently initiating direct physical action.[62]

4. The expression of hope that is found in verse 13, where the psalmist declares לוּלֵא הֶאֱמַנְתִּי לִרְאוֹת בְּטוּב־יְהוָה בְּאֶרֶץ חַיִּים, presumes that Yahweh will act before the psalmist's life is directly endangered. Again, this suggests that this is not yet the case, though it is assumed to be imminent.

Taken together, these factors suggest that it is psychological distress that is reflected in the second half of the psalm. This does not mean that we are therefore required to read the opening verses in these terms alone. They remain a statement of confidence that can be generally applied, and verses 7-14 have then taken up their theme in a prayer for protection from violence that is currently experienced psychologically but which will move over into physical violence if any charges made are deemed to be proved. Throughout the actual prayer for protection (verses 7-9) it is assumed that only Yahweh can protect the intercessor in such a situation. That is why the final verse can encourage a hopeful waiting[63] on Yahweh throughout the current ordeal. Yahweh is seen as the one who is able to provide protection in the current psychological assault, and in the physical attack that may follow.

In summary, we can affirm that the opening part of the psalm (verses 1-6) provides a platform that expresses confidence in Yahweh's ability to provide protection for the righteous in all conditions of violence. Verses 7-14 are then an application of this confidence to a specific instance of violence. The violence experienced is currently psychological in that it derives from the threat of the imminence of physical violence, though this situation is still perceived as one of violence. It is in this situation of violence, both current and potential, that the protection of Yahweh is summoned.

Response to Violence

The response to violence here follows the same pattern as the other psalms in this section. In the midst of the oppression, the psalmist appeals to Yahweh for deliverance, expressing the request that he bring deliverance (verse 7) from the distress. No attempt is made to have some retributive action on the part of the psalmist justified. Rather, the plea to Yahweh is allied with expressions of confidence that assert that the right to deal with this situation belongs to Yahweh alone.

This response in this psalm goes beyond that of Psalm 3 in one important

---

[62]In passing, we should note that this use of חָמָס is indicative of the fact that the term can describe an experience as violence even when no physical action has taken place.

[63]For the element of hope in waiting reflected in the verb קוה, cf. Walther Zimmerli, *Man and His Hope in the Old Testament*, London: SCM Press, 1971, 6ff, and 33ff for specific reference to Psalm 27.

respect. There we also saw the theme of hope present, though the element of security was related only to the specific situation faced. Here, the benefits of trust in Yahweh are extended so that his protection is understood to be active in all aspects. Although the complete psalm now speaks to a specific situation, it does so from the perspective of a general encouragement towards trust in Yahweh as the protector. It is his protection that is sufficient in all circumstances, and although the prayer for protection relates that to a specific circumstance, the faithful are taught through this psalm that the only acceptable response to Yahweh is finally to trust in his protection. It is thus suggested that human activism that goes beyond such trust that is expressed through prayer is unnecessary since the protection offered by Yahweh against all forms of violence is alone sufficient. Indeed, in light of the opening affirmations of Yahweh's saving power, it is a denial of the faith to seek to overcome the enemies on one's own.

The final encouragement (verse 14) points to the canonical function of the psalm in that it urges a hopeful waiting on Yahweh. It is thus a final reminder of the need to put the faith that is expressed in the opening verses in practice, no matter what form of oppression is suffered. The psalmist's own context thus indicates the type of situation in which such faith in God is to be summoned and applied. By including this psalm in their collection, the final editors have therefore also suggested that the confidence indicated in verses 1-6 has an application in real experience, an experience that now models such trust in Yahweh in the midst of oppression as the appropriate response to all forms of violence. How the faithful are to experience this deliverance remains unstated. They are, however, assured that a hopeful waiting on Yahweh is the appropriate response to violence in all its forms.

Psalm 35

Form Critical Discussion

As with Psalms 3 and 27, the discussion of the *Gattung* of this psalm has been less than helpful. However, where there were essentially only two choices available for Psalm 3, the diversity of metaphors that are found in Psalm 35 has provided a range of options. Thus, the speaker could be the king or a private individual. The *Sitz im Leben* could be one of military conflict, false accusation or sickness. The multi-dimensional use of language within the psalm permits this range of options, and is perhaps the primary reason for the uncertainty in the form critical analysis of the psalm.

A good case can be made for seeing this psalm as a prayer for protection. Once this point is established a finer analysis can be attempted. The following points need to be particularly noted:

1. The opening imperatives of verse 1 (רִיבָה, לְחַם) specifically

summon Yahweh to act. This clearly pre-supposes a situation of current distress that requires his protection, an interpretation that can be amply demonstrated in the body of the psalm. This is especially so in the balance of the summons to Yahweh to act in the rest of the first three verses, and especially in the fact that he is summoned to act against those who contend (ריב) and wage war (לחם) against the psalmist. This is notably clear in the petition that is addressed to Yahweh at the end of verse 3, אֱמֹר לְנַפְשִׁי יְשֻׁעָתֵךְ אָנִי. It is the protection of Yahweh that is sought.[64]

2. The imprecation against the enemies (verses 4-8) includes a reference to the "net" spread by the enemies for the psalmist. Irrespective of the type of violence that this implies, it indicates that the prayer comes out of a situation of current distress.

3. The picture of violent witnesses (עֵדֵי חָמָס) in verses 11-16 describes a situation of current oppression, from which Yahweh is summoned to act and rescue the psalmist.

4. In verses 19-21 there is a further description of the activities of the enemies in which they gloat over the psalmist and devise accusations that have no basis in reality. In verses 22-25 Yahweh is summoned to act in response to this situation by rising to the psalmist's defence. We note especially the summons addressed to Yahweh in verse 23:

הָעִירָה וְהָקִיצָה לְמִשְׁפָּטִי
אֱלֹהַי וַאדֹנָי לְרִיבִי

Although the language is that of the court, it is utilised to portray Yahweh as the defender of the psalmist.

All the above elements are consistent with the interpretation of Psalm 35 as a prayer for protection. On the other hand, this psalm differs from Psalms 3 and 27 in that the element of trust is expressed in more uncertain terms.[65] Other elements, however, are less than clear. Fundamental to our concerns here are two questions that arise from the text - is the supplicant a royal figure or a private individual? Secondly, is the protection that is desired part of the prayers of the accused, or is a wider base of protection sought? We will address these questions in turn.

Once again, Eaton has argued that this is a clearly royal psalm, a position that he takes on the assumption that the military language of the opening verses is to be taken literally.[66] If we follow this line of interpretation, then we need to see the psalm as envisaging a situation external to Israel that is both military and legal. According to Craigie, the *Sitz im Leben* of the psalm is one in which the king faces the threat of war from foreign powers who use a supposed

---

[64]Cf. Miller, *They Cried to the Lord*, 141.
[65]Brueggemann, *Message of the Psalms*, 63.
[66]Eaton, *Kingship*, 41f; cf. Craigie, *Psalms 1-50*, 285f.

violation of a treaty agreement as the basis for launching the battle.[67] The psalm would then be a prayer uttered in the temple prior to the departure for battle. However, the argument in this instance is less than persuasive, since it means relegating all the other metaphors within the psalm, which are abundantly present, to a secondary position. Eaton and his supporters are unable to provide any suitable reasons for doing so, and at some points (e.g., the interpretation of the violent witnesses) the argument is determined by a pre-conceived setting more than the evidence of the text. In fact, there is nothing in the psalm that would, taken on its own, suggest a royal interpretation. We can, therefore, only agree with Broyles when he says that,

> The royal interpretation tries to read most of the psalm's language as literal by positing a treaty background for the various episodes of the psalm. Such an attempt, however, appears strained.[68]

In the absence of any evidence that clearly points to a royal interpretation, we shall read this psalm as being one of a private individual. Even within this approach, however, all is not clear.

Croft argues that the psalm needs to be read as one reflecting a court situation, perhaps reflecting a situation of one who is falsely accused.[69] This reading is certainly stronger than that of Eaton and the royal school since the references to violent (or ruthless) witnesses (עֵדֵי חָמָס) in verse 11 seem to describe an actual rather than metaphorical situation. Further, the psalmist's request in verse 24, שָׁפְטֵנִי כְצִדְקְךָ יְהוָה אֱלֹהָי, is also strongly suggestive of a judicial context. However, there is insufficient material in the psalm to suggest that this represents an actual court situation. As we noted in Psalm 27, the presence of references to false accusations does not necessarily mean that this is a prayer of the accused. Further, to include a psalm within the prayers of the accused we need to see the resolution of the accusation as the central issue in the psalm. This does not appear to be the case here, especially when we note that the psalm also lacks a declaration of innocence or any indication of what the charge might be. In this case, the prayer is not aimed at the resolution of the charge but rather at protection from those making the accusation. Although a false accusation may well provide the context from which the psalm originated, it is a prayer for protection from the enemies, not an institutional prayer of the accused.[70]

Other options are also available. Thus, we should note the references to a previous time of illness on the part of the adversaries during which the psalmist

---

[67]Craigie, *Psalms 1-50*, 286.
[68]Craig C. Broyles, *The Conflict of Faith and Experience in the Psalms: A Form Critical and Theological Study*, Sheffield: JSOT Press, 1989, 193.
[69]Croft, *Identity*, 63, 142. Cf. Delekat, *Asylie*, 114ff.
[70]Cf. J. W. Rogerson and J. W. McKay, *Psalms 1-50*, Cambridge: Cambridge University Press, 1977, 160f.

interceded for them. These are now contrasted with the position of the psalmist having stumbled (verse 15). This could suggest that the *Sitz im Leben* of the psalm is to be understood instead as one of sickness. However, the breadth of possibilities makes it almost impossible to be specific. As with Psalm 3, we appear to be dealing with a psalm which uses such a high proportion of metaphorical language that it is impossible to penetrate back to an original *Sitz im Leben*. Illness may lie in the background of the psalm, but its resolution is not the central concern of the psalm.

The presence of such an extensive body of metaphors does at least suggest that we are dealing with a psalm that chooses to express itself in non-literal ways. This in turn would indicate that we are dealing with a situation, again similar to that of Psalm 3, where a high proportion of stereotypical language is used, but used in such a way as to suggest that the metaphors have become stock language.[71] If this is so, then the redactional processes through which the Psalter has developed virtually force us to read the psalm as one of an ordinary individual seeking that Yahweh provide protection from a group of enemies.

Since the lament proper occurs in verses 11-16 we should seek something of the situation of the psalm there. Again, the weight of metaphor makes the determination difficult, but the situation would appear to be one of betrayal by former friends. Since the tenses here would suggest current action, it would seem that their assault on the psalmist is current, though ill-defined.[72]

Structure

The structure of the psalm is also suggestive of it being primarily a prayer for protection. It is generally agreed that the psalm contains three main units, each element of which is itself a prayer for protection in some sense, though it is now integrated into the whole.[73] Thus, although the focus of protection is different in each section, the emphasis remains. That each section is to some

---

[71] Kim, *Rapid Change*, 219f, again points to the high level of language drawn from the holy war tradition. However, the holy war language is essentially limited to verses 1-10 and some elements of the appeal in verses 17-27.

[72] Erhard S. Gerstenberger, *Psalms Part 1 With an Introduction to Cultic Poetry*, Grand Rapids: Eerdmans, 1988, 150, rejects such a reading because it presupposes an element of autobiography in the psalm that his cultic approach does not recognise. However, this ignores the function of the canon in providing instruction on prayer through the psalms. For a psycho-analytical reading of the psalm, cf. J. Gerald Janzen, "The Root *škl* and the Soul Bereaved in Psalm 35", *JSOT* 65 (1995), 55-69.

[73] The compositional history of the psalm is not clear. Oesterley, *Psalms*, 215, suggests that although it is all by the one author, it was not written at the same time. Hossfeld and Zenger, *Die Psalmen*, 215ff, argue that the basic psalm consisted of verses 1-6 and 11-16, the balance of the psalm being added after the exile. Although these suggestions may explain the difficulties faced in determining the psalm's *Sitz im Leben*, our task is still to interpret the psalm as a whole.

extent a separate prayer for protection is also apparent from the fact that each one ends with a vow of praise related to the preceding plea.[74] Aside from these elements, the psalm's structure is rather loose. It is easier to see the major units than the development within them.

Accordingly, we may outline the psalm according to the following divisions:

1. A prayer for protection in which military imagery is dominant, verses 1-10.

2. A prayer for protection in which legal imagery is dominant, verses 11-18.

3. A prayer directed against the enemies, verses 19-28.[75]

Given the movement between the sections of the psalm, it will be necessary to consider the nature of violence in each separately before attempting to describe the ways in which the whole comes together.

Nature of Violence

Because of the highly metaphoric language used in verses 1-10, the exact nature of the violence described is difficult to determine with any certainty. Thus, although the initial imperative, רִיבָה, may seem to be more closely related to the situation of the law court, it is adapted here to the military language used in the balance of verses 1-3. There may be a hint of the language of holy war in the summons for Yahweh's assistance,[76] though the evidence for this is by no means clear. What is important for our purposes is to note that the assistance is sought from Yahweh. He is the one who is to provide protection from those who attack the psalmist.

As we have noted, the extent of metaphoric language in the opening verses makes it very difficult to be certain about the nature of the violence from which Yahweh is to provide protection. Indeed, it is probable that the language in this instance is deliberately ambiguous. Yahweh is summoned to provide protection from any form of violence - the language of warfare being a suitable metaphor for all types of violence that can be experienced. The use of the metaphor of warfare does, however, add vigour and colour to the situation, suggesting the seriousness of the threat from the actions of the enemies. Equally importantly, the use of the imperfect tense to describe the activities of the enemies in verse 1 suggests that the psalmist is currently experiencing whatever violence is being enacted.[77] That is why the psalmist needs the assurance of Yahweh's salvation (verse 3).

---

[74]Compare verses 10, 18, 28.

[75]Cf. D. C. van Zyl, "Psalmhermeneuse en Psalmberyming", *NGTT* 29 (1985), 64.

[76]So Dahood, *Psalms 1-50*, 210, who derives בְּעֶזְרָתִי from the Ugaritic root '*zr* II, "lad, warrior" rather than the Hebrew root עזר.

[77]One could also read the verbs as iterative, in which case the sense would be one of continued assault.

A more specific situation of violence may be presupposed by the imprecation of verses 4-8 where it is indicated that the enemies have sought the psalmist's life (נֶפֶשׁ), specifically by the laying of a net and the digging of a pit. All of this is related to the plots the enemies are alleged (verse 4) to be making against the well-being of the psalmist (חֹשְׁבֵי רָעָתִי). However, the language is again full of metaphor, so an actual situation is difficult to determine. The implication may be that physical violence has been attempted against the psalmist or that there has been some sort of psychological assault made, though either one may result in the death of the psalmist. Both possibilities would fit the application of the *lex talionis* in the imprecation proper of verses 5-8. That the *lex talionis* lies behind the imprecation seems to be indicated by the fact that it employs metaphors for persecution that may lead to death, which is precisely the experience of the psalmist at the hands of the enemies.[78]

The context of the violence in verses 1-10 is thus ambiguous, and in the final form of the psalm perhaps deliberately so. The violence described may be either physical or psychological, though both cases may lead to the physical suffering of the psalmist, even to the point of death. On balance, the apparent imminence of physical violence may suggest that the major form here is psychological, but this is not to be pressed. In either situation, though, the psalm models a prayer in which Yahweh alone is the one summoned to provide protection. The inference is that his protection is sufficient for all circumstances, no matter the form of violence employed. The dominant metaphor of warfare may suggest that the protection offered is primarily physical, but if so it certainly does not exclude the possibility of other forms of protection.

A more specific form of violence would appear to be indicated in verses 11-18. The dominant metaphor here is that of the law court, though it is not used exclusively.[79] These verses are of particular importance for the interpretation of the psalm since they represent the actual lament. Verses 1-10 have provided a necessary background to the lament, but as we have seen they do not allow us to penetrate to the actual situation of the psalmist. Although metaphor is still used in these verses, an actual situation may be perceived behind them. The legal metaphor of describing the enemies as עֵדֵי חָמָס[80] (verse 11) governs our reading of the actions of these former friends throughout the section.

---

[78] Allan M. Harman, "The Continuity of the Covenant Curses in the Imprecations in the Psalter", *RTR* 54/2 (1995), 64-72, tries to link the imprecations in the psalms to the covenantal curses in the Pentateuch. Although he does not treat Psalm 35 (a curious omission), the failure to include the element of the *lex talionis* greatly weakens his presentation.

[79] It is notable that the verb יִשְׁאָלוּנִי in verse 11b is used with the technical sense of questioning a witness in a court of law. T. H. Gaster, "Short Notes", *VT* 4 (1954), 73, derives this from Akkadian usage.

[80] The identical idiom is used in Psalm 27:12.

Although verse 13 speaks of the former friends lying in wait for the psalmist's נֶפֶשׁ, the subsequent references in the lament proper would suggest that this is to be understood in terms of the psychological assault that they bring to bear upon the psalmist. This would seem to be indicated by the approach of the enemies in questioning the psalmist on areas of ignorance (verse 11), together with the offering of evil in response to good. If we follow the translation of the NIV and see a reference to slander in verse 15 we would have fairly conclusive evidence that this section of the psalm operates out of a setting of psychological assault.[81] However, the extent of the textual difficulties here and in verse 16 are such that we cannot be certain of such an interpretation.[82] One could equally well follow a more literal reading and see a reference to "smiters", a reading that is more suggestive of a physical attack. However, in the context of a dominant metaphor of a court case it is not necessary to interpret the language literally, and a reference to "smiters" could be a metaphor for the false accusation referred to in verse 11.[83]

Since this is the nearest that the psalm comes to literal language in describing the situation being faced then it follows that we should allow it to shape our reading of verses 1-10 rather than follow Eaton and allow a literal reading of these verses to shape the lament proper. The psalmist is thus suffering under the weight of accusations, something that could result in death. At this stage, however, it is only the psychological distress of accusation that is felt, though this may well lead to physical suffering. It is the possibility of physical suffering as a result of these accusations that leads to the current suffering. This suggests that although there is a present state of distress, Yahweh's protection is being sought before the violence becomes worse and takes a directly physical form. Such violence is imminent, and its very imminence acts as a form of psychological violence against the psalmist.

The complaint takes on an intriguing feature in verse 17 with the psalmist's cry of "how long", in which it is implied that Yahweh has been lax in exercising his role as protector. There is, perhaps, an indication of some anger towards Yahweh in such a situation (אֲדֹנָי כַּמָּה תִּרְאֶה, verse 17a).[84] Nevertheless, this simply provides a further ground for appeal in verse 17b, with the request that Yahweh rescue the psalmist's נֶפֶשׁ from the enemies. It is a means by which Yahweh is incited to act rather than an attempt to have

---

[81]NIV seems to be strongly influenced by Dahood, *Psalms 1-50*, 214. The evidence offered by Dahood in this context, again based on supposed Ugaritic parallels, seems particularly slight. Craigie, *Psalms 1-50*, 285, is particularly harsh in his criticism of such a reading, and is doubtful if such a sense is found in Ugaritic.
[82]Cf. D. Winton Thomas, "Psalm XXXV. 15f", *JTS* 12 (1961), 50-51.
[83]Cf. Kissane, *Psalms*, 156.
[84]Brueggemann, *Message*, 64f.

personal violence in retribution accepted.[85]

In verses 19-28 we then have the specific prayer against the enemies. The methods used to attempt to persuade Yahweh vary, but they all depend upon the foundational belief that the right of retribution belongs to Yahweh alone. Within this request, though, we note that the principle of *lex talionis* is still operative. Thus, although Yahweh is summoned to rise in the psalmist's defence (verse 23), an element which includes pronouncing judgment on the psalmist (presumably a declaration of innocence,[86] though the last line of verse 24 indicates that this is part of the means of protection), the actual request in verse 26 is that they should suffer some form of humiliation for what they have done. The request is therefore that the enemies should receive punishment from Yahweh, a punishment that is experienced in a variety of possible forms. However, all are related to those forms of violence that they have inflicted upon the psalmist. At this stage, it is essentially humiliation that has been suffered by the psalmist, and that is what is now sought from Yahweh against the enemies. Again, human retributive violence is rejected, whilst Yahweh's protection is sought instead. This is based on the belief that he alone can act in retribution. The requested retribution remains, however, in Yahweh's domain, though what is sought is still controlled by the *lex talionis*.

The pattern of violence reflected in Psalm 35 is therefore more complex than that of either Psalms 3 or 27. The opening section (verses 1-10) could be understood as referring either to physical or psychological violence. The evidence there was not entirely clear, though it established the pattern followed throughout that only Yahweh could deal with violence. The identification of the nature of violence became clearer in the second and third sections of the psalm. It was the imminence of physical violence, and therefore the threat that it generated, that suggested that the current assault is experienced psychologically. The possibility of physical violence remains, and in some sense it is this violence that generates the psychological violence that is experienced. The response that is requested from Yahweh could be understood physically or psychologically, but in either case it is limited in extent so that it is to be equivalent to that which the enemies have carried out against the psalmist.

Response to Violence

The response to violence in Psalm 35 is more complex than that seen in the other psalms examined in this chapter so far. The reason for this lies in the range of possible settings, plus the fact that each section of the psalm was to some extent in itself a discrete prayer for protection. We noted that verses 1-10 used metaphors that reflected a balance between psychological and physical

---

[85] Broyles, *Conflict*, 195.
[86] Cf. Kraus, *Psalms 1-59*, 392.

violence whilst verses 11-18 addressed violence that was principally psychological in nature. The final section of the psalm was open to both forms. Adding to the complexity is the fact that this psalm also features an expression of concern over Yahweh's tardiness in providing protection, even if this was used more as a motivation for action by Yahweh than anything else.

All these features need to be considered within the psalm as a whole, irrespective of its compositional history. Such a reading would suggest that verses 1-10 are now seen as providing a general backdrop to the specific situation, one in which Yahweh is summoned to act in any situation, with the underlying belief being that the only acceptable defence against such attacks is Yahweh himself. This is then applied to the specific situation indicated in verses 11-18. Although the experience reflected here is primarily one of psychological torment caused by false accusation, it is understood that it could become directly physical. The protection that is sought is then to be understood as an application of the general principle introduced in verses 1-10. Protection in all circumstances is to be sought from Yahweh alone.

Yahweh is summoned to act in this case of assault because that is the acceptable approach irrespective of the violence experienced. Yahweh may, at times, be slow to act, but this does not provide a motive for acting in retributive violence. It is rather a situation in which one has further grounds to approach Yahweh to act. This final approach is outlined in verses 19-28. Since Yahweh alone may act in retribution, and in this instance retribution is the means of protection, then he is summoned to act. Although this section contains imprecations against the enemies, they are controlled by the *lex talionis*, as was the case in the earlier imprecation in verses 4-8. Yahweh's protection may be sought, but not in such a way as to see greater harm inflicted on the enemies than they themselves sought to inflict.

This psalm thus provides a model of prayer for protection in which the retributive action of Yahweh is necessary. It suggests that the faithful may indeed seek Yahweh's action against oppressors irrespective of the form of violence, even if this means that some retributive action is necessary. But this is to be seen and understood as an application of the protection that he provides, protection in which the faithful must trust. This is so even when there is no immediate sign of Yahweh's activity in providing protection.

Psalm 55

Form Critical Discussion

The determination of the exact genre, along with many other questions, is a problem that remains unanswered in this psalm. This may stem in part from the difficulty of the text, whose "jagged, hectic character"[87] "makes it certainly one of the most difficult psalms to."[88] Difficulties in analysis naturally reflect themselves in other issues of interpretation. A number of different *Gattungen* have thus been proposed for the psalm, though none has received universal assent. Similarly, the basic unity of the psalm has been called into question. Since this latter issue has affected the ways in which the prayer is read, we need to consider this question before considering the issue of the *Gattung* of the psalm.

The most substantial assault on the unity of the psalm was by Briggs, who proposed two original psalms consisting of (1) a prayer for deliverance (verses 2-3, 5-9a), and (2) imprecations on both treacherous foes (verses 9b-12) and a treacherous friend (verses 13-16a, 21-22, 24ab). To both of these original psalms, extensive glosses have been added, all of which modify the intent of the psalm to some extent.[89] Although the question of glosses is clearly a separate matter, the presence of both a prayer for deliverance from oppression and imprecations against foes in the one psalm is by no means indicative of originally separate psalms. Indeed, Psalm 54, in which Briggs finds only minor glosses,[90] includes both of these elements, albeit in a less developed form.[91] The fundamental division proposed by Briggs is thus less than persuasive.[92]

A more commonly held division is one that was first proposed by Gunkel, in which the psalm is seen as consisting of two main blocks that were originally separate - verses 2-19b + 23 and verses 19c-22 + 24. According to Gunkel, the fact that these originally separate units were joined was quite accidental, with the first half of the psalm being an affirmation of confidence and plea, whilst the second half is understood as a new complaint. Quite how one accounts for the place of verse 23 on this suggestion is uncertain since an accidental joining of units would presumably leave the text of each as a block.

A slightly simpler version of this theory is adopted by Anderson[93] and Kraus,[94] who see verses 2-19a and 19b-24 as being the two originally separate psalms. This approach has the obvious virtue of not forcing us to consider the reasons for the placement of verse 23, but we still need to question the validity

---

[87]Eaton, *Kingship*, 74.
[88]D. J. Human, *Die Begrip 'Berit' in 'n Aantal Klaagpsalms; 'n Perspektief*, unpublished DD dissertation, University of Pretoria, 1993, 83 (my translation). The Afrikaans reads "maak dit seker een van die moeilikste psalms om te analiseer."
[89]Briggs, *Psalms* 2:19f.
[90]Briggs, *Psalms*, 2:16f.
[91]The prayer for deliverance in Psalm 54 occurs in verses 3-4, whilst the imprecation is in verse 7.
[92]Kissane, *Psalms*, 1:236, appropriately comments on Briggs' suggestion that "there is really no reason why a prayer and an imprecatory passage should not find a place in the same poem."
[93]Anderson, *Psalms*, 412.
[94]Kraus, *Psalms 1-59*, 519f.

of the exegesis that sustains this division. The main arguments raised in support of such a division are the apparent disorder in the verses and the sometimes odd shifts in pronouns and tenses. The force of these arguments must be noted, but they must be placed in the context of what is an admittedly very difficult text.[95] The textual difficulties are by no means limited to the break at verse 19, and it is equally possible to account for the changes that we find in the psalm by pointing to the apparent emotional distress that is present throughout. In addition, Tate points to the presence of a word play on the roots מוט (verses 4 and 23) and ירד (verses 16 and 24).[96] The fact that these word plays occur across the division proposed by Gunkel may suggest the original unity of the psalm.[97] Even if the psalm is the result of a redactional process, whether intentional or accidental, it is the whole psalm that we need to interpret. Given that the psalm as it stands is coherent and shows elements that link both parts, we shall read the finished psalm as a whole.

Granted that it is possible to read the poem as a whole, this still leaves open the question of the *Gattung* of the psalm. Again, there have been a wide range of proposals. Eaton and Croft both treat the psalm as royal,[98] an approach which is developed with reference to a specific incident in David's life by Goulder.[99] Eaton is fairly cautious in his assessments, pointing to the presumed situation behind the psalm rather than the specific evidence of the text as pointing towards a royal identification.[100] It is especially the presumed situation of battle (verses 19 and 22)[101] that is alleged to indicate that the individual who speaks throughout the psalm is the king. Similarly, Mowinckel sees the psalm as a

---

[95] The one exception to this view is Mitchell Dahood, *Psalms II*, Garden City: Doubleday, 1968, 30, who finds the psalm to be a happy hunting ground for the application of the grammar of North West Semitic languages. According to Dahood, these factors indicate that the verses are in logical order and that there are no actual problems with the tenses of the psalm. As appealing as this position might be, it has to be admitted that the support for many of his proposals seems extraordinarily slight. Indeed, we shall note several points where Dahood has subsequently been forced to adapt earlier positions, which suggests that the text is indeed more difficult than he initially suggested.

[96] Tate, *Psalms 51-100*, 56.

[97] Note the structural analysis of Human, *Die Begrip 'Berit'*, 82ff. While this analysis does not necessarily prove the psalm to be an original unity, it certainly requires us to read it as a coherent whole.

[98] Eaton, *Kingship*, 74, though in the "less clear cases", Croft, *Identity*, 126f, is more confident of the royal origin of the psalm.

[99] Michael D. Goulder, *The Prayers of David (Psalms 51-72)*, Sheffield: JSOT Press, 1990, 96ff. Goulder relates the psalm to David's retreat to Olivet following Absalom's coup (2 Samuel 15:13-37).

[100] Eaton, *Kingship*, 74.

[101] Cf. Birkeland, *Evildoers*, 32 and, idem, *Die Feinde*, 234ff.

Prayers for Protection 79

national psalm of lament in which the "I" is really the nation.[102] Other options are also canvassed, though generally only to highlight the uncertainty that is there.

In dealing with the arguments for a royal identification of the psalm we are confronted with issues similar to those that we have seen elsewhere. Apart from the battle allusions, we should also note the apparent concern with societal issues in verses 10-12. These could also be seen as indicating that the speaker is identified as a national figure.[103] However, such factors are by no means determinative. We need to note that the psalmist speaks of the wound inflicted by a former friend, suggesting that personal betrayal is at stake, although the former friend is also included among the wider circle of enemies (verse 16). The expression of such emotions sits awkwardly with a royal interpretation, and the proposal that the former friend was a counsellor like Ahithopel which is necessary to defend the royal interpretation[104] is forced. It is doubtful that such an interpretation would have arisen had there not been a previously determined decision to interpret the psalm as royal. A similar observation needs to be made in terms of the references to battle in verses 19 and 22. Both references are set in wider contexts that indicate that the actions of the enemies were initiated by the former friend. As such, it is far more likely that the references to battle are metaphors for the type of experience endured by the psalmist rather than to a literal experience of warfare.

A royal interpretation is therefore not necessary, and in a peculiar way the placement of the psalm among the prayers of David (Psalms 51-72) requires that it be read as the words of an individual. While the overall argument of Goulder's *The Prayers of David* is not finally convincing, he has at least recognised the central canonical intention of this collection of psalms in their attempt to define a direct relationship with David's life - even if in Goulder's assessment the period in David's life is not the one indicated by the titles! In this construal, David does not function as a cultic figure, as one would expect for a royal psalm, but rather as a representative individual within Israel.[105] The ascription thus requires a democratised reading of the psalm so that we finally hear in it an individual's declaration of trust in the midst of adversity. It is, admittedly, portrayed as the experience of one who is king, but it is the personal dimension of David's experience and not the royal that provides concrete guidance on how individual Israelites may express their experiences before God. The title expressly moves the reader away from a royal reading that is associated with the cult and shifts the psalm into the dimension of the individual. Greater specificity than that in terms of the *Sitz im Leben* that gave

---

[102]Mowinckel, *Psalms in Israel's Worship*, 1:219.
[103]Cf. Croft, *Identity*, 127.
[104]So Croft, *Identity*, 127. See Kirkpatrick, *Psalms*, 307, for a critique of the association of the friend with Ahithopel.
[105]Cf. Miller, *They Cried to the Lord*, 83.

rise to the psalm is not possible given the rather general nature of the language that is used.[106]

Taking the fact that we can identify this as a psalm of an individual and not a royal figure, we also need to consider the evidence that would indicate that this is a prayer for protection. In this respect, the following points need to be noted:

1. The opening appeal (verses 2-4) summons God to act because of the actions of the enemy. This is particularly clear in the opening words of the psalm proper:-

> Hearken to my prayer, O God,
> do not withdraw from my plea,
> attend to me and answer me.

The actions of the enemy against the psalmist generate a feeling of oppression. The need for God to act and provide protection is highlighted by the psalmist's desire to flee (verses 5-9), something that it was presumably impossible to achieve. Hence God is summoned to provide protection against the enemy.[107]

2. In verses 10-12, God is specifically summoned to act against the wicked. This is made particularly clear in verse 10:-

> Destroy, O Lord, divide the tongue,[108]
> for I see violence and contention in the city.

Although the wicked remain ill-defined at this stage, it is clearly the case that the psalmist seeks protection from them because of the ways in which they assault the social order.

3. In verse 16 there is an impersonal summons to bring death to the enemies of the psalmist:-

> Let death overcome them,
> let them go down to Sheol alive,
> for evil finds a lodging in their midst.

Although the previous verses (13-15) were addressed to the false friend, it seems clear that in this instance we have returned to a direct address to God.

---

[106] Bellinger, *Psalmody and Prophecy*, 42.

[107] Against Delekat, *Asylie*, 177ff, there is nothing here to indicate that asylum is sought. It is, rather, the impossibility of asylum that is at issue, which is why God is summoned to provide protection. Cf. Beyerlin, *Die Rettung*, 25f.

[108] See below, "Nature of Violence", for a discussion of this translation.

Prayers for Protection 81

These elements are all suggestive of the fact that this is a prayer for protection. However, we should also note that the element of trust is also present to a marked degree, so that in both verses 17-20 and 23-24 it is this motif that has become dominant. This is particularly clear in verse 23:

> Cast your cares on Yahweh
> and he will uphold you,
> he will never let the righteous stumble.

The psalm clearly shifts as it progresses from a prayer for protection and moves towards the Songs of Trust. However, since these affirmations of trust occur in a context in which God has first been summoned to act, it seems that they are subordinated to the initial element of the prayer for protection. Although the psalm therefore has something of a mixture of form critical elements, the dominant ones would appear to relate to the individual's prayer for protection. Accordingly, we may treat it as such.

Structure

Just as there has been considerable debate over the form critical classification of this psalm, so also the structure has been a matter of some uncertainty. In part, this uncertainty stems from the difficulties of the text itself, though certain conclusions seem to be based more on what is *not* in the text than what is.[109] Whatever the difficulties posed by the text, our primary task here is to understand it as it currently stands. In doing so, we must still allow for its awkward nature, a factor that suggests that any proposed structure needs to be held lightly. Superficially attractive suggestions, such as that of Kissane, that the psalm consists of three stanzas of nine verses each are accordingly doubtful.[110]

In view of the difficulties posed by the text, it seems best to simply outline the major movements of the thought of the psalm. Even here, though, not all the divisions are absolutely clear. For our purposes, ignoring the superscription, the following broad outline will suffice:

1. A plea for God to hear the psalmist's prayer (verses 2-4) along with a complaint about current circumstances (verses 5-9).

2. A description of the activities of the enemy, concerning which God is summoned to act (verses 10-16).

---

[109] A number of commentators point out that Gunkel's proposed separation of verses 19ff requires a substantial re-writing of the text. Cf. Kissane, *Psalms,* 1:236.

[110] Kissane, *Psalms* 1:236. The suggestion requires that verses 21-22 be placed after verse 15, which is not necessarily, as he maintains, "their natural position."

3. Expressions of trust in the midst of uncertainty (verses 17-24).[111]

It is readily apparent that this is a somewhat simplistic outline of the psalm,[112] and that certain structural issues are not, therefore, addressed. It is, however, sufficient for our purposes in that it isolates the different expressions of violence from one another.

Nature of Violence

Although the whole *Sitz im Leben* of the psalm would seem to indicate a situation of widespread oppression, the language and motif of violence are only explicitly dealt with in verses 10-12 and again in verse 24. Nevertheless, both of these passages need to be understood within the wider context of the psalm as a whole, especially since the opening plea is rooted in the anger of the enemy. This suggests that the balance of the psalm contains the response to the violence that is being experienced. Accordingly, the whole of the psalm needs to be investigated so that those sections that deal explicitly with violence can be understood.

As mentioned, the opening section of the psalm (verses 2-9) makes no explicit reference to violence. There is, however, considerable evidence of its effect upon the psalmist. Unfortunately, the exact situation in which the psalmist is placed by the actions of the enemy is unclear due to the occurrence in verse three of the unusual verb אָרִיד. A bewildering array of suggestions as to its meaning is available. Kraus derives the word from the root רדד,[113] and sees this as essentially the equivalent of אבד. On the other hand, Dahood initially understood the word as an aphel imperative from ירד,[114] though he subsequently revised his opinion and derived the word from ארה.[115] None of these suggestions is entirely satisfactory, and we need to be content with acknowledging that the verb indicates that the psalmist is undergoing some form of oppression, something that is in any case apparent from the parallelism.

A clearer picture of the psalmist's situation begins to emerge in verses 4-6, though it must be acknowledged that there are further textual difficulties here.

---

[111]Cf. N. A. van Uchelen, *Psalmen II*, Nijkerk: G. F. Callenbach, 1977, 103f. Curiously, van Uchelen recognises this as the final literary form of the psalm, though he also recognises the division proposed by Kraus.

[112]Apart from the complex analysis of Human, *Die Begrip "Berit'* (see above), one can also note the more detailed structures proposed by Gerstenberger, *Psalms*, 223, and Tate, *Psalms 51-100*, 56. However, although such finer analyses are useful, they do not make any further contribution to our purposes here.

[113]Kraus, *Psalms 1-59*, 518. This in itself requires an emendation to אורד, since he recognises that as the text stands the root would appear to be רוד, something he judges to be unlikely.

[114]Dahood, *Psalms II*, 30.

[115]Mitchell Dahood, "Philological Observations on Five Bib Texts", *Biblica* 63 (1982), 390-94.

Prayers for Protection

The psalmist's prayer seems to arise out of the verbal assault of the enemy (מִקּוֹל אוֹיֵב), an assault that is coupled with some further form of oppression. Although Dahood initially argued that this is "staring" from the enemies,[116] presumably resulting in a sense of psychological torment, he subsequently emended this position to understand the word to mean "press", resulting in a translation of the line as "[I am] constrained by the presence of the wicked."[117] Neither of these suggestions is particularly plausible. The first requires a meaning in Ugaritic that is by no means clear, whilst the second requires the presence of a broken construct chain, something that only Dahood and his students are generally willing to recognise. More plausible is the suggestion of Kissane that we ought to emend עָקַת to זְעָקַת.[118] This suggestion requires the addition of only one consonant, and is the sort of emendation that is easily justified. The simplest option, though, is to presume an Aramaism, since the root עוק can be understood as being more or less equivalent to the Hebrew צרה (cf. Amos 2:13).[119] If we follow this line of interpretation, then the psalm presents a situation in which the words of the enemy create a sense of oppression in the psalmist, suggesting that the words themselves are threatening some form of violence. In doing so, they create a sense of dread in the psalmist, indicating that at the psychological level they have already begun the process of assault. This will be made explicit in verse 5 where the psalmist speaks of "the terrors of death." The fear of imminent physical violence is generated by the speech of the enemies, creating a situation of psychological violence.

Indeed, it is possible that the enemy is portrayed as attempting to hunt the psalmist down through hostile speech in the last part of verse 4,[120] though the evidence for this meaning of שטם is not clear.[121] Although the exact sense of the word cannot be established, the parallel in Job 16:9 strongly suggests that it reflects hatred that is put into action of some sort, most likely pursuit or persecution.[122] The compound picture of the actions of the enemy that we see in verses 3-4 is thus one where a verbal assault is set against the psalmist, resulting in the psalmist's present distress. Although the enemy pursues the psalmist in this way, it leaves open the prospect that more direct physical

---

[116]Dahood, *Psalms II*, 31f, deriving the hapax עָקַת from the Ugaritic ʿq, which he translates "eyeball."

[117]Mitchell Dahood, "'A Sea of Troubles': Notes in Psalms 55.3-4 and 140:10-11", *CBQ* 41 (1979), 604f.

[118]Kissane, *Psalms*, 1:239. Oesterley, *Psalms*, 285, goes further and reads מִזַּעֲקַת, but it is difficult to see how this level of corruption could have occurred.

[119]So Kraus, *Psalms 1-59*, 518.

[120]Cf. Anderson, *Psalms*, 413, and Tate, *Psalms 51-100*, 52.

[121]The main evidence for this reading comes from Job 16:9. On the use of the verb there, cf. David J. A. Clines, *Job 1-20*, Dallas: Word, 1989, 370. John E. Hartley, *The Book of Job*, Grand Rapids: Eerdmans, 1988, 260, suggests that it has the meaning of "hate actively."

[122]Goulder, *Prayers of David*, 96.

violence is to follow. This violence is most likely the אָוֶן that is spoken of. It is currently experienced psychologically, but a physical manifestation is considered imminent.

The effect of this assault on the psalmist becomes clear in verses 5-6. These verses build up the sense of dread that has been apparent in verses 3-4, but express them in terms of the psychological experience of the psalmist. That these verbal assaults may lead to further physical violence is indicated by the reference to the "terrors of death" (אֵימוֹת מָוֶת)[123] that have fallen on the psalmist, which are a part of the surrounding horrors. It is from this situation that the psalmist desires to flee, though this is not possible.[124] Because the psalmist is unable to flee from the situation, the protection of God is called forth.

Further textual difficulties are found as we move into the second major section of the psalm (verses 10-16). An immediate problem is encountered in the translation of verse 10. If we assume that the image of the fleeing bird is maintained from verse 9, then a suitable meaning can be found, though the text requires extensive surgery.[125] It is more probable though that there is a shift at this point, so that verse 10 is a direct address to God. If we follow this line of thought, then it is probably necessary to translate בַּלַּע as "destroy" and not as BDB suggests, "confuse", since it elsewhere has the meaning of swallowing that leads to destruction.[126] If we accordingly translate the first two lines of the verse as "Destroy O Lord, divide the tongue", then there is probably a reference to the experience of the Tower of Babel in which both destruction and the division of language occur. The reason for this request lies in the actions of what is now a group of undefined enemies who have brought trouble (אָוֶן, verse 4) upon the psalmist and who are responsible for the חָמָס וְרִיב in the city (verse 10).

Although the material so far has suggested that the primary manifestations of violence against the psalmist are psychological in nature, there is a broadening of the focus here. In this part of the psalm there is violence that is parallel to the psychological assault in the opening verses, and that would seem to be some form of social violence, brought about by the creation of contention within the society (verses 10b-12). This assault on the structures of society is

---

[123]The phrase itself could also be "deadly terrors", though that would be consistent with our exegesis. More importantly, we need to recognise the possibility that מות is an example of a dittograph, in which case it is only terrors that overwhelm the psalmist (so Tate, *Psalms 51-100*, 52). However, the LXX's δειλία θανάτου would seem to support the MT. If the reading of the MT is a dittograph, it is one that has probably caught the sense of what was intended anyway.

[124]Van Gemeren, "Psalms", 393, suggests that this is the result of physical paralysis induced by psychological trauma.

[125]Cf. Kraus, *Psalms 1-59*, 519f.

[126]Tate, *Psalms 51-100*, 52.

apparent in verse 12 from the fact that the market square of the city[127] has become a place of violence and contention. It is specifically in response to the attack on the social order that the request for destruction is made in verse 10, though it is also linked in verses 13ff to the actions of the former friend. For our purposes, it is sufficient to note that what is significant is that this is a request directed to God and not something that is taken on by the psalmist personally. Violence is not an individual right. Indeed, the fact that such a prayer can be uttered is already moving the psalm towards the statement of trust with which it ends.

That which is placed in God's hands is both the response to the social disorder and the actions necessary against the former friend. In this light, the imprecation of verse 16 would seem to cover both the false friend and those who attack the social order. Although the violence that is sought against these enemies is extreme since the psalmist seeks their death, it is notable that once again the Psalter refuses to sanction human retributive violence. The matter is submitted to God in the prayer and left at that point. Further, since "the enemy" in verses 2-4 seems to be the false friend who has generated the terrors of death within the psalmist, and since Sheol is here perceived as a place of wickedness, it would seem that the prayer is still controlled by the *lex talionis*, though perhaps not to the extent that we have seen elsewhere. The enemy has brought death into the realm of the psalmist, and it is this same experience that the psalmist asks God to bring into the realm of the enemy. What is apparent is that physical violence against the enemies is sought because they have brought about physical suffering through psychological and social violence, both of which have affected the psalmist. In addition, the perceived aim of their violence was to bring about the death of the psalmist, and the prayer accordingly asks that they suffer that which they sought to inflict.

Textual difficulties continue to confront us as we move into the third main division of the psalm. Direct violence occurs here as an explicit motif only in verse 24 with the affirmation that God will "bring down the wicked." However, its presence is felt even in the declarations of trust that build up to this reference, especially in the use of warfare as a metaphor in verses 19 and 22. It is notable that here again, the motif of violence is seen as something that belongs to God. The warfare metaphor in verses 19 and 22 refers once more to the activities of the enemies of the psalmist. That these references are specifically defined in terms of speech is entirely consistent with the actions of the enemy in the opening verses of the psalm. Warfare is thus a suitable metaphor for the verbal assault on the psalmist, indicating the force of the conflict.

The response to this situation is essentially one of trust, faith that Yahweh

---

[127]Dahood, *Psalms II*, 30, understands this as a foreign city. This is possible, but by no means necessary.

does respond to the cry for help.[128] The psalmist accepts that the activities of the enemies will continue, but asserts that trust in God is necessary. Such trust leaves retribution to God. In particular, verse 24 speaks of retributive violence since the fate of the אַנְשֵׁי דָמִים וּמִרְמָה (verse 24) seems to be a case of the judgment of God fitting the crime. Their actions brought the possibility of death within the ambit of the psalmist. This, the psalmist hopes, is what God will accordingly do to the enemy. Although their assault has been experienced psychologically and socially, it manifests itself physically. The psalmist trusts God to bring about the necessary response to this situation.

We can therefore note the presence of two major types of violence in this psalm. The opening section of the psalm reflects psychological violence as it describes the terrors brought about by the verbal assault of the enemy. The second section of the psalm then reflects primarily social violence that is brought about by both the wicked and the former friend. The form of violence in the third section of the psalm is less specific. What is clear, however, is that the response of God is meant to fit the crime of the perpetrators of violence. Throughout the psalm, therefore, there is an expression of acceptance for Yahweh's violence and a rejection of the violence of the enemy. Equally, personal retributive violence is denied.

Response to Violence

Psalm 55 shows the close link between the Song of Trust and the prayer for protection. It arises out of a complex set of circumstances in which oppression comes from a variety of sources, at least one of which is the actions of a formerly close friend. It reflects a situation in which the psalmist is assaulted through the words of the enemy and the manipulation of the social order. Both of these elements bring about a situation of suffering because both bring violence into the experience of daily life. Violence may thus manifest itself in different ways, but under none of these circumstances does the psalmist claim the right to act in vengeance on the enemy. Rather, in the midst of considerable pressure and uncertainty of experience, the psalmist expresses the view that the only option is trust in God. Trust is possible because God alone retains the right to retributive violence, and because he alone is the one who can deliver the psalmist from the present circumstances.

The response to the violence that is experienced is accordingly twofold. First, the psalmist summons Yahweh to come and provide protection against all

---

[128] The tense of the response of Yahweh in וַיִּשְׁמַע קוֹלִי is uncertain. Normally, the waw consecutive imperfect refers to a past action, but Leslie McFall, *The Enigma of the Hebrew Verbal System*, Sheffield: Almond Press, 1982, 18, regards this as one of 30 examples of this construction having a future sense. Therefore, the psalmist could be expressing trust on the basis of a past action of God, or could simply be expressing trust that God will act.

forms of violence. Psalm 55 is significant in this respect in that it is the only prayer for protection that responds to violence brought about in the social order as well as that which the psalmist personally experiences. This violence is, as we have noted, something that is presently experienced, but is also seen as potentially worse than the current experience. It is the imminence of physical suffering that generates psychological suffering. Although the psalmist's own desire was to flee from the personal assaults, this was not possible. The violence of the city itself is equally not something from which one can flee. In both circumstances of violence, God's protection is sought.

The second element is closely related to the first, and that is the strong element of trust. The circumstances of the psalmist would not ordinarily have suggested that a positive outcome was likely, but in spite of that the psalm moves progressively towards a more clearly defined declaration of trust, with the last line providing the climax - וַאֲנִי אֶבְטַח־בָּךְ. This suggests that the summoning of God's protection is not perceived as a final attempt at solving the difficulties, but rather as the only choice, one that leaves no other alternative. Because the right of retributive violence belongs to God alone, trust is the only option available to the faithful under all such circumstances of oppression.

Psalm 56

Form Critical Discussion

The determination of the *Gattung* of this psalm poses a number of difficulties, though the range of options is less than at other points. We may, however, begin by noting the following considerations that suggest that we need to interpret it as a prayer for protection.

1. The situation of the psalmist would appear to be one of unrelieved distress. This element is apparent from the psalm's opening plea (verses 2-3) which refers to warlike opponents who are attacking the psalmist. It is in this context of oppression that God is summoned to offer succour to the psalmist with the opening plea:

Be merciful to me, O God, for people[129] pursue me,
all day they press the attack.

2. In addition, the description of the oppression in verses 6-7 and the subsequent imprecation (verses 8-9) both suggest that Yahweh is being summoned to defend the psalmist. This is particularly apparent in the plea

---

[129] In light of the subsequent use of רַבִּים, it is best to treat אֱנוֹשׁ as a collective noun.

of verse 8 which asks God not to let the enemy escape.

Both of these elements are typical of the prayer for protection. On the other hand, there is also a dominant note of confidence that runs through the psalm, especially in verses 4-5 and again in verses 10-12 that could almost see the psalm treated as a Song of Confidence. However, this psalm is similar to Psalm 55 in that the confidence, although rooted in God still seems to come out of the initial cry for deliverance. As such, the key concern of the psalm, even though it is expressed in terms of confidence, is a prayer for protection from the enemies.[130]

Equally problematic is the identification of the speaker. Once again, Eaton has identified the speaker as the king, though he places this psalm in his category of "less clear cases."[131] His arguments are not, however, particularly substantial, and depend more upon circumstantial evidence than anything within the psalm that could be described as explicitly royal. He is accordingly cautious in his assessment of the psalm.[132] Croft is more certain that this is a royal psalm, regarding it as a prayer for assistance in battle because of the use of martial language (notably in verses 2-3), and more specifically because of the reference to the end of the enemies, described as nations (עַמִּים), in verse 8.[133] Although he notes Anderson's point that עַמִּים could simply be a cultic term[134] he argues that the absence of other material that is explicitly non-royal means that we are to read this as a royal psalm. Such a method of argument is doubtful in the extreme. An absence of non-royal material does not suggest that the psalm is therefore to be regarded as royal. A royal interpretation must be demonstrated as the most probable interpretation of the martial language utilised by the psalm, something for which Croft provides no information. In fact, in the absence of any material that is explicitly royal, the balance of proof should lie in the direction of those who want to read it as being royal. Although the language of the psalm may well contain some royal vestiges, we can agree with Tate when he observes with respect to its language that it "has sufficient ambiguity to become meaningful for any reader."[135]

A more specifically "royal" treatment of the psalm is offered by Goulder,

---

[130]Cf. Gerstenberger, *Psalms*, 226f.

[131]Eaton, *Kingship*, 75.

[132]Dahood, *Psalms II*, 41, also supports a royal interpretation, claiming that there are points of contact between verses 2, 3, 7 and 8 and the royal psalms. Although he subsequently asserts a royal interpretation (page 44), none of the alleged points of contact are made explicit.

[133]Croft, *Identity*, 115.

[134]Anderson, *Psalms*, 423. Alternatively, Sabourin, *The Psalms*, 247 makes the reasonable observation that "a private individual may have prayed for the liberation of the Israelite nation from foreign domination." Whilst neither of these interpretations is necessarily correct, they both indicate that the presence of the term itself is by no means a decisive marker for assigning this psalm to the royal group.

[135]Tate, *Psalms 51-100*, 68.

who places the psalm within a group (51-72) which he believes were written for David's Passion narrative, and in the particular case of this psalm his flight from Olivet to Mahanaim.[136] A great deal of conjecture is necessary for his theory to work as a whole, though his method at least has the benefit of taking the titles of the psalms seriously.[137] However, even if his reading is correct it still means that the psalm is a prayer of an individual rather than a truly "royal" psalm. On this interpretation, David would function as an individual in distress rather than a king participating in an annual rite or leading the nation's army into battle. If anything, attention to the title, with its explicit placement of the psalm within David's life, leads one to read the psalm as the words of an individual, and not as a royal psalm.[138] Again, the final editors have provided a means for reading the psalm that addresses the individual rather than the king. David's function in the title is thus as a representative Israelite and not as the king.

Additional and more pressing arguments for regarding the psalm as a prayer of an individual can be found within the text itself. In particular, it is to be noted that the enemies are said to be in pursuit, even conspiring against the psalmist's life (נֶפֶשׁ, verse 7). This pursuit comes out their twisting of the psalmist's words (verse 6). An assault that is based on a verbal misrepresentation is unlikely to represent a genuinely military situation. It is far more likely that the military terminology is used metaphorically, as indeed it is in all the psalms in this group, so that planned assaults on the psalmist's life are to be regarded as a manifestation of some form of verbal assault. However, the lack of references to an actual accusation means that this is not related to the institutional psalms of the accused.[139] Rather, it is a prayer of an individual suffering a loss of social prestige and torment as a result of the actions of others within society.

Structure

Although the form critical questions surrounding the psalm are complex, its basic structure is relatively clear. There is some dispute about the relative boundaries of the sections of the psalm, but these need not detain us here.[140] For our purposes, we need only consider the major sections of the psalm, noting the ways that the reflections on the experience of violence are developed through

---

[136] Goulder, *Prayers of David*, 109ff.

[137] Albeit concluding that although they are worthwhile guesses, they are still not actually correct!

[138] The situation is thus similar to that which we noted in Psalm 55.

[139] Cf. Beyerlin, *Die Rettung*, 25f.

[140] Cf. Paul R. Raabe, *Psalm Structures: A Study of Psalms with Refrains*, Sheffield: JSOT Press, 1990, 98ff for a detailed assessment of the elements of structure related to metre and a comparison of the different ways of dividing the psalm.

the prayer for protection and the interspersed affirmations of hope.[141]

Briefly, we may note that, apart from the title, the psalm consists of 5 major sections, all of which in some way reflect on the motif of violence. Setting aside the title, we may outline the psalm as follows:-

1. The psalm commences with an entreaty to God for deliverance from unspecified enemies (verses 2-3).

2. The entreaty then moves into the first declaration of trust (verses 4-5), a declaration which, if it is not actually a refrain in the strict sense, still repeats all of its major concerns in verses 11-12a.

3. In spite of the positive question with which verse 5 ends, we return to the theme of the persecution of the psalmist in verses 6- 7, with the actions of the enemies now formally described for the first time.

4. As a result of these actions, the psalm then records a prayer in verses 8-9 that is specifically summoning God to act. In particular, this prayer calls God to act both against the enemies and on the psalmist's behalf.

5. From verse 10 onwards the tone of the psalm changes, having a stronger emphasis on the motif of hope amidst the violence, including a vow of praise. The hope itself comes to a clear expression in verse 14, though whether the hiphil perfect הִצַּלְתָּ is to be understood as a certainty of God hearing the request or a reflection on a previous deliverance from danger that provides confidence in light of the present situation is not clear. In either case, the psalmist feels confident of Yahweh's deliverance from the present situation.

Nature of Violence

Since the motif of violence is so firmly woven into the fabric of the psalm we shall have to consider its interpretation in each section. This approach will shed some light on the relationship between the currently envisaged situation and the motif of hope, and thus indicate something of the response to violence that is modelled here.

The motif of violence is introduced immediately when we move into the body of the psalm, though the title would also indicate some violence in terms of the Philistines seizing (בֶּאֱחֹז) David in Gath. The opening plea for God's grace (חָנֵּנִי אֱלֹהִים, verse 1) is set in the context of people[142] pursuing the psalmist, possibly desiring to crush the psalmist, depending on the sense we

---

[141]It is possible that verses 5 and 11-12 constitute a refrain (so Raabe, *Psalm Structures*, 91), though the wording is not quite identical at each point, leading Kraus, *Psalms 1-59*, 525, to reject such a possibility.

[142]As noted above, although verse 2 uses the singular forms אֱנוֹשׁ and לֹחֵם, the fact that verse 3 speaks of "many" (רַבִּים) indicates that these references are to be understood collectively.

give to שֹׁאֲפַי (verse 2).[143] The word could refer to an intense pursuit, or to a desire to crush someone, though on any interpretation it is indicative of intense persecution. This is given a military twist in verse 2b, where a warrior is pictured as pressing in (יִלְחָצֵנִי) on the psalmist. The terminology at this point could be understood in purely literal terms, and the repetition of terms in verse 3 gives no necessary indication that at this stage we are to read the psalm in any other sense. Only Dahood's suggestion on the possibility that שׁוֹרְרָי is to be given the sense of my "slanderer" or "defamer"[144] may provide an alternative perception, but this meaning of the word is by no means clear.[145] The opening picture of violence would thus appear to be primarily physical in its emphasis, though this would also include some degree of psychological distress. We shall need, however, to note the ways in which verse 6 adapts this perception.

The first occurrence of the refrain-like material in verses 4-5 then responds to this situation. It affirms that trust in God is what is necessary when facing violence, whether real or potential. When, in the context of trust in God, the question is asked, מַה־יַּעֲשֶׂה בָשָׂר לִי, the presumed answer is that no form of human violence can overcome the protection of God that has been summoned. Trust is all that is necessary. The placement of this material immediately after the initial plea is of particular importance, for it affirms that God has in some sense already dealt with the hubris of the enemies. Retributive violence in response to any form of violence is therefore unnecessary.

The actual nature of the assault on the psalmist only becomes clear in verses 6-7. Only here are the actions of the oppressors described in non-metaphorical language, specifically in terms of some form of verbal assault. The interpretation of verse 6 is complicated by a number of textual problems.[146] In spite of the impressive range of alternatives available, the MT can still be considered as intelligible if we regard יְעַצֵּבוּ as derived from עצב II, "twist,

---

[143]In context, the parallelism with the second member's reference to the pressing of an attack would suggest "crush" as the more probable translation. Commentators are divided, though we are fortunate in that the sense given to the word here does not markedly alter the nature of violence that is described.

[144]So Dahood, *Psalms II*, 42. The linguistic evidence for this is examined earlier in the same volume, on pages 25f. Dahood is followed by Tate, *Psalms 51-100*, 65, and NIV.

[145]The word occurs at a total of 6 points, all in the psalms - 5:9, 27:11, 54:7, 56:3, 59:11 and 92:12. Although the wider context of psalms 5, 27, 56 and possibly 59 includes some element of verbal assault, this element is absent from Psalms 54 and 92. In addition, the immediate context, especially that of the parallelism, does not require the sense of "slander" in any instance. Although the word clearly has some sense of oppression, the usage in the Psalms does not require the sense of slander, though slander may well be included in the wider body of oppression reflected by the word.

[146]*BHS* notes that LXX seems to presume a consonantal variation, with יתעבו for the MT's יעצבו. Other readings also exist. Similarly, the pronominal suffix on דְּבָרָי may have arisen as a result of dittography.

shape".[147] The specific actions of the oppressors that are described here are therefore those of twisting the words of the psalmist. Taken in conjunction with the parallel references to a conspiracy against the psalmist in verses 6b-7, the actual situation faced would appear to be one of a conspiracy against the life (נֶפֶשׁ) of the psalmist. This is well brought out by the NIV's translation:-

> All day long they twist my words,
> they are always plotting to harm me.
> They conspire, they lurk,
> they watch my steps,
> eager to take my life.

This is perhaps done through the spreading of a false report based on a distortion of what the psalmist has said. At this stage, physical violence has not been directly enacted by the enemies, though the twisting of the psalmist's words would reflect something that is currently causing psychological distress. Such distress seems to be linked to the goal of the enemies, which is the death of the psalmist. The physical violence intimated by verses 2-3 is here given a psychological twist, but the fundamentally physical nature remains since this is the perceived goal of the violence. This in turn suggests that the worst violence is perceived as being imminent, which is why God's protection is specifically summoned. Nevertheless, this points to a present experience of psychological violence.

The psalmist's imprecation against the enemies is then recorded in verses 8-9. In spite of the textual difficulties posed by both verse 8[148] and verse 9,[149] the general thrust of the imprecation is clear enough, though some of the elements here remain uncertain. What is clear is that God is summoned to bring down (הוֹרֵד, verse 8) the enemies, with the enemies here personified as nations through the use of cultic language.[150] Essentially, appeal is made to God as the divine judge, so that he is the one who is to act, not the psalmist. The "bringing down" of the enemies would appear to be the passing of the death penalty on them, in which case the prayer is controlled by *lex talionis*, since the stated aim of the enemies is the death of the psalmist.[151]

The motif of violence is much less pronounced in verses 10-14, reflecting

---

[147]The decision of BDB to place the gloss for this psalm under עצב I, "hurt, pain, grieve", has surely contributed to the contemporary confusion, though the range of ancient alternatives indicates that the difficulty has long been felt.

[148]Cf. Tate, *Psalms 51-100*, 67, for the text followed here.

[149]Cf. G. R. Driver, "Psalm LVI. 9 'Thou Tellest My Wanderings'", *JTS* 21 (1970), 402-403.

[150]With Anderson, *Psalms*, 423.

[151]This would also indicate that God's anger is in parallel with the pursuit of the psalmist by the enemies mentioned in verses 2-3.

the fact that God as the divine judge has now been summoned to act. There is a strong sense of assurance here that God will indeed act against the enemies, an assurance of what could be known about one's relationship with God.[152] The point to which these verses build is that in the midst of oppression and violence the matter is to be committed to God. No human violence is considered sufficient to overcome the protective power of God. God's intervention, through his word,[153] transfers the psalmist to the realm of life.[154]

In summary, we can note that Psalm 56 summons God's protection in a situation of predominantly psychological violence. The psalmist suffers from a misrepresentation of speech by the enemies, a distortion that is part of a perceived plan on their part. The aim of this plan is the death of the psalmist. There is therefore some current action against the psalmist, but also the imminent possibility of death. That is why the psalm uses the language of physical violence in verses 2-3, though without denying that the principle form of violence currently experienced is of a psychological nature.

Response to Violence

In spite of the numerous textual problems that it provides, this psalm is therefore to be interpreted as one in which the psalmist is seeking God's protection in the midst of intense oppression. The poet is portrayed as currently suffering psychological torment as a result of a misrepresentation of what has previously been said, though this is apparently also causing physical suffering. This misrepresentation means that the psalmist's well being is under a virtual state of siege, a situation complicated by the fact that the goal of the enemies is presented as the psalmist's death. The psalm thus reflects a situation of predominantly psychological violence, but one in which physical violence is imminent.

Because of this situation, we have the prayer of verses 8ff. The situation is one that the psalmist perceives as dire, but Yahweh alone provides a model of help. Thus, Yahweh can be asked to bring these enemies down, a request that is rooted in the *lex talionis* since it essentially asks that Yahweh do to the enemies what they are attempting to do to the psalmist. The threat of death that they have brought to the psalmist must now be brought to the enemies. Further evidence for this is seen in the fact that this summons occurs in the midst of a forensic representation of God. Once again, therefore, the psalm refuses to justify human violence in response to an attack. Rather, the right of retributive violence is seen as belonging to Yahweh alone.

The strongly developed declarations of trust provide a further nuance to this

---

[152]Miller, *They Cried to the Lord*, 130.
[153]James L. Mays, *Psalms*, Louisville: John Knox, 1994, 208, describes this as the "Old Testament gospel."
[154]Kraus, *Psalms 1-59*, 527.

psalm as a theological reason is given for the hope of this protection. Hope in Yahweh, and more specifically in his word,[155] is portrayed as a sufficient shelter from all forms of human violence. No human assault can overcome this defence. Indeed, the psalm affirms that it is this word that has already acted in moving the psalmist from death to life. God's violence in retribution is appropriate and sufficient, and in spite of the tension between the present experience and what is affirmed about God, it is the affirmation of God's saving power that is central.

The psalm thus seeks to model a prayer of protection, in which the right to violence is given over to Yahweh in a judicial context, a context that stresses the justice of his actions. In doing so, it not only renounces human violence in retaliation, but seeks to assure other worshippers that no other action is necessary. One must trust God, and summon his help. That is all. The worshipper who now uses this psalm is summoned to take the same position. Indeed, the fact that the psalm's conclusion (verses 13-14) looks to the setting of congregational worship indicates that from the outset the psalm was understood to have a teaching function, in which the psalmist's own thank offerings (תּוֹדֹת) become a means of instructing others.[156]

The final response to violence that is modelled here is therefore not only one of trust, but also one that seeks to make that trust something that is declared as a means of instruction to others in the worshipping community. One expression of trust in a context of oppression thus becomes more than a personal response - it becomes a type of the response that the community as a whole is meant to follow.

Psalm 64

Form Critical Discussion

In comparison with the other psalms studied in this chapter, the discussion of Psalm 64 is marked by a fair degree of agreement. The majority of scholars have seen this as the prayer of a private individual, though there are some dissenting voices to be considered. A further issue that needs to be considered is the relationship of this psalm to the institution of the psalms of the accused.

Although the majority of scholars place this psalm among the prayers of private individuals, Mowinckel regards the "I" of this psalm as a national figure, presumably the king.[157] In following this line of approach he clearly

---

[155]Presumably the word of judgment sought in verse 9, since verse 10 claims this as evidence that Yahweh is on the side of the psalmist.
[156]Cf. Knight, *Psalms*, 1:260.
[157]Mowinckel, *Psalms in Israel's Worship*, 1:220.

reflects the influence of his student Birkeland.[158] However, once we accept that there is no need to see the enemies in the Psalms as necessarily being foreign powers, the need for such a reading falls away. It is surely significant to note that in this particular instance, Eaton finds nothing more than analogy to the royal psalms and accordingly denies that the speaker is here a royal figure.[159]

A variant to the interpretation of the speaker as king is that offered by Briggs[160] (and to a lesser extent Weiser[161]) who interprets the speaker as the nation of Israel. Unfortunately, Briggs provides no evidence for seeing the psalm in these terms. In the absence of anything that is of a specifically national character it seems best to follow the majority opinion and understand the psalm as the prayer of a private individual.

That this is a prayer for protection would seem to be clearly established by the following:-

1. Verse 2, makes a specific summons to God to hear the voice of the psalmist and to provide protection (תִּצֹּר) from the dread generated by the enemies. Similarly, verse 3 asks that God hide (תַּסְתִּירֵנִי)the psalmist from the schemes of the wicked.

2. As the rest of the psalm works itself out from this opening plea, the fact that this is a prayer for protection would seem to be clearly established. We should, however, specifically note that verses 4-7 describe in some detail the activities of the enemies from which protection is sought. The activities of the enemies in this part of the psalm are likened to a hunter trapping prey. This provides a clear motivation for the protection of God to be applied.

We must, however, also consider the context that generates the need for protection. Although Bellinger considerably overstates the position in asserting that most commentators link this psalm to a situation of false accusation, there is still a considerable body of support for this position.[162] This line of interpretation is most fully developed by Delekat,[163] though Kraus seems to indicate some degree of support for it.[164] Delekat finds traces of priestly oracles that are associated with a period of incubation in the psalm, especially in verses 8-11. There is, in addition, the fact that the psalmist is associated with the צַדִּיק (verse 11), which may suggest a legal background. On this basis, it can be argued that the psalm needs to be interpreted as a prayer for protection against

---

[158]Birkeland, *Evildoers*, 22.

[159]Eaton, *Kingship*, 86. Cf. Croft, *Identity*, 144, though he gives no reasons for including this psalm among the prayers of private individuals.

[160]Briggs, *Psalms* 2:76ff.

[161]Weiser, *Psalms*, 457f.

[162]W. H. Bellinger, Jr, *Psalms: Reading and Interpreting the Book of Praises*, Peabody: Hendrickson, 1990, 67.

[163]Delekat, *Asylie*, 67ff.

[164]Kraus, *Psalms 60-150*, 23f.

false accusers.

In support of the association with the psalms of false accusation, we should note that the major actions currently attributed to the enemies in the psalm are all associated with speech, and that their speech is linked to injustice. In addition, the psalm retains the contrast between the wicked (verse 3) and the righteous (verse 11), a contrast that is naturally part of language relating to false accusation. However, there is nothing in the psalm itself to suggest that the psalmist has sought refuge in the temple,[165] so the attempt to link it to the institution of the prayers of the accused seems gratuitous. It is dependant upon a range of presuppositions that the text itself does not support. In addition, and perhaps more importantly, there is no appeal in the psalm for Yahweh to judge the case, something that is a defining mark of the institutional psalms of the accused, and neither is there a specific affirmation of innocence by the psalmist. This is not to deny that false accusation plays a part in the psalm; but its function is not linked to the institutional form of such prayers. The psalm is therefore more likely to be a psalm that makes use of the motif of false accusation, but in a non-institutional manner.[166] The recognition of this factor leaves open the possibility that the prayer seeks protection in a wider range of areas, as may be hinted at in verses 6-7.[167] Accordingly, the psalm is to be interpreted as a prayer for protection by an individual Israelite. This is a classification that may include the element of false accusation, but only as a part of a broader range of areas in which protection is sought.

Structure

Although the text of the psalm is in poor condition, especially in verses 7-8, its major literary movements are clear enough. Apart from the title in verse 1, the psalm can be outlined as follows:-

1. An initial plea for God's help and protection from the actions of the enemies (verses 2-3).

2. A description of the activities of the enemies in verses 4-7. This description provides the reason for the psalmist's need as it flows immediately from the plea for protection from these enemies.

3. Verses 8-9 then provide a reflection on the certainty of God's actions on behalf of the afflicted against the enemies.[168]

---

[165] Bellinger, *Psalmody and Prophecy*, 55f.

[166] So Beyerlin, *Die Rettung*, 30 and Tate, *Psalms 51-100*, 133.

[167] The text of verse 7 is unfortunately very difficult, and a clear interpretation of its function is therefore difficult to achieve.

[168] The interpretation of this section is somewhat uncertain because of the unusual use of the waw consecutive imperfect in these verses. We shall argue below that it is an expression of confidence that comes out of the fact that God has been summoned to act in the initial plea.

4. The psalm closes with a final summons to praise Yahweh, a summons that is based in what is perceived as the natural response to his intervention.

Apart from these features, there is also a degree of artistry in the way in which certain key terms that describe the actions of the enemies are also used to describe the actions of God, though there is surely some sense of irony intended in doing so. Thus, both the enemies and God are portrayed as hunters, and both shoot "suddenly" (פִּתְאוֹם)[169]. God's judgment also matches the crime, since the words used by enemies, the current source of distress (verse 4), will be their undoing (verse 9). This suggests that verses 2-7 and verses 8-10 are consciously presented as being in parallel to one another. Nevertheless, in examining the nature of violence we will follow the broader movement outlined first, though the implications of this pattern of paralleling will need to be considered.

Nature of Violence

The initial plea of the psalmist fails to provide any clear evidence of the nature of the persecution that is being experienced. The words,

> Hear, O God, as I voice my complaint,
> from the dread of the enemy protect my life,

are general enough to cover a range of situations, although they do suggest a situation of some urgency. What they do indicate, however, is that God is summoned to protect (תִּצֹּר) the life of the psalmist from the terror (מִפַּחַד) of the enemies.[170] The seriousness of the threat posed by these enemies is such that the life (חַיָּי) of the psalmist is under threat. Exactly how this threat could become reality is not stated, though it is noted in verse 3 that the enemies are involved in various plots and schemes (סוֹד,[171] רִגְשַׁת). The enemies are thus portrayed as actively working against the life of the psalmist.

The evidence is suggestive of the possibility that the main weapon that they currently employ is the use of words. Their words clearly cause terror on the part of the psalmist indicating that their current actions reflect the inflicting of some sort of psychological torment. Such an interpretation may also be borne out by the fact that the enemies are also called פֹּעֲלֵי אָוֶן (verse 3). The exact meaning of this phrase has been the matter of some dispute, but the association with the pronouncing of a curse seems clear, even if the link with sorcery is

---

[169] Though there is a spelling difference through the use of *matres lectionis*.

[170] Although verse 2 only uses the singular form אֹיֵב, the use of the plural in verse 4 indicates that the singular is used here with a collective force. Cf. McCullough and Taylor, "Psalms", 335.

[171] Since סוֹד can refer either to the plot or the process of plotting, a translation such as "conspiracy" is necessary here. Cf. Tate, *Psalms 51-100*, 133.

difficult to sustain.¹⁷² If so, the enemies are portrayed as currently inflicting psychological torment on the psalmist through their plots and words, and this may also include a curse. However, the violence is not of a purely psychological nature since these actions also pose a threat to the psalmist's life. The use of these techniques merges the psychological and physical dimensions of violence, though it also suggests that the worst elements may still come. It is the fact that physical violence of some sort is imminent along with the reference to the terror caused by the enemy that suggests that the major form of violence here is psychological in nature.

The merging of these dimensions of violence is continued in the description of the enemies in verses 4-7. Throughout, they are presented through the metaphor of a group of hunters, though in their case their sword is their tongue and their arrows are poisoned words.¹⁷³ It is also notable that their actions are carried out in secret (verse 6), all of which is suggestive of the nature of the conspiracy that they enact against the psalmist. However, although there is a cluster of violence-related terms in this section,¹⁷⁴ the use of metaphor throughout makes it difficult to see any development of it taking place since its presentation in the initial plea. It serves more to present a characterisation¹⁷⁵ of the enemies that is consistent with the initial plea than to develop the motif of violence any further. The enemies' violence is a mixture of the psychological and the physical, though the threat throughout is that, as hunters, they have not yet finished in the stalking of their prey. This is suggestive of the fact that although their violent actions against the psalmist have so far been to create a condition of psychological dread, it is physical death that is actually sought. The imagery of ambush and the stalking of the psalmist contribute to the psalm by developing the reader's awareness of the fact that there is a continued process of hunting going on in which the "trophy" is the death of the psalmist. Again, there is a mingling of psychological violence and the threat of further physical violence, in which the worst of the physical violence is perceived as being imminent. Indeed, its very imminence is what causes the psychological suffering.

The major shift in the psalm occurs in verses 8-10. The text now focuses on

---

¹⁷²Cf. Kraus, *Theology*, 135f. He points to parallels with Egyptian execration texts and therefore suggests the possibility of some form of curse. Kraus is prepared to move from the curse into magic, a shift that was not too great in the ancient world, though he finally settles on describing the פֹּעֲלֵי אָוֶן as those who do what is "uncanny."

¹⁷³Cf. Dahood, *Psalms II*, 104, for the interpretation of מָר as "poison."

¹⁷⁴Thus, the speech of the enemies is compared with weapons such as arrows or a sword (verse 4), whilst their actions are portrayed as a violent ambush of the upright (תָּם). The imagery is adapted to that of hunting in verse 6, though there is no development in terms of the nature of violence described.

¹⁷⁵The closing line of verse 7, וְקֶרֶב אִישׁ וְלֵב עָמֹק, may therefore be intended as a conclusion on the character of the enemies rather than a general statement, though in the current context it remains obscure.

God's violence in response to the violence of the enemies. A major interpretative problem confronts us here in the use of waw-consecutive imperfects, a grammatical form that is, to say the least, unusual in such a context. Although Bellinger takes these verbs as clear evidence of the "certainty of hearing",[176] such a meaning needs to be established, especially when we note the fact that the waw-consecutive imperfect is not elsewhere used in a "certainty of hearing" context.[177] Bellinger treats the verbs here as having a future sense, though one would normally treat such verbs as having a past sense. Clearly, this poses a major grammatical difficulty.

Four major options seem to be available in the interpretation of these verbs. These are:-

1. The verbs function as optatives. When read in this way, these verses represent the wish of the psalmist.[178] As such, they are virtually a continuation of the prayer of verses 2-3. This has the effect of making verses 4-7 little more than a commentary on the opening prayer. Although this is a possible interpretation, it seems to ignore the role played by the *waw* as a conjunction.

2. We may treat these verbs as past actions, describing what God has done.[179] Although this is the most immediately attractive view grammatically since it follows the most common use of the waw-consecutive, it stumbles in the context of the psalm. If this is what God has already done, then the initial prayer for protection becomes meaningless - why pray for God to do what he has already done? If one was to respond that what is sought is a continuation of what God has already done, then it becomes apparent that we are already moving beyond the interpretation of these verbs as only describing something in the past tense.

3. These verbs may be read as the equivalent of the so-called perfect of certainty.[180] Such verbs have a future reference, and would certainly reflect a "certainty of hearing." The difficulty with this view is that it almost requires that there be a speech from a cultic prophet after verse 7 since otherwise there is no obvious basis for the certainty.[181] In addition, although the imperfect may be used in parallel with the perfect of

---

[176]Bellinger, *Psalmody and Prophecy*, 56.

[177]Cf. Tate, *Psalms 51-100*, 131.

[178]So McCullough and Taylor, "Psalms", 337f.

[179]So Kraus, *Psalms 60-150*, 24f, Weiser, *Psalms*, 458.

[180]This is presumably the view of Bellinger, *Psalmody and Prophecy*, 56, though he does not provide a grammatical comment on the text. A grammatical defence of this position is provided by Kirkpatrick, *Psalms*, 359, who also points to a parallel with verse 4.

[181]If we are correct in interpreting Bellinger at this point, then there would be an odd conflict between his rejection of the role of cultic prophets and his interpretation of the psalm.

certainty or in a subsequent point in a narrative, it is not otherwise used to express a certainty on its own.[182] If the psalm presumes the activity of a cultic prophet, then there may well have been a context suitable to the use of these imperfects, but it is difficult to sustain an interpretation of the psalm that requires something additional that cannot be proved.

4. The consecutive may be taken as future, expressing some degree of assurance, but falling short of absolute certainty.[183] This is an attested use of the consecutive imperfect,[184] and leads to the waw being read as a mild asseveration. In all, this is the best option since it not only takes the context into account, but it is also grammatically consistent.

If this interpretation of the verbs is correct, then the psalmist does not express certainty in what God will do, but the statement is also more than a wish. One could, perhaps, characterise it as a statement of probability, and thus translate the *waw* as a hopeful "surely!". Within this presentation of God's actions, though, there is a tension held between what God will probably do (verse 8) and the likely, though natural, outcome of the actions of the enemies (verse 9).

God's anticipated action is the shooting of an arrow at the enemies, something that is surely intended as a counterpart to the arrows that had been shot by the enemies, though this time these are the arrows of justice. The punishment is clearly equal to the crime, an application of the *lex talionis*. There is, in addition, the apparent fruit of the enemies own wickedness in verse 9. The moral order of creation is also assumed to be operative, so that their own actions bring about their end.[185] There is thus justice in God's direct action, but also in the moral universe that exists, something that in the Old Testament is rooted in the theology of creation. In that sense, it is still God who brings the enemies down, but in this instance the means is less direct than in verse 8. It remains, however, an expression of the *lex talionis*, and it is the twofold expression of it that leads to the summons to praise in verses 10-11. What God achieves in the protection of the innocent, whether through direct action or the moral order of creation, provides a basis upon which all may be summoned to come in praise.

In summary, we can observe that it is the combination of the terror caused by the words of the enemies, whether or not these are the words of a curse, in conjunction with a threat of some sort against the psalmist's life that defines the violence of this psalm. References to "terror" naturally point to psychological violence, though this must be seen in context. The terror is generated by the

---

[182]GKC §106n.
[183]So Tate, *Psalms 51-100*, 131.
[184]GKC §111w.
[185]The text here is once again quite difficult, with seeming differences in number and gender. With Bellinger, *Psalmody and Prophecy*, 56, it seems best to see the actions of the enemies as bringing about their own downfall. Cf. Rogerson and McKay, *Psalms 51-100*, 70.

further threat of physical violence. As long as it remains in the realm of the threat, though, it only affects the psalmist as psychological violence.

Response to Violence

This psalm is entirely consistent with the other psalms we have examined in this group. The violence is currently experienced psychologically through the plots of the enemies, but tends towards a physical manifestation given the image of them stalking the psalmist. More importantly, the full force of the violence is yet to be felt, and it is into this context that God is summoned to act. Again, there is no place in this prayer for human retribution, apart from that which is the natural outcome of the plots of the wicked. The right to violence on behalf of the upright (נָקָם) belongs to God alone. Accordingly, he is summoned to act on behalf of the righteous, with the expectation that this action will be governed by the *lex talionis*. The fact that God may not act, which we suggested is implicit in the choice of tense in verses 8-10, does not change this fundamental position.[186]

The new dimension that this psalm adds is that of incorporating God's position into the moral order of creation. The psalmist therefore expresses,

> the conviction that the deepest and most closely guarded secrets of those opposed to his [i.e. God's] way are to be fully and utterly exposed.[187]

In such a universe one must accept God's right of response, but also recognise that this may come about either through direct action or through the order of creation. In either case, though, the right of response belongs to God alone, and it is this belief that God will act in some way that generates the praise of the righteous. The hope that God will act, however, is also the basis on which the psalmist summons the congregation to praise. The final verse is clearly intended to instruct the congregation, guiding them to adopt the position taken by the psalmist. In the face of danger and violence, they too are to place their trust in Yahweh and take refuge in him (וְחָסָה בּוֹ). From this flows praise, a praise in which all are instructed and invited to participate.

---

[186] An analogy may be drawn to the statement of Shadrach, Meshach and Abednego in Daniel 3:16ff. God is there seen as able to act if he chooses, but even if he does not act it is not the right of the three friends to respond.
[187] Durham, "Psalms", 299f.

Psalm 143

Form Critical Discussion

Amongst those following a cultic interpretation of the psalms, it is generally agreed that the speaker in this psalm is the king,[188] probably one facing a situation of an invading enemy, though possibility of the presence of a pagan lord remains.[189] Again, it cannot be denied that the language here may have been originally royal. However, the decision of the final editors to remove most directly royal rubrics suggests that a different line of interpretation is now suggested for the psalm. Further, given the absence of even a military metaphor, the main foundations for a royal interpretation of the psalm are less than secure. If, as many scholars suggest, the psalm is post-exilic,[190] then the use of terms such as עַבְדֶּךָ (verse 2) to describe the supplicant may simply be an example of democratised language. Even if this date is not provable, and arguments based on a proposed date for a psalm have an unfortunate propensity towards circularity, there is no reason why an ordinary Israelite may not be described as a servant of Yahweh. The absence of any specifically royal language accordingly leads to the conclusion that this psalm is to be read as the prayer of a private individual. However, even with this conclusion established a number of factors remain unclear.

The situation of an individual falsely accused could provide an appropriate *Sitz im Leben* for the psalm. Specifically, we should note that in the initial prayer, the psalmist requests of Yahweh וְאַל־תָּבוֹא בְמִשְׁפָּט אֶת־עַבְדֶּךָ. It must be admitted, however, that if this psalm is a prayer of the accused then the language is much less precise than the other psalms that we identified in chapter 2 as making up this group. In particular, the absence of an appeal for a declaration of innocence stands against such an interpretation. Further, in verse 2 the psalmist admits guilt[191] in a generalised sense, making the observation כִּי לֹא־יִצְדַּק לְפָנֶיךָ כָל־חָי. Such an affirmation is contrary to the pattern that

---

[188] Eaton, *Kingship*, 64, placing the psalm in his "clearly royal" group. Cf. Johnson, *The Cultic Prophet and Israel's Psalmody*, 266ff, and Croft, *Identity*, 124. Croft, is more guarded than the others in making this identification.

[189] Birkeland, *Die Feinde*, 280-295 and, *idem*, *Evildoers*, 34.

[190] Anderson, *Psalms*, 926, points to numerous allusions to earlier psalms in support of this conclusion. Walther Eichrodt, *Theology of the Old Testament*, 2 vols, London: SCM Press, 1961, 1967, 2:399, points to the developed concept of sin as being typical of the post-exilic period.

[191] It is probably this factor that led to the treatment of the psalm in classical Christian theology as one of the Seven Penitential Psalms. The psalm is not strictly penitential, but the element of confession means that this is not an inappropriate element. Cf, Kittel, *Die Psalmen*, 428.

Prayers for Protection

is evident in the institutional[192] psalms of the accused since the procedure there is to deny guilt.[193] It does seem that the situation is dire, but no specifics are offered for the setting.[194] False accusation may indeed be a part of the background of the psalm, but it is not the primary experience of the psalmist.

The classification of this psalm is made more difficult by the way it almost collects pieces out of the tradition of the lament.[195] Although the evidence in this instance is less compelling than at other points, the best position is still to interpret this psalm as a prayer for protection from the violence of enemies. The main evidence for this classification is found in the introduction and conclusion to the psalm, though other elements are certainly capable of being interpreted in a manner favourable to this position. In particular, we should note the following points in favour of the inclusion of this psalm in the classification of the Prayers for Protection:-

1. The opening two verses specifically summon Yahweh to action on behalf of the psalmist in response to the prayer that is offered. The pattern is established by the opening words of the psalm proper:-

> Yahweh, hear my prayer,
> hearken to my plea for mercy.

Immediately following this prayer for Yahweh's intervention is a declaration of the actions of the enemy against the psalmist. This includes references to the hostile pursuit that the enemy carries out against the psalmist (verse 3). A request for protection is clearly sought.

2. The psalmist's request for a swift answer from Yahweh (verse 7) is cast in terms of the alternative being a journey to the pit, which is a synonym for death. The psalmist is therefore seeking an answer from Yahweh where such an outcome will not have to be faced.

3. In verse 9 Yahweh is summoned to rescue (הַצִּילֵנִי) the psalmist from the enemies. The nature of such a plea in a context where, as we shall argue, the full force of violence is still to be unleashed suggests that this is a prayer for protection.

4. In verse 11, Yahweh is summoned to preserve the life (תְּחַיֵּנִי) of the

---

[192]Cf. Beyerlin, *Die Rettung*, 36f. He notes that the request for an oracle in verse 8 suggests a cultic setting, but not as a part of the institution.

[193]Although not treated in this study due to an absence of references to violence, this is particularly evident in Psalm 26, though it is also apparent in the psalms treated in chapter 2.

[194]Cf. Durham, "Psalms", 452.

[195]The interpretation is even more complex if with, for example, Oswald Loretz, *Die Psalmen II: Beitrag der Ugarit Texte zum Verständnis von Kolometrie und Textologie der Psalmen, Psalm 90-150*, Neukirchener Verlag: Neukirchen-Vluyn, 1979, 359, we regard the psalm as a composite of two separate pieces in verses 1-6 and verses 7-12. However, we shall argue in "Structure" (below) that this is an unnecessary position.

psalmist, a request that is paralleled by a petition that seeks the deliverance of the psalmist from the current distress (מְצָרָה).

These elements clearly indicate a desire for Yahweh's protection from the enemies, with the opening and closing petitions forming something of an inclusion to the psalm as a whole. The strong requests in the opening and closing verses especially tend to support the interpretation of this psalm as a prayer for protection, but it is also clear that the other elements of the psalm can be interpreted in these terms. In this respect, it is notable that the psalm uses the imperative a total of 9 times (three times in verse 1, two times in both verses 7 and 8 and once each in verses 9 and 10), and that in every case it is directed to Yahweh. Since this is a prayer, that sort of linguistic feature is not particularly remarkable. What is notable, though, is the fact that 6 of these imperatives (those of verses 1, 7 and 9) are used in the context of requests for Yahweh's protection from the enemies. The other three are in terms of the psalmist's desire to hear from Yahweh and respond faithfully to him. Since the presence of imperatives tends to indicate the central petitions of the prayer, such a concentration of verbs in the area of a request for protection and deliverance may be taken as further evidence that we should treat this psalm as a prayer for protection.

Structure

Before we can move on to consider the structure of the psalm *per se*, we need first to consider the possibility that Psalm 143 is a composite of two separate psalms, with verses 1-6 and 7-12 being originally separate. Loretz argues in support of such a position that we should note the following:-[196]

1. Verses 1-6 are mostly in a 3+3 meter, whilst verses 7-12 are 3+2. The סֶלָה at the end of verse 6 could therefore be significant.

2. Verses 1-6 can be read as a lamentation (*Klagelied*), whilst verses 7-12 can be understood as a petition (*Bitte*).

Although these points are noteworthy, they are not finally persuasive. The normal structure of the lament is such that it leads to a petition, so this shift is to be expected. Further, there is some evidence of an inclusion in verses 1-2 and 11-12, since in both instances the psalmist's self-description before Yahweh is as עַבְדֶּךָ, whilst Yahweh is summoned to act "in your righteousness" (בְּצִדְקָתֶךָ).[197] Coetzee also points to a substantial body of shared vocabulary across both halves of the psalm, again suggesting its original unity.[198] Finally, we should note that to achieve the regular division in meter it

---

[196] Loretz, *Die Psalmen II*, 359.
[197] Allen, *Psalms 101-150*, 284. Cf. Coetzee, *Die Spanning*, 248.
[198] Coetzee, *Die Spanning*, 247, points to נַפְשִׁי (verses 3, 6, 8b, 11 and 12a), רוּחִי (verses 4 and 7), צִדְקָתֶךָ (verses 1b and 11), עֲנֵנִי (verses 1b and 7a), אוֹיֵב (verses 3, 9

is necessary to delete verse 3bβ, and in any case the irregularity of meter could be a conscious poetic device.[199] These elements suggest that while there are clear distinctions to be drawn between verses 1-6 and 7-12 they are not sufficient to demonstrate a division of the psalm. The validity of these distinctions also has the effect of rendering invalid Kissane's suggestion that the psalm is to be treated as containing three strophes of five lines each.[200] Such a structure is a triumph of style over content.

An alternative approach, but one that still sees the psalm as a composite, is adopted by Lindström. He suggests that there was an original poem consisting of verses 1, 3-4, 6-8b, 9 and 11-12. To this have been added verses 2, 5, 8cd and 10, all of which reflect either the motif of a confession of guilt or trust in Yahweh.[201] The effect of the removal of these elements is that the psalm is more specifically a prayer for protection, but one that is now somewhat more general in that the petitions for Yahweh's instruction and judgment are removed, as also is the reflection on what Yahweh has done in the past. Lindström's observations have some validity in that the elements he deletes fit the traditional definition of the genre of the lament poorly. In addition, the removal of these elements means that the petitions for Yahweh's protection from future sins are all removed, creating a more uniform piece. However, the benefits obtained through this approach may be more in bringing the psalm into line with the standard categories than in the actual interpretation of the psalm itself.

Lindström's arguments can all be countered. The fact that there is a clear inclusion with verses 1-2 and 11-12 is strongly suggestive of the authenticity of verse 2. Similarly, reflection on what Yahweh has done in the past as a basis for a current prayer for protection is also found in Psalm 27:1-3, so verse 5 is not form critically unacceptable. The position of verses 8cd and 10 is less clear, though it is notable that Psalm 51:12-19 seeks Yahweh's restoration along with a prayer to be led in Yahweh's ways. Therefore, although the elements removed by Lindström are form critically unusual, they can all be paralleled. The evidence adduced by Lindström is thus ambiguous, and it is best to treat the psalm as originating more or less as we now have it.[202] Even though it demonstrates a certain level of form critical novelty, the psalm is coherent as it stands before us now.

Accordingly, we need to outline the psalm as it currently stands. The observation that there is a shift after verse 6 indicates that there is a primary

---

and 12) and עַבְדֶּךָ (verses 2 and 12b). He also points to some commonly used roots, though these are not necessarily as significant.

[199]Oesterley, *Psalms*, 566.
[200]Kissane, *Psalms II*, 309.
[201]Lindström, *Suffering and Sin*, 123ff.
[202]Even if Lindström is correct, we would still need to interpret the psalm in its canonical form.

division of the psalm at that point, as may also be borne out by the סֶלָה. However, within the division of verses 1-6 as the lamentation and verses 7-12 as the petition we need to note other elements that make up these sections. Broadly, we can outline the whole psalm as containing five main units, three in verses 1-6 and two in verses 7-12. Even in summary form, it will be seen that these units point to the unity of the psalm. The units are:-

1. Introductory plea for deliverance in which the psalmist expresses a desire for relief (verses 1-2).
2. Description of the actions of the enemies and the effect of these actions on the psalmist (verses 3-4).
3. A reflection on the works of Yahweh as the one who can help (verses 5-6).
4. Petition for help, flowing from verse 6, emphasising the elements of trust and the need to walk in the ways of Yahweh (verses 7-8).
5. New petitions, summing up the earlier elements that have come before (verses 9-12).[203]

Nature of Violence

That this is a prayer that comes from a context of oppression is apparent from the opening words. The introductory plea (verses 1-2) summons Yahweh to action on behalf of the psalmist. It is a situation where grace is needed. In this situation, the psalmist prays to Yahweh וְאַל־תָּבוֹא בְמִשְׁפָּט אֶת־עַבְדֶּךָ. In comparison with the Prayers of the Accused, such a statement is remarkable. The Prayers of the Accused envisage a court situation with a declaration of innocence before Yahweh, whereas here the psalmist essentially asks Yahweh not to commence legal proceedings.[204] The protection that is sought is therefore clearly understood as something that flows from the grace of Yahweh, and not from the righteousness of the psalmist.[205] There is a clear contrast that is drawn between the judgment of Yahweh, which is right but expressed through faithfulness, and the actions of the enemies. The presumption is that should Yahweh choose to act against the psalmist, then he would be entirely right in doing so.[206] This understanding is central to the whole of the psalm.

The violence of Yahweh's judgment against the psalmist, should he choose to exercise it, would thus be entirely correct. The form that this violence would take is unstated, and is perhaps to be understood in terms of what is finally requested against the enemies in verse 12. What enables the psalmist to come

---

[203] On this structure, cf, J. P. M. van der Ploeg, *Psalmen II*, Roermond: J. J. Romen and Zonen, 1974, 465.
[204] Cf. Johnson, *The Cultic Prophet and Israel's Psalmody*, 267.
[205] Rogerson and McKay, *Psalms 101-150*, 169.
[206] Brueggemann, *Message*, 104 appropriately comments that the psalmist "seeks graciousness, not justice, for justice will not suffice."

before Yahweh is the clearly expressed trust in his אמנה and צדקה (verse 1). Yahweh's faithfulness, expressed in righteousness, means that he is understood as refraining from entering into the violence of an unnecessary legal judgment with the psalmist. What is significant is that we therefore begin the psalm from the perspective of the potential of Yahweh's judgments, a perspective that already assumes that the right to violence belongs to Yahweh alone. Even before we are alerted to the actions of the oppressors, the psalm has therefore opened up its central perspective on violence, which is an affirmation of the fact that this right belongs solely to Yahweh.

The actual context of oppression within the psalm is introduced in verse 3, though the opening כִּי links it back to the prayer for Yahweh's grace in verse 2.[207] The context of the enemy is initially introduced (verse 3) in the singular. The use of the singular here is unclear. We could take it as a reference is to a single enemy throughout, it could be used as a collective throughout, or finally we could understand the presence of a ringleader among a group of enemies.[208] A good case can be made for any of these options, and the evidence is not finally conclusive,[209] though the weight of scholarly opinion would appear to be behind a collective interpretation,[210] and that interpretation is tentatively followed here. Whichever option is followed, it is clear that the psalmist is experiencing considerable distress. Not only do we have an obvious situation of persecution (כִּי רָדַף אוֹיֵב נַפְשִׁי, verse 3), but also a clear situation of violence. In this context the psalmist expresses the feeling of being crushed to the ground (דִּכָּא לָאָרֶץ חַיָּתִי). The language used in verse 3 is certainly strong, but it remains general.

Perhaps the only hint of something specific is the fact the enemy has caused the psalmist to dwell בְמַחֲשַׁכִּים, which may be an allusion to prison.[211] Certainly the experience of being in prison would fit in with the description of the emotions found in verse 4, and we may tentatively adopt this line of interpretation. If this is an allusion to prison, it is to be identified with the pit (בוֹר, verse 7), so that the aim of the enemy is the death of the psalmist.[212] Since

---

[207]It is perhaps this element that saw this psalm traditionally treated as one of the seven penitential psalms. Cf, Norman H. Snaith, *The Seven Psalms*, London: Epworth, 1964, 102ff.
[208]Dahood, *Psalms III*, 323, takes אוֹיֵב as death. Such an interpretation seems odd as it loses the force of the simile in the second half of verse 3.
[209]Although the case for a single enemy throughout may seem odd, we should note that the fact that אֹיְבַי is treated as a plural is purely as a result of Masoretic accentuation. The phrase כָּל־צֹרְרֵי נַפְשִׁי in verse 12, which clearly must be plural, would then be seen as a generalising statement. The parallelism would then by synthetic rather than synonymous.
[210]Cf. Anderson, *Psalms*, 927.
[211]So Kraus, *Psalms 60-150*, 537.
[212]The use of the perfect here is perhaps indicative of the certainty of the outcome of the enemy's actions unless Yahweh acts in deliverance.

this has obviously not happened, it is obvious that the actions of the enemy have not as yet reached their potential conclusion. Although conformity to the pattern of the other psalms in this group cannot be a determinative argument, the fact that the psalm can be interpreted along these lines is at least suggestive that this may be the most appropriate approach. If this is correct, then this psalm is probably like the other prayers of protection in the fact that the worst elements of violence have not yet been faced.

The violence experienced by the psalmist is thus both physical and psychological. It is psychological since that is the distress that the psalmist currently feels, but it also represents a situation of potential physical violence. Indeed, it is the potential nature of this physical violence that creates a situation of psychological violence. Certainly, verse 4 highlights the elements of psychological distress that are being experienced, with the descriptive references to the failing of both רוּחַ and לֵב. The violence of the enemy is thus currently manifested psychologically, but the failing of these elements of life also suggest a degree of physical distress, with illness perhaps to be understood as the physical manifestation of the violence.[213] Again, violence that was originally enacted psychologically can become physical violence.

Direct references to the motif of violence fall away in both the reflection on Yahweh's works (verses 5-6) and the petition for Yahweh's help (verses 7-8). Nevertheless, even though the motif is not explicitly present, it is dealt with in both of these sections. As we noted above, the petition flows out of the reflection on Yahweh's works, and since their development of the motif is essentially the same we shall treat them together. Both the reflection on Yahweh's actions in the past and the petitions which are presented in verses 7-8 are rooted in the initial plea for Yahweh's protection in verses 1-2. The psalmist reflects on what Yahweh has done, perhaps in the holy war tradition and in personal experience, and recognises that the right to act against the enemies belongs to Yahweh alone. This is not, therefore, something open for a human to claim. Hence, we note the sense of urgency in the appeals for Yahweh's assistance in verses 7-8, and especially so since death seems imminent, as is apparent from the reference to the possibility of going to the pit.[214] What is significant from our point of view is that this reflects a rejection of human retributive violence, since that right belongs to Yahweh alone.

This perspective is further developed by the initial petitions in verses 9-10. The request for rescue in verse 9 (הַצִּילֵנִי) essentially re-iterates the request of verse 1, but an interesting perspective is added by verse 10. The request for

---

[213]This does not mean that we should treat this psalm with the Psalms of Sickness (which we will examine in chapter 4), since deliverance from sickness is not the central theme of the psalm.

[214]It is possible that the request for Yahweh's decision to be known in the morning reflects a situation of a vigil of some sort (so J. W. McKay, "Psalms of Vigil", *ZAW* 91 (1979), 241f), though this does not substantially affect the position argued here.

Yahweh's instruction and guidance are not to be understood as generalised statements, but in the context suggest that what the psalmist must learn is related to Yahweh's ways of deliverance, and it is in this path that one must walk. Again, this is a rejection of human retributive violence, since it assumes that Yahweh delivers and that it is the task of the faithful to follow this way. This presumes that walking in such a path is the harder direction to follow since it must be learned, but it is also understood as being the only option open to the faithful.

The motif of violence is again reflected in the psalmist's final petition to Yahweh in verses 11-12. What is striking here is that the psalmist's plea for vengeance is based on Yahweh's חֶסֶד,[215] along with the final declaration of fidelity in which the psalmist claims to be the servant of Yahweh. The language here is also harsh, as the psalmist asks Yahweh to apply the death sentence to the enemies in general. The concern is thus with an oppressing community, all the members of which need to be judged. In asking Yahweh to apply the death sentence to the enemies (note the presence of both the roots צמת and אבד), the psalmist would again appear to be asking for the *lex talionis* to be applied. In verses 3- 4 and 7 the psalmist has indicated that death was approaching, and that if death comes it will be as a result of the actions of the enemies. The prayer thus asks Yahweh, as the one who truly judges both the psalmist and the enemies, to apply that same sentence to all the enemies as they sought to apply to the psalmist. This means that they should suffer from the same physical and psychological violence with which they have afflicted the psalmist. As judge, only Yahweh may do this, not the psalmist.

In summary, we have suggested that the dominant form of violence that is currently experienced by the psalmist is psychological. The evidence for this is seen directly in the references to the failing of the basic faculties of life (לֵב and רוּחַ, verse 4) as a result of the accusations made by the enemy. It is also seen in the fact that the presumed goal of the enemies was the death of the psalmist. The bringing of such pressure to bear is suggestive of future physical violence, but represents current psychological violence since it has contributed to the illness of the psalmist. In response, the psalmist asks that the enemy receive an appropriate punishment from Yahweh, one that is equivalent to that which they have inflicted on the psalmist.

Response to Violence

Psalm 143 thus stands with the rest of the psalms that we have examined in that it assumes that the right to retributive violence belongs to Yahweh alone. Its special contribution lies in its understanding of the justice with which Yahweh acts in these instances. In this respect it stands close to the Prayers of the Accused that we considered in the last chapter. Yahweh has the right to act in

---

[215]It is notable that the word sought in verse 8 is also related to Yahweh's חֶסֶד.

violence because he alone does so on the basis of צדקה and חֶסֶד. It is on this basis that the psalmist is able to petition Yahweh for protection from assaulting enemies.

The violence inflicted on the psalmist is not yet physical in the sense of a direct physical assault, but even though it is therefore of a psychological nature it still manifests itself physically. In any case, the aim of the enemies is perceived as being the death of the psalmist, so no matter the form the goal of the violence is physical. In such circumstances the psalmist seeks Yahweh to act in vengeance, and specifically that he will do to the enemies what is equivalent to that which they have sought to do themselves. The prayer is thus controlled by the *lex talionis*. In seeking this intervention from Yahweh, the psalmist is also conscious of the need to walk in Yahweh's ways, for if Yahweh acts with justice then it is necessary to act appropriately before him.

The response to the violence is thus complex. It involves a submission to Yahweh in all respects - in responding to the violence experienced, and in life, so that Yahweh's righteousness might be seen. This involves the additional requests for instruction. There is, perhaps, a hint of theodicy in these requests for instruction that we find in verses 8b and 10. Although they still affirm that the only appropriate response to violence is to commit the matter to Yahweh as judge, they also seek guidance from Yahweh on the obviously vexing issue of how one should live in such a context. Trusting Yahweh may be the theologically appropriate thing to do, but it is clearly not something that comes naturally. The psalmist's requests are thus an attempt to receive guidance on how one lives within the tension that is obviously present. Yahweh is sought, but what is currently experienced is oppression from enemies. These requests for instruction are not a means of undermining expressions of trust, for that is where the psalm ends. But what they seek is an understanding that can be lived out on how Yahweh acts to provide protection. But even when one cannot understand, the psalm models a faith in Yahweh that puts trust before full understanding. It is, as Brueggemann has observed,

> [a] guileless faith throwing itself without reservation on the good intention of God.[216]

In doing so, it models a faith that lives between the tension of what God can do and what is often experienced, suggesting that neither can be denied, and that both must be confessed.

Conclusion

The psalms examined in this chapter represent a diversity of original settings. Although they are uniform in the fact that they all seek the protection of

---

[216] Brueggemann, *Message*, 104.

Yahweh against the oppression of enemies, they do so out of a range of differing contexts. There is also a diversity of responses to violence, but they are all related to a common core. It is this common core that is of particular importance, since it points to the theology that was responsible for the original collection of the psalms and the instruction that they were meant to provide. It is these common features that we need to bring together here. The following need to be highlighted:-

1. In each case, the psalmist was under attack from enemies whose assault at this stage had not yet reached the climax. The situation in which God's protection was sought always assumed that the worst assault of the enemy was imminent, and would thus exceed what had been done already. Consistently, the pressure that had been applied by the enemies was of a psychological nature, though this often had physical manifestations, particularly illness that is associated with a sense of dread. Psalm 55 varied from this pattern only in that it also noted the effects of social violence. The danger that was assumed to be imminent was consistently physical violence, most commonly the death of the psalmist. It was the imminence of this threat that created a current context of psychological violence. In these psalms, we therefore see a fusion taking place between the psychological and physical dimensions of violence, though they are still separable, with the principal physical violence always viewed as imminent.

2. Although retribution against the enemies was sought in every case, the approach that was consistently adopted was one where the psalmist asked that God be the one to act in vengeance. At no point did the psalmist's seek God's approval for their own acts of personal retributive violence. There was thus a consistent theological position that denied the right of human violence. How God would actually act is not clearly spelled out, though it is probable that the intention of the editors was only to instruct in a basic attitude, not to provide an assured means of seeing situations of violence settled.

3. The retribution that was sought was consistently governed by the *lex talionis*. At no point did the psalmist pray that God would inflict harm upon the enemy that exceeded that which the enemy had brought to the poet. Again, we note that the prayers model an approach where the means by which this is to be achieved are left open. Instruction is provided in an attitude of prayer, rather than on how it is to be answered.

The consistency of these elements across the whole of the prayers for protection indicates that they reflect a fairly fixed response to violence. Further, this pattern is entirely consistent with that which we saw to be present in the prayers of the accused. Always, the prayers for protection assume that the right to violence belongs only to God, and that the only right that the oppressed have in response to violence is to commit this cause to God.

It might, of course, be noted that this is precisely what we would expect in a situation of a prayer for protection. It is because one needs the protection of God that one comes in prayer. However, the elements that we have noted go beyond that level of expectation. It is not necessary that the psalmist cede the right of retribution to God alone, nor that there be a limit to the counter-violence that is sought. These factors suggest rather that there was a consistent policy in the selection of psalms for inclusion in the Psalter. In the process of forming the book of Psalms, the instructional value that was sought by the editors is accordingly one that seeks to affirm that, in the midst of oppression and the suffering of violence, the only valid human option is to present one's case to God.

CHAPTER 4

Psalms of Sickness

Introduction

Overview and Critique of Research

The exact determination of what constitutes a psalm of sickness is not always clear. Indeed, psalms that reflect such a context normally have features associated with some of the other *Gattungen* found in the Psalter. In reality, of course, since the psalm of sickness is fundamentally a sub-classification within the individual laments we should not expect otherwise.

The leading questions on the history of research in this area have been related to the question of the extent of the psalms of sickness and the relationship between the illness and the perceived role of sin in generating the suffering. Since this second question does not bear on our present purpose, we may leave it to one side.[1] However, the first question is of considerable importance for us since its answer tends to define our research limits.

As is well known, Gunkel assigned most of the individual laments to a context of illness,[2] a position that was initially followed by Mowinckel. This position was subjected to a radical scrutiny by Birkeland, who virtually denied illness any place within the psalms of lament in terms of the prayers of individuals.[3] Instead, Birkeland tended to see the prayer of a king, indicating a

---

[1]What might be called the traditional position is that there is a close relationship between suffering from illness and sin. This position is taken, for example, by Mowinckel, *The Psalms in Israel's Worship*, 2:1ff. However, this has recently been challenged by the thesis of Lindström. In *Suffering and Sin*, he argues that Psalms do not support such a position. The truth, perhaps, lies somewhere in between. It is notable, however, that Lindström is consistently forced to delete those passages in the Psalter that seem to oppose his hypothesis. For a sketch of how a mediating position on this issue might be developed, cf. Michael L. Brown, *Israel's Divine Healer*, Grand Rapids: Zondervan, 1995, 133ff.
[2]Gunkel, *The Psalms*, 20.
[3]Birkeland was originally more open to the possibility in *Die Feinde*, but by the time he wrote *Evildoers* his position on the enemies as foreign powers had become so settled

situation where his illness reflected the weakness of the nation. On this interpretation, there are no individual prayers that arise from a context of illness. Although Mowinckel's later works showed a great deal of influence from Birkeland, he still felt constrained to observe that in reacting against Gunkel, Birkeland had gone "a little too far in the opposite direction."[4] He believed that there were still some individual psalms that reflected a situation of illness, though not to the extent proposed by Gunkel.[5] This mediating position of Mowinckel on the extent of illness is that which is essentially followed here. One cannot assume that an individual lament arises from a context of illness, but neither can one rule it out. As always, it needs to be determined on a case by case basis.

Method of Approach

In seeking to assess the contribution of the prayers of sickness to the issue of responses to violence within the psalms of the individual we will need to consider three central issues in determining which psalms need to be considered. They are:-

1. Is the speaker in the psalm a private individual, or is it the king? In every case this issue will have to be raised as a result of the arguments of those who assign a major role to the king.

2. Is illness a central issue within the psalm? We have already had occasion to note places where there is reference to illness, as for example in Psalm 143. For the psalm to be considered within this group, however, illness would need to be a central issue. We will, accordingly, need to seek evidence that points to this, especially that there should be points in the psalm where at least some of the petitions relate to the illness.

3. Does the psalm reflect a situation where the psalmist is suffering some form of violence at the hand of enemies? The need to pose this question would suggest that not all of the petitions of a given psalm can be related to the illness, since some would need to refer to the violence as well.

Taking this as our basic methodology for identifying psalms of sickness where the motif of violence is clearly apparent, we shall argue that Psalms 38 and 69 are psalms of sickness reflecting a situation of violence. We may accordingly treat them here. Since there are some proponents of a royal interpretation for each of these psalms, it will be necessary in each case to justify their inclusion.

What we will argue in this chapter is that the psalms of sickness mostly deal with the effects of psychological violence that has been experienced during the

---

that there was little scope left for the prayer of an individual regarding a situation of illness. On the ways in which his position changed, cf. *Evildoers*, 41ff.

[4] Mowinckel, *The Psalms in Israel's Worship*, 2:2 n.2.

[5] Mowinckel, *The Psalms in Israel's Worship*, 2:1ff.

period of affliction with illness. This is primarily seen as having been caused through the words of the enemies. A modification introduced in these two psalms, though, is that they both reflect the belief that the present illness was inflicted as a result of physical violence from Yahweh. However, the main concern is with the violence of the enemies. The intercession of the psalmist in each case also assumes that a greater level of violence may be expected from the enemies. The expected result of this is normally the death of the psalmist. In that respect, the psalms of sickness are quite similar to the prayers for protection. However, they lack the strong element of trust that marked those prayers.[6] It may further be argued that these psalms associate the activity of human violence only with the wicked. The option of the righteous is to commit their cause to Yahweh instead. Unlike the prayers for protection, then, the element of trust is not strongly expressed as a component of the response to violence, but we shall argue that it is implicitly present. Accordingly, it will be seen that these psalms provide models of prayer for those who, in a period of illness, suffer persecution from enemies.

Psalm 38

Form Critical Discussion

With the notable exceptions of Croft and Birkeland,[7] who understand the speaker in the psalm to be the king, and Briggs,[8] who sees the speaker as the nation, there is general agreement that this is a psalm that reflects the experience of an individual who is facing illness. In particular, the psalm has traditionally been included among the seven penitential psalms[9] because of the psalmist's apparent belief that the illness is something inflicted by Yahweh in response to sin (note especially verses 3-4).[10] In addition, the psalmist

---

[6]The element of trust may, of course, still be formally expressed, as in Psalm 38:16. However, it plays a far less significant role in these psalms than the prayers for protection.
[7]Croft, *Identity*, 128f, Birkeland, *Evildoers*, 43f.
[8]Briggs, *Psalms*, 1:335ff.
[9]Cf. Snaith, *The Seven Psalms*, 43-46.
[10]Cf. R. Kelvin Moore, *An Investigation of the Motif of Suffering in the Psalms of Lamentation*, unpublished Th.D dissertation, New Orleans Baptist Theological Seminary, 1988, 40ff. A radically different position is adopted by Lindström, *Suffering and Sin*, 239ff. He argues that the elements that reflect an attitude of penitence, verses 4bd, 5-6b and 19 are all additions to the text. They were intended to add the theme of penitence to the psalm as a part of a *relecture*. Although he is able to point to literary critical factors that could support such a conclusion, his argument seems dangerously close to having been determined by his prior conclusions. From the perspective of a canonical approach to the psalms, one would also need to add the fact that what is

experiences a sense of personal desolation as a result of rejection by friends, an experience that is only directly paralleled in Psalm 88. In view of the alternative assessments of the psalm that are available the evidence for the individual interpretation will need to be considered.

It is unfortunate that Croft provides very little in the way of argumentation to support his royal interpretation of the psalm. His main points in support of this position are the descriptions of the enemies and the assumed close relationship with God in verses 10, 16 and 23.[11] Exactly how these elements point to a royal interpretation of the psalm is not clear, and Croft himself only asserts that they lead to the possibility of the psalm being royal.[12] Birkeland is more convinced, and his central point is also the position of the enemies with reference to the psalmist. He points to the fact that the enemies are portrayed as constantly seeking the life of the psalmist (verse 13), and argues that the sickness of the psalmist is what generates their enmity. It is, he suggests, because the king of Israel is sick that the enemies become active, although the psalm also betrays the king's awareness of the plans and speech of these foreign powers.[13]

There is no great force to these arguments, and it is particularly notable that Eaton does not find any evidence for a royal interpretation here. The argument is based on the close relationship between the psalmist and Yahweh. This is presumably, then, based on the use of the word אֱלֹהָי (verse 16) and the expression אֲדֹנָי תְּשׁוּעָתִי (verse 23). Perhaps the element to which Croft refers in verse 9 is the fact that the psalm indicates the total awareness that God has of the psalmist's needs. Assuming that this is a correct interpretation of Croft, and as noted he does not point to the particular features of these verses that support his argument, we would have to say that there is nothing particularly royal among them. Any Israelite who was addressing Yahweh in prayer could use these sorts of expressions. In fact, the argument would appear to be circular – certain terms are declared to be "royal", and their presence then makes the psalm royal, thus proving that these expressions are royal. The flaw in such reasoning is apparent. The stronger argument is clearly that which refers to the description of the enemies, though it will again be necessary to point to some circularity of argument.

Since Croft does not argue the case from the description of the enemies but

---

finally determinative for the theology of the Psalms is their finished shape, not a theoretical reconstruction of an *Ur-Psalm*.

[11] Croft, *Identity*, 128f. Croft gives the references for the close relationship between the psalmist and God as verses 9, 15 and 22. They are adapted here to the verse numbering of the MT rather than the EVV. Unfortunately, Croft does not indicate exactly what it is in these verses that is indicative of a royal identification. They are simply listed.

[12] Croft, *Identity*, 128.

[13] Birkeland, *Evildoers*, 43.

Psalms of Sickness 117

merely asserts it, we shall focus our attention on the position of Birkeland.[14] There are two central planks to his argument.

1. The enemies are portrayed as constantly seeking the death of the psalmist. Specifically, they plot against the psalmist when they hear about the illness. In this respect, Birkeland considers it significant that the verb הגה is used in verse 13, the same verb that is clearly used of the plots of nations against an Israelite king in Psalm 2:1.

2. The friends of the psalmist stay away, something that would be part of traditional practice. However, it is noted that the friends have not become enemies. This is felt to be significant in that it leaves the presentation of the enemies within the normal stereotypes, leading to the conclusion that there is "no reason why they cannot be interpreted as *gōyîm*."[15] Following this argument through, if the enemies are indeed *gōyîm* then the psalmist must be the king.

Again, the argument here is not persuasive. It works on the assumption that if one cannot prove that the enemies are not *gōyîm* then they must be foreign powers. Such an argument misplaces the burden of proof. A more direct response is also possible, strongly suggesting that these enemies are not *gōyîm*, and that the speaker is not the king. It should be noted, of course, that demonstrating that the enemies are not foreign powers does not prove that the psalmist is not the king, though it does markedly reduce the probability. A king may, after all, have enemies who are internal. However, the presence of internal enemies would indicate that the king functions more as a private individual within the psalm rather than as a royal figure. In this particular psalm, the absence of any clearly defined royal features predisposes us to a private reading.

We should therefore note that there is nothing in the psalm that consciously portrays the enemies as national figures. Although Birkeland is correct in noting that the friends who stay away are not the enemies, it is also apparent that their actions are paralleled with those of the enemies in verses 12-13. Birkeland acknowledges that the friends are individuals, and the nature of the parallel would suggest that the enemies are also to be understood as private individuals. Not only are the enemies not explicitly identified as foreign powers, but the balance of probabilities from the parallelism would suggest that they are private individuals.

Once we see that the enemies may be individuals, then the absence of any specifically national references makes a royal interpretation improbable. The use of the verb יֶהְגּוּ cannot on its own indicate this since the breadth of the

---

[14]In all probability, Croft is here dependant upon Birkeland, though there is no direct reference. Since in *Die Feinde* Birkeland was prepared to concede that the psalmist here was a private individual, we shall consider only his position in *Evildoers* where he had revised his earlier position to come to a royal interpretation.

[15]Birkeland, *Evildoers*, 44.

root הגה's semantic range[16] means that it cannot be limited to plots against a king.

The alternative position of Briggs, that the speaker in the psalm is the nation, is also lacking in argument. It is notable, however, that in order to achieve this interpretation he finds it necessary to delete verses 2-6 and 19 as glosses to what was originally a complaint psalm.[17] These verses are, of course, intensely personal, and were principally responsible for the inclusion of this psalm among the seven penitential psalms,[18] though even with their removal it is still possible to see the speaker as an individual. Curiously, in his exegesis Briggs seems to treat the psalmist as an individual, though this is perhaps a personification of the nation.

The identification of the speaker as the nation of Israel would require that both the friends and the enemies be interpreted as foreign powers. It is not necessary that verses 2-6 be original to the psalm for it to be a psalm of an individual, though their presence would be decisive. Unfortunately, Briggs does not indicate what it is about the friends and enemies that lead to them being identified nationally. One could assume that the friends were bound by a treaty to Israel but had failed to act in response to the enemies, but such assumptions move beyond the direct evidence of the text itself. There are no hints in the text to suggest such an interpretation, and they are accordingly to be considered as individuals. This means that the most likely interpretation of the psalm is still that the speaker is a private individual, and not the nation personified. It shall be further argued in the section on the structure of the psalm that there is a close relationship between verses 2-5 and 18-23 in the psalm, a factor that suggests the originality of these verses. A national interpretation of the psalm is therefore to be considered unlikely.

In light of the rejection of the royal and national interpretations of the psalm, an individual interpretation becomes most probable. That this is a psalm of an individual suffering from some form of illness[19] and reflective of a situation of violence becomes apparent when we consider the following:-

1. In verses 2-9 the psalmist describes a series of symptoms, all of which are related to the absence of bodily health (especially verses 4 and 8). This is clearly suggestive of a context of illness.

2. The actions of the enemies in verses 13, 17 and 20-21 are described

---

[16]Compare, for example, the radically different uses of the verb in Psalms 1:2 and 2:1. Further, even though the verb obviously can be used in terms of a conspiracy against a king by the nations, the possibility still exists that the language has been democratised. Context must finally be determinative.

[17]Briggs, *Psalms*, 1:336.

[18]Briggs finds other glosses in the psalm, but they are relatively minor and do not affect the classification of the psalm.

[19]Attempts to identify the illness (such as that of Kraus, *Psalms 1-59*, 411, who suggests leprosy) achieve nothing. We know only that the psalm reflects a serious illness.

in terms of their desire to see the death of the psalmist. They are also said to set traps and desire the ruin (verse 13) of the psalmist, all of which comes from their hate. A situation of violence is clearly apparent.

3. In some sense, the actions of Yahweh against the psalmist are also reflective of violent activity. This becomes apparent in the use of the image of Yahweh in verses 2-3 as the archer who pursues the psalmist, inflicting illness as the punishment for sin.

All of this thus indicates that we need to treat this psalm as a prayer of sickness. Although it is possible that it was composed as a part of an institution of prayers for the sick,[20] this does not primarily affect its canonical role. The very presence of such a psalm in the canon assigns it an instructive purpose, though this is now generalised so that the psalmist becomes a representative speaker in a context of illness. The areas in which the psalmist now acts as a representative will be investigated below when we consider the nature of violence.

Structure

Although most commentators are agreed about the importance of the 22 verse format of the psalm as an alphabetising feature[21] (though it is not an acrostic), the exact divisions of the psalm are not generally agreed. As van Gemeren notes, the psalm's structure "is not transparent because of the lack of movement."[22] In spite of this, certain key factors can be noted.

First, we can observe a close relationship between verses 2-5 and 18-23. Verses 2-3 are a direct appeal to Yahweh not to rebuke the psalmist, whilst verses 22-23 are also a direct appeal to Yahweh, this time not to forsake the psalmist.[23] Both are negative pleas, based on a vocative of יהוה and אַל + imperfect, though the word order is slightly different in terms of the location of the vocative. However, the common grammatical features as well as the shared central concern indicate that these verses form an inclusion in the psalm. In addition, verses 4-5 and 18-21 also show elements that are in parallel to one another. In particular, it is notable that verses 4-5 attribute the current suffering to sin in a context where the psalmist sees illness as Yahweh's discipline. In verses 18-21 there is the additional element of the confession of such sin where this confession is seen as necessary because of the present suffering. Although these verses also include the element of the actions of the enemies, so the

---

[20]So, e.g., Rogerson & McKay, *Psalms 1-50*, 181, though they concede that it may have had a wider application. Craigie, *Psalms 1-50*, 302f is more cautious. Alternatively, illness could be used metaphorically, but this does not seem markedly to affect the canonical function.
[21]E.g. Dahood, *Psalms 1-50*, 234.
[22]van Gemeren, "Psalms", 306.
[23]Cf. van Uchelen, *Psalmen I*, 253.

parallel is only partial,[24] they still indicate a close relationship between the opening and closing verses of the psalm. The reasons for the inclusion of the material on the enemies at this point will also need to be considered. However, this evidence points to the basic structural unity of the psalm.

Recognising the basic unity of the psalm, we can best outline its contents in terms of its progression of thought. Although there is still divergent opinion as to the psalm's structure, and setting the title to one side, we may broadly outline the psalm as follows:-[25]

1. A plea to Yahweh that he might relent from the effects of his anger. This anger is manifested in the illness of the psalmist, the symptoms of which are then described (verses 2-9).

2. A description of the sufferings of the psalmist relative to the actions of others, but one that recognises the need to wait on Yahweh (verses 10-17)

3. A confession and closing prayer for deliverance from illness and the enemies (verses 18-23). A particular emphasis here is to motivate Yahweh to act on behalf of the psalmist.

Nature of Violence

The motif of violence is directly expressed in two different forms within this psalm. On the one hand, there is the violence enacted by Yahweh in inflicting illness on the psalmist. On the other, there is pattern of human violence in the main body of the psalm, something especially apparent in verse 13, though the prayer of verses 14-17 is essentially a response to it. There is also an implicit request for divine violence against the enemies in verses 18-23. Thus, we shall suggest that the closing prayer brings together both of the aspects of violence that are reflected in the earlier parts of the psalm.

The violence described in verses 2-9 is exclusively that of Yahweh, enacted against the psalmist. However, the greater emphasis in this section of the psalm is on the results of this violence. This is evident when we note that verses 2-3 describe the actions of Yahweh against the psalmist, whilst verses 4-9 are a description of its effects. However, the violence of Yahweh is still a central concern of the psalm, and it is notable that the violence that is attributed to Yahweh is consistently physical in its nature. Given the fact that the psalm

---

[24]And the chiasmus of van Gemeren, "Psalms", 306f, accordingly fails to finally convince. In addition, his treatment of verses 6-13 as one unit of thought seems improbable.

[25]Cf. N. H. Ridderbos, *De Psalmen*, Kampen: J. H. Kok, 1962, 410ff. Hossfeld & Zenger, *Die Psalmen I*, 241ff, offer a slightly more complex analysis, though it broadly agrees with the analysis offered here. The only substantial difference is their preference for a break after verse 15 rather than verse 17. However, the motive for Yahweh's action is really only introduced in verse 18, not 16, so the above analysis is to be preferred.

assumes that the current illness is the result of Yahweh's violence, it could hardly be otherwise.[26]

It is notable that the prayer asks that Yahweh cease from his present actions against the psalmist. This is significantly different from the prayers for protection in that in those psalms the psalmist sought Yahweh's action against the enemies. Here, it is Yahweh's violence that is the problem, and in the absence of any higher authority to whom one can appeal, the psalmist asks that Yahweh cease. The underlying assumption in the appeal, though, is that Yahweh is fundamentally right in acting in this way. This becomes apparent when we note that Yahweh is said to act in anger (קֶצֶף) and wrath (חֵמָה). In the wider witness of the Old Testament, it is consistently the case that the wrath of God is generated by the sin of humanity, whether it be the sin of the nation of Israel, other nations, or of an individual. Such wrath is consistently directed against the sinner, whether the sinner be identified corporately or individually.[27] This wider usage suggests that, even before there is an explicit confession of sin such as we find in verse 19, there is an implicit acknowledgment of the justice of these actions of Yahweh.[28] In any case, verse 4 will make it clear that Yahweh's actions are predicated on the basis of the psalmist's sin.

The perceived justice of these actions also becomes apparent when we note that the language of Yahweh's arrows piercing the psalmist is derived from the language of theophany,[29] where lightning has eventually been expressed metaphorically as the arrows of God. This leads in turn to the use of such language to describe an action of God in discipline against another. Whether or

---

[26]Even if Lindström, *Suffering and Sin*, 239ff, is correct in asserting that the references to sin are later additions, the fact remains that the current psalm does make such a link.
[27]G. A. F. Knight, *A Christian Theology of the Old Testament*, revised edition, London: SCM Press, 1964, 122f. Some of the conclusions that Knight derives from this observation are not to be supported, but the observation itself seems well founded.
[28]Craigie, *Psalms 1-50*, 303, rightly points out that the psalmist's perceptions as recorded here are not necessarily correct. That is, the psalmist perceives that Yahweh, as omnipotent, must have caused the current illness, but there is no objective evidence available to test such a perception. Although this is a more helpful approach to the pastoral problem that appears to be generated than that of Lindström, *Suffering and Sin*, 239ff, it must still be observed that the psalmist's perception is consistent with what is observable elsewhere. Whether or not Yahweh is the cause of the illness described is not of relevance to this study. What is of relevance is the fact that the psalm presumes that should Yahweh choose to act in this way it would be an entirely appropriate expression of divine violence.
[29]Jeffrey J. Niehaus, *God at Sinai: Covenant and Theophany in the Bible and Ancient Near East*, Grand Rapids: Zondervan, 1995, 305. Although Niehaus notes that this language is in fact an adaptation of Baal theophanies, his argument suggests that the place of Sinai in the theology of the Old Testament and the fact that subsequent theophanic language has been expressed in terms of Sinai is indicative of the justice of Yahweh's actions. Dahood, *Psalms I*, 235, prefers an association with Resheph to Baal, but the effect is the same.

not the psalmist is aware of the theophanic background to the language is not clear, but the presence of justice in theophany suggests that the metaphor that developed from it would also assume such justice. There is thus no protest here against the actions of Yahweh. They are accepted as just. At the same time, however, there is a paradox in that the psalmist asks that Yahweh no longer act in this disciplinary manner. This assumes that although Yahweh is just, he is also merciful.[30] The paradox is thus that the psalmist accepts the justice of Yahweh's violence whilst at the same time seeking mercy that it may continue no more.[31] Unlike the violence of enemies, one cannot protest against the violence of Yahweh, but one may still seek mercy.

It is immediately apparent when we move into verses 10-17 that we are in a different context of violence. No longer are we concerned with the just violence of Yahweh, but rather with the unjust violence of the enemies. In the context of verses 10-13, the actions of the enemies that are introduced here are essentially parallel to those of the former friends. All have failed to provide comfort for the psalmist in the midst of suffering. We must, however, distinguish between the enemies and the former friends.[32] Although the former friends avoid the psalmist because of the sickness[33] they do not formally act against the psalmist. However painful their actions may have been, they are not in themselves actions of violence. They are distinguished from the group mentioned in verse 13 who are portrayed as hunters who seek the life of the psalmist. It is these enemies who are the focus of the greater part of verses 13-17.

Such a context would also suggest that the primary form of violence that is currently experienced here is psychological. It is not that the enemies seek the life of the psalmist, but rather that the snares they lay against the נֶפֶשׁ of the psalmist (verse 13) are an assault on general well-being and not a physical attack. Such an interpretation would seem to be borne out by the fact that the verbal roots that occur in the second half of the verse, דבר[34] and הגה, are both primarily related to speech. The enemies *speak* of the psalmist's destruction,

---

[30]Cf. H. C. Leupold, *Exposition of the Psalms*, Grand Rapids: Baker, 1969, 310.

[31]This would be a further example of the conflict pointed out by Broyles, *Conflict*, where God is seen as both the cause and the solution to a situation of distress. For the effect of this in the resolution of the conflict, cf. Broyles, *Conflict*, 224f.

[32]Against Kraus, *Psalms 1-59*, 412, it seems best to distinguish between the former friends and the enemies. The basis for this distinction lies in the fact that the enemies are spoken of in abstract terms in verse 13, whilst there is an immediacy in the description of the friends in verse 12. So, van Gemeren, "Psalms", 309.

[33]The "wounds" (נגע) of verse 12 are typically those brought about by a weapon, and are thus a reference back to the metaphor of Yahweh's arrows that cause illness. Craigie, *Psalms 1-50*, 304 see this as being more the paranoia of the ill than reality.

[34]Dahood, *Psalms 1-50*, 236, understands דבר as the equivalent of the Akkadian *duppuru*, "drive away." Such an interpretation regularises the meter to some extent, but does so through the use of a doubtful cognate. It is not clear how a Hebrew speaker would have recognised this usage.

and it is through speech that they seek to lay traps against the psalmist's life. This does not deny that the psalmist may have experienced such an assault physically since psychological suffering may manifest itself in this way, but the expression of violence is primarily aimed psychologically. This is brought out with particular vigour by the NEB's translation of verse 13:-

> Those who wish me dead defame me,
> those who mean to injure me spread cruel gossip,
> and mutter slanders all day long.

However, just as we noted in the prayers for protection, the psalmist perceives that the intent of these actions is not limited to the infliction of psychological distress. The fact that the aim of the enemies remains the taking of the psalmist's life (נֶפֶשׁ) is indicative of the fact the psychological torment is understood as a prelude to actual physical violence. It is thus understood that the wounds inflicted by Yahweh have opened up the possibility of these actions by the enemies, but whilst Yahweh's activity is perceived in a positive sense as discipline (note the use of the verbal roots יכח and יסר in verse 2), the actions of the enemies are judged negatively. The psalmist thus rejects humanly initiated violence, whilst accepting that which is begun by Yahweh. This factor is seemingly hinted at by the request that the enemies not be allowed to gloat over the fallen psalmist (verse 17).

Such a complex of responses explains the direction taken in verses 18-23 in which the psalmist summons Yahweh to act against the enemies. The poet perceives, and makes explicit, that personal sin has brought about the violence of Yahweh. This is expressed forcefully in verse 19:-

> My iniquity I declare,
> I am troubled by my sin.

This confession is made in the context of the injuries inflicted by Yahweh and the actions of the enemies, both of which cause pain that the poet perceives as leading to an imminent death.[35] The troubling element, though, is still the activities of the enemies, those who hate the psalmist (verse 20). The central charge against them is made in verse 21, that they repay the good purposes of the psalmist with evil. No addition is made to the description of their violence.

The psalmist's final intercession in verses 22-23 is shaped by this context, but it refrains from asking for a specific action from Yahweh against the

---

[35] It is difficult to unravel the actions in verses 18ff. Some seem to be those of Yahweh, others those of the enemies. However, it seems best to assume that at this point they are presented as a complex whole. One might also note the observation of Durham, "Psalms", 249, that the "progression of thought [is] disjointed." Conversely, and rather oddly, Terence Collins, "The Physiology of Tears in the Old Testament: Part II", *CBQ* 33 (1971), 189, regards the psalm as the work of "a careful craftsman."

enemies. The psalmist then asks in verse 22 not to be forsaken by Yahweh (אַל־תַּעַזְבֵנִי יְהוָה אֱלֹהָי), a statement effectively paralleled by the urgent summons for help in verse 23 (חוּשָׁה לְעֶזְרָתִי). But there is no petition beyond this. It is as if the psalmist finally asks for nothing more than that Yahweh be shown to be saviour-either by overcoming the enemies or the illness. All that is sought is the help of Yahweh.

In summary, we can observe that the psalm as a whole thus demonstrates a complex conception of violence. The violence of Yahweh against the psalmist is accepted as just because of the psalmist's sin, whilst the violence of the enemies is rejected because it is not consistent with Yahweh's disciplinary purpose. Yahweh's violence is experienced physically, though it is understood as bringing important psychological elements such as guilt to the fore. On the other hand, the violence of the enemies is currently experienced psychologically through the effects of defamation, but it is understood that this is a step towards physical violence, the seeking of the psalmist's life.

Response to Violence

The response of the psalmist is consistent with the general pattern observed so far. That is, there is no attempt to personally retaliate for the violence received. Although vindication is sought (note the plea that the enemies may not exalt themselves over the psalmist in verse 17), it is sought only in a context of confession (verse 19), and a desire that Yahweh should be the source of redemption. Personal violence is thus rejected because the expectation of deliverance from sickness and persecution is found only in waiting on Yahweh.[36]

Apart from its conformity to the normal pattern, however, the psalm introduces two elements. The first is that it accepts the justice of Yahweh's violence against the psalmist. Although the possibility of such violence was hinted at in Psalm 143, it now becomes explicit. We will note that Psalm 69 retains this feature. Elsewhere, we only have to deal with violence on one front, which is the violence of the enemies. The response to Yahweh's violence is, however, consistent with what we have seen elsewhere. Other psalmists pray for Yahweh's violence against the enemies who attack them. The logic of Yahweh's right to violence is continued here with the additional factor that those who experience it need to accept it, noting its disciplinary nature. The justice of Yahweh's violence is thus accepted in the response to it, and it accordingly summons a confession from the psalmist.

The other novel element, something that is unique to this psalm, is that there is no prayer for action against the enemies. What is sought is simply the help of Yahweh in a context of violence, that Yahweh be shown to be the psalmist's saviour. Here, however, is a particularly profound understanding of the

---

[36]Eichrodt, *Theology*, 2:309.

Psalms of Sickness

common position of the psalms, that only Yahweh has the right to act in violence. No specific action is sought – instead, Yahweh is informed of the particulars of the case. The assumption behind this is that Yahweh will then act appropriately to restore the psalmist in all dimensions of suffering.

Therefore, we can suggest that the inclusion of this psalm within the book of Psalms points to the didactic function that the editors of the Psalter had in forming their collection. It has become a model of the type of prayer that is to be prayed by the faithful in times of illness and affliction from others. The psalm thus models a prayer that acknowledges Yahweh's right to violence whilst rejecting human violence. The faithful are thus instructed once more to commit their cause to Yahweh alone. But they are also instructed to recognise that if Yahweh deals with them, then that violence must be accepted. Yahweh's violence has a reforming purpose that is not present in the violence of the enemies.

Psalm 69

Form Critical Discussion

The difficulties in classifying Psalm 69 are manifest. It has been classified as a national psalm, a royal psalm and an individual psalm. Although we shall argue that this is a psalm of an individual, we need to consider the case for the alternatives.

The national interpretation of the speaker is offered by Briggs[37] and Mowinckel.[38] As Mowinckel does not indicate the basis for his position, we shall note the argument of Briggs.[39] He claims that the figure who suffers in the psalm is "doubtless the ideal community," something patterned on the suffering figures of Psalm 22 and Isaiah 53.[40] Again, though, we must deal with the fact that Briggs asserts his interpretation rather than arguing it. It is, however, difficult to see how the national interpretation could be arrived at on the basis of the text as it now stands, and it is to be noted that Briggs carries out some extensive textual surgery.[41] Further, there is a strongly personal element to much of the psalm, notably in the sense of familial alienation expressed in

---

[37]Briggs, *Psalms*, 2:112ff.
[38]Mowinckel, *The Psalms in Israel's Worship*, 1:219.
[39]Probably, Mowinckel is led to this conclusion because of the influence of Birkeland's assessment of the identification of the enemies.
[40]Briggs, *Psalms*, 2:113.
[41]Briggs, *Psalms*, 2:112ff, divides the psalm into two originally separate, glossed poems that have been woven together. The extent to which this division leads to the national interpretation is unclear. A case against this division will be made in the discussion of structure.

verse 9, or the experience of being mocked in verse 13. These elements strongly resist a national interpretation of the psalm, and it is accordingly to be rejected. The speaker in the psalm is an individual, though that individual could be a national or private figure.

As always, a strong minority contends that the speaker in this psalm is the king. Eaton places it in his "clearly royal" group, although he admits that a substantial part of the psalm "is so 'individual' as almost to conflict with the communal references" that are necessary for his identification. He resolves this difficulty by pointing to Egyptian references in which the king becomes the representative penitent for all.[42] Eaton also points to elements that he believes to be more specifically "communal" within the psalm. These are especially in the thanksgiving at the end of the psalm where the concerns become those of the worshipping community.[43] The royal interpretation is developed further by Croft, who sees the psalm as a king's prayer before battle.[44] In particular, he feels that the reference to an enemy camp (אָהֳלֵיהֶם) in verse 26 is suggestive of such an interpretation.[45]

Again, we must acknowledge that this is a possible interpretation of the psalm, but it is doubtful that the final editors wished to assign it such a position. The absence of any clear rubric that assigns the psalm a royal status suggests that we need to seek a different interpretation to appreciate its canonical role. In fact, we can go further than this in denying a royal approach, and suggest that there is positive evidence in the text to refute the royal interpretation.

Central to the recognition of the fact that this is not a royal psalm is the situation pre-supposed by the conclusion of the psalm, verses 36-37. Although the integrity of these verses is often questioned, we shall argue in "Structure" (below) that they form a coherent part of the psalm as a whole. In any case, they indicate the function of the text available to the final editors. There is good evidence available here to suggest that this part of the psalm (at least) must have been written either in the exile or the period immediately after it. In particular, we should note the statement of verse 36:-

---

[42] Eaton, *Kingship*, 51ff. Cf. Birkeland, *Die Feinde*, 92f, for examples from the Amarna Letters.
[43] Eaton, *Kingship*, 51ff.
[44] Croft, *Identity*, 117f. Cf. Birkeland, *Evildoers*, 32. Birkeland's position is entirely dependent upon his interpretation of the enemies as foreign powers. As this position depends upon his wider argument on the identification of the enemies rather than the specific evidence of this psalm, an interpretation that we have already rejected, we shall not attempt to directly refute his interpretation.
[45] Johnson, *The Cultic Prophet in Israel's Psalmody*, 386ff, takes a similar line, except that he believes that the psalm is a prayer of a cultic prophet for a king who was defeated in battle. This is essentially an extension of the royal interpretation, and cannot be substantiated unless the prior arguments of Eaton and Croft can be proved.

> For God will save Zion,
> he will rebuild the cities of Judah.

Although Kidner suggests that this may refer to the time of Hezekiah,[46] it is far more plausible that we have here a reference to Judah after the fall of Jerusalem.[47] A psalm composed when there are no longer kings in Judah can hardly be a part of the royal cult (Eaton) or a king's prayer before war (Croft). Apart from this, we should note that there is nothing in the psalm that is specifically royal unless we have previously defined certain items as constituting a "royal style." The prayer of a private individual is thus a much more probable reading of the psalm.

An alternative "royal" reading is once again proposed by Goulder, who links it with the final stages of the Succession Narrative. In the case of Psalm 69, however, he is considerably more tentative than in his treatment of the other psalms in his book, but he does link it to Sheba's rebellion (2 Samuel 20).[48] The "hints" that he finds for this are, unfortunately, somewhat insubstantial. However, the reading of Goulder has something in common with the highly conservative commentators who have wanted to see David as the author of the psalm[49] in that it represents David as the archetypal individual in Israel rather than as a royal figure. The same is true of those who have seen Jeremiah as the author of the psalm,[50] though there is little to be said in favour of such an identification. It is simply a case of attempting to identify the individual behind the psalm, something that is now impossible. The psalmist is a representative Israelite. More than that cannot be said.

Even with that question answered, we have not determined the actual situation of the psalm. Two major options have been proposed for the actual context of the psalm – either it is a prayer of someone who is accused, or it is a prayer that comes out of illness. As we shall seek to demonstrate, the two options are not incompatible with one another, but only one is primary.

The interpretation of the psalm as a prayer of the accused was proposed by Schmidt,[51] and he has most notably been followed by Kraus[52] and Delekat.[53]

---

[46]Kidner, *Psalms 1-72*, 249.

[47]So, e.g., J. H. Coetzee, "Lyding 'Om U Ontwil' in Psalms 44 en 69", *Skrif en Kerk* 9 (1988), 7.

[48]Goulder, *Prayers of David*, 217.

[49]E.g. Kidner, *Psalms 1-72*, 245ff, Leupold, *Psalms*, 500f and J. Ridderbos, *De Psalmen I*, 205f. Those holding to Davidic authorship are normally forced to concede that the final verses are a subsequent addition.

[50]E.g. Delitzsch, *Psalms*, 315ff and Kirkpatrick, *Psalms*, 396ff. The logical inconsistencies in Delitzsch's case were pointed out by his near contemporary, J. J. S. Perowne, *Commentary on the Psalms*, Grand Rapids: Kregel, 1989 (original 1878), 543, though the option is still canvassed. There is, indeed, a hint of openness to this position still in Rogerson & McKay, *Psalms 51-100*, 92.

[51]Schmidt, *Das Gebet*, 32ff.

The basis for this interpretation of the psalm is the declaration in the last part of verse 5:-

> That which I did not steal
> I am forced to restore.

The implication here is clearly that the psalmist claims innocence against an accusation of theft. Kraus buttresses this line of interpretation by suggesting that the references to the miry pit in verses 2-3 can be interpreted on the basis of an Akkadian parallel as a reference to a prison. The example of Jeremiah 38:6f also indicates that the pit could be utilised as a means of imprisonment in Israel,[54] though it is also arguable that the specific context of that narrative may indicate that this was an unusual means of punishment.

The situation here, however, is complicated by the fact that the psalmist does not make an absolute claim of innocence, but in verse 6 actually admits guilt, consistent with the pattern of Psalm 38.[55] While it is true that the confession is of a general nature, such confessions are contrary to nature of the prayers of the accused where the primary concern is establishing the innocence of the psalmist. As we noted in the case of Psalm 143, the presence of such a confessional factor allows us to see that the psalmist has been accused, but accusation is not the primary concern of the psalm.[56]

There are a number of elements of distress reflected in the psalm, each of which builds a cumulative picture of the suffering of the psalmist.[57] However, the following factors are suggestive of the fact that illness is the primary context of the psalm:-

1. In verse 21 that the psalmist declares the central nature of the

---

[52] Kraus, *Psalm 60-150*, 60.

[53] Delekat, *Asylie*, 134-141. He develops this thesis considerably further than the others, supposing that illness led the psalmist to commit a robbery, the proceeds of which allow the psalmist to make a donation to the temple to speed recovery. The rejection of this by the enemies leads to a variety of consequences that make the illness worse. Although this interpretation has the admirable advantage of linking illness with the accusation, it surely goes well beyond the evidence of the text itself. Lindström, *Suffering and Sin*, 326, rightly regards this as "fantastic."

[54] Kraus, *Psalms 60-150*, 61.

[55] Lindström, *Suffering and Sin*, 327f, deletes the whole of 6-13 from the psalm. This would obviously nullify our argument against Schmidt and Kraus. However, we shall argue in "Structure" for the coherence of the psalm as a whole, so the objection falls away. Cf. Broyles, *Conflict*, 40.

[56] Cf. Broyles, *Conflict*, 123ff, who points to a number of points of contact between these two psalms.

[57] Birkeland, *Evildoers*, 32, places the oppression in the context of warfare. However, the explicit statements that are made suggest that the elements alluding to warfare are to be understood metaphorically.

affliction as illness of some sort, declaring:-

> Reproach has broken my heart and I am sick,
> I sought sympathy, but there was none,
> for comforters, but there were none.

Given the close linguistic relationship between verses 10 and 21[58] in which the words used to describe the actions of the enemies are now used to describe the effects of illness, we must assume that there is a close relationship between the oppression and the illness.

2. We may further note that the psalmist is described as one wounded by Yahweh (verse 27), a description similar to that of the ill psalmist in Psalm 38.

3. Since illness is further utilised as an element in the prayer for retribution (note the desire for the affliction of the enemies in verse 24) it seems best to treat the psalm with the psalms of sickness, though in reality it moves beyond the one genre.

Violence is also a motif that occurs at a number of points within the psalm. Although it is only explicit in the psalmist's prayer for retribution (verses 23-29), leading to the call that the enemies be "blotted out from the book of life" (verse 29), it is also implicit in the earlier parts of the psalm. This is especially clear in the description of the enemies' activities in verse 5 and the subsequent prayer in verses 7-13. It is, therefore, appropriate to treat the psalm at this point.

Structure

Anyone who reads through this psalm can only be struck by the notable change that takes place after verse 30. Up to this point we have a classic lament psalm, one in which the psalmist expresses the sort of difficulties that are typical of the genre. From verse 31 through to the end of the psalm (verse 37) though, we are confronted with something more typical of the personal thanksgiving. Although no reason is given, the psalm suddenly shifts at verse 31 to a declaration of intended praise:-

> I will praise the name of God with song,
> I will magnify him with thanksgiving.

The extent of the change that this demonstrates becomes apparent when we note the declaration of verse 30:-

---

[58]Leslie C. Allen, "The Value of Rhetorical Criticism in Psalm 69", *JBL* 105/4 (1986), 579 and J. H. Coetzee, "Die Funksionering van Spanningselemente in 'n Aantal Klaagpsalms", *NGTT* 30 (1988), 14.

> I am poor and suffering,
> may your salvation help me O God.[59]

This shift from lament to thanksgiving is suggestive of the fact that we have a decisive break in the structure of the psalm at this point. In broad terms, we can affirm that verses 2-30 form the primary lament, and verses 31-37 a vow of praise to God.[60]

Accepting this as the primary division of the text, we need to consider a number of suggestions that have been made regarding the unity of the psalm. Since verses 36-37 are the most widely disputed element, and also central to our rejection of a royal reading for this psalm, we will consider them first. Apart from that, we also need to consider the radical separation of elements proposed by Briggs[61] and the removal of verses 6-13, as proposed by Lindström.[62]

Although the integrity of verses 36-37 is often raised, it is most often done through an observation that they "may be a later addition", or some such similar phrase,[63] rather than through a detailed argument. Those committed to Davidic authorship usually feel the need to see these verses as an addition,[64] since the references to Judah alone and the rebuilding of the cities do not fit the period of David.[65] However, this position is not limited to entrenched conservatives.[66]

Allen has noted the presence of an inclusion between verses 31 and 37, especially in respect of the use of שֵׁם with reference to God, whilst there is also an alliterative word play based on מ-שׁ that runs through verses 34-36, with שֹׁמֵעַ in verse 34, שָׁמַיִם in verse 35 and שָׁם in verse 36.[67] The presence of these elements across the whole of verses 31-37 strongly suggests the integrity of the whole section, requiring us to read verses 36-37 as an integral part of the text. Although these verses do not reflect on the motif of violence, their presence is

---

[59] The NEB translates verse 30 as an expression of confidence. However, this seems unlikely when we note the larger structure of the psalm. Cf. Coetzee, *Die Spanning*, who sees verse 30 as transitional between the two main sections of the psalm. As Allen, "Rhetorical Criticism", 582, has shown, תְּשַׂגְּבֵנִי must be a jussive, not an imperfect, which requires that the break come after verse 30.

[60] Cf. Anderson, *Psalms*, 499 and Allen, "Rhetorical Criticism", 578.

[61] Briggs, *Psalms*, 112ff.

[62] Lindström, *Suffering and Sin*, 327ff.

[63] E.g. Anderson, *Psalms*, 499.

[64] So Kidner, *Psalms 1-72*, 249. Leupold, *Psalms*, 509, makes an attempt to defend these verses as authentic to the psalm along with a defence of Davidic authorship, though his case is hardly convincing.

[65] Curiously, Goulder, *Prayers of David*, 228, makes no comment on these verses. This is odd since they would seem to undermine his thesis.

[66] E.g. Briggs, *Psalms*, 2:113.

[67] Allen, "Rhetorical Criticism", 580.

Psalms of Sickness 131

still important for our assessment of the psalm's genre.

Although verses 2-30 have generally been regarded as a unit, there have also been challenges to their unity. The most significant challenge was that of Briggs, who saw the psalm as a composite. Leaving aside those verses that were seen as glosses, Briggs saw two psalms, consisting of a prayer (verses 2-3, 5, 7, 14b-16, 17-19 and 31-32) and the lamentation of a sufferer (verses 8-13, 20b-26 and 28-29).[68] Equally substantial cuts are proposed by Lindström, who argues that the original psalm contained only verses 2-5, 14-18 and 30-32, the remainder being the result of a thorough redactional revision.[69]

It is not necessary to consider the arguments for these positions in full. If the coherence of the finished psalm can be demonstrated then we shall be justified in reading it as a whole. Again, the study by Allen strongly mitigates against those who would remove sections from the psalm. He notes the presence of two units in verses 2-30 of roughly equal length that pivot on verse 14. The two halves of the psalm run a very close parallel to one another, repeating certain key terms as a part of a rhetorical structure. Admittedly, verses 14c-19 fit his scheme awkwardly,[70] but Coetzee has shown that they form a "plea for rescue" with links to both verse 2a and 30b-37.[71] The psalm thus forms a coherent whole, and we can therefore read it as a unity.

Although the analyses of Allen and Coetzee highlight some of the major strategies used by the psalm, our purposes can be best advanced through a more traditional analysis that shows the development of thought through the psalm. Accordingly, we may outline the psalm in six main sections as follows:-

1. The psalm begins with a plea for deliverance in which the psalmist confesses guilt, but asks that God act as saviour (verses 2-6).

2. The psalm then describes the psalmist's circumstances, ending with a plea that God will answer with salvation (verses 7-13).

3. The psalmist then petitions Yahweh for rescue from foes, repeating much of the contextual material of verses 2-6 (verses 14-19).

4. Verses 20-22 then provide a description of the psalmist's humiliation at the hands of the enemies.

5. This is followed by an imprecatory prayer that asks that the enemies be denied the normal elements of life, just as they have been denied to the psalmist. This prayer ends with a description of the psalmist's own

---

[68] Briggs, *Psalms*, 2:112f.
[69] Lindström, *Suffering and Sin*, 329. It is, perhaps, not surprising that the verses deleted include all those that would conflict with Lindström's central thesis.
[70] Allen, "Rhetorical Criticism", 533 argues that they are a sub-unit in the A x B insertion pattern, and thus a consistent part of the psalm.
[71] Coetzee, *Die Spanning*, 170 (my translation). The Afrikaans reads "smeking om redding." With Coetzee, the position followed here is that the minor break occurs after verse 13, not in the middle of 14, though with Allen the major break is seen after verse 30, not 29. These are, however, minor differences in two fine analyses of the psalm.

condition as the final motivation (verses 23-30).

6. The psalm closes with a vow of praise, one that encompasses both the psalmist's own experience and summons all to come in praise (verses 31-37).

Nature of Violence

The opening section of the psalm serves to introduce many of the primary themes that are found in it. Although the psalmist's own experience of violence is only recorded directly in verse 5, it is apparent that verses 2-4 provide something of the context for it. The description of the psalmist's circumstances is unclear in that it does not provide a clear identification of the situation. The image in verses 2-3 of the watery depths and the experience of sinking down into them shows great affinity with Psalms 40:3 and 88:6, 8-9. This suggests that it is a stock metaphor in Hebrew poetry for suffering that approaches death.[72] Given that the psalm contains elements relating to illness and accusation, it is possible that this opening section is left deliberately vague because of the need to leave open the full range of suffering.[73] However, the use of the metaphor in both Psalms 40 and 88 relates to illness, so it may well be that the psalm commences with a stock metaphor for illness, but intentionally modifies it to include false accusation in verse 5. What is clear is that these verses thus introduce the theme of the psalmist's suffering, providing a context for all that follows.

As mentioned, however, the first direct reference to violence occurs in verse 5. In spite of certain textual difficulties,[74] the main thrust of the verse is clear.

> More than the hairs of my head are those who hate me without reason,
> numerous are those who would destroy me,
> that which I did not steal I am forced to restore.

The psalmist affirms that there is no reason for the present opposition. There are, however, false accusations made, suggesting that the psalmist had stolen goods.[75] The violence that is currently experienced here is essentially

---

[72]Goulder, *The Psalms of the Sons of Korah*, 201ff interpreted the references to the pit in Psalm 88 as referring to a ritual involving a priest at Dan being lowered into a cistern for the night. Accordingly, in *The Prayers of David*, 221, he believes that we may have a reference to a similar rite here. However, there is little evidence to support such a view, and none external of the psalms themselves that unambiguously supports this interpretation. A metaphoric interpretation is therefore preferable.

[73]Cf. Tate, *Psalms 51-100*, 196.

[74]מַצְמִיתַי is frequently emended, especially with reference to the Syriac, though the MT is still possible. Cf. Tate, *Psalms 51-100*, 188f.

[75]Such an allegation may also lie behind the gossip of those in the gate in v13.

psychological. This is apparent from the fact that the psalm refers only to hatred (שְׂנְאֵי) and the fact that the enemies desire the destruction of the psalmist. It would seem that at this stage they have not actually physically assaulted the poet. They have, however, created an element of dread in the psalmist, a dread that anticipates something worse taking place. The aspect of sickness may also mean that their assault has some current physical dimension as the outcome of the psychological assault, though the exact relationship of the illness to the actions of the enemies is never made clear within the psalm. What is clear, though, is that the desire of the enemies for the destruction (indicated through the use of the hiphil participle מַצְמִיתַי) is such that the psalmist perceives that direct physical violence as such cannot be far behind. The situation is thus one in which psychological violence has created a state of dread in the psalmist with the awareness that extreme physical violence may soon follow.

The motif of violence is not directly reflected in the description of the psalmist's circumstances (verses 7-13), though the scorn which is endured is mentioned. This section is, however, shaped by the psalmist's response to the violence described in the previous section of the psalm. Further, it provides a context in which we may place the poet's suffering. The psalm portrays the psalmist as a representative sufferer, but not one who suffers for others. Rather, the hope that is expressed in verse 7 is that the psalmist's current experience will not lead to others who trust in Yahweh being disgraced:-

> Do not let those who hope in you
> be shamed (יֵבֹשׁוּ) because of me,
> Lord Yahweh of hosts.

The implication of such a prayer is that the psalmist perceives that should the violence of the enemies prove too much then others who hope in Yahweh in the same way will also be put to shame, presumably indicating that they would suffer as the psalmist has done.[76]

The psalmist's own condition is described in verses 8-9 in terms of rejection and scorn. Although these are not themselves necessarily expressions of violence, the earlier references to the activities of the enemies would suggest that they are related to their assault. In particular, verse 20 subsequently affirms:-

> You know my reproach,
> my shame and my humiliation,

---

[76]Cf. Oesterley, *Psalms*, 330.

all my foes are before you.[77]

This would indicate that the actions of the enemies are related to the scorn heaped on the psalmist. On the other hand, verse 13 locates at least some of the scorn among the songs of the drunkards in the gate, so we cannot make a precise equation that identifies the scorn with the psychological dimension of the assault of the enemies.

The particular element that is said to have generated the scorn for the psalmist, and presumably the actions of the enemies as well, is the psalmist's zeal for Yahweh's house, which is most likely a reference to the temple.[78] It is this linkage that allows the psalmist to claim to be suffering for the sake of Yahweh. In particular, this indicates that the psalmist's sufferings are to be seen in terms of the righteous sufferer, of the one who takes up Yahweh's cause to such an extent that the enemies of Yahweh have now become the enemies of the psalmist.[79]

A notable element in this section is the trust that is implicitly present throughout. The whole context of the prayer is one of hope in Yahweh as the deliverer, although at this stage all that the psalm has provided is a basis for Yahweh to act. Alienation and suffering are said to occur because of the psalmist's zeal, but these have come about because of the poet's trust in Yahweh.

The element of trust becomes clearer in the third section of the psalm (verses 14-19). Here we have a prayer that Yahweh would redeem the psalmist from the current suffering. In particular, it is deliverance from the enemies that is sought, as is apparent from verse 15:-

> Deliver me from the mire,
> do not let me sink.
> Let me be delivered from those who hate me (מִשֹּׂנְאַי),
> from the watery depths.[80]

What becomes immediately apparent from this plea is that the psalmist has

---

[77] The verse is textually difficult. The translation offered scans the verse as 3 + 2 + 2, a rhythm that is somewhat irregular, though it is arguable that it also occurs in verse 33, which is also a direct address to Yahweh. Anderson, *Psalms*, 505, observes that the verse seems overloaded, but is uncertain as to what has been misplaced or is missing. Since the meter of the psalm is somewhat irregular anyway, we can retain the MT.
[78] In light of the references to the fall of Jerusalem in verse 36, it is likely that the psalmist's zeal must have been for the re-building of the temple in the early post-exilic period. Cf. Kraus, *Psalms 60-150*, 60f.
[79] Cf. Coetzee, "Lyding", 6f.
[80] Tate, *Psalms 51-100*, 190, suggests that the niphal cohortative אִנָּצְלָה sets up a factitive – passive sequence, justifying the parallel of "mire" with "those who hate me."

integrated the experience of illness with the oppression of the enemies, though the reference in verse 27 to "those whom you (i.e. Yahweh) wound" would also suggest that the psalmist sees Yahweh as responsible for the illness. These two elements are kept in tension throughout the psalm. In addition, the prayer focuses solely upon Yahweh's ability to save. The situation of the psalmist is such that individual effort will not result in deliverance – only the action of Yahweh can do that.

The psalmist's plea is grounded in the character of Yahweh. In particular, it is the goodness of Yahweh's חֶסֶד[81] and the greatness of his compassion (רַה<) that motivates the psalmist (verse 17). These elements provide the motivation for the deliverance that is sought. The motivation is still controlled by the psalmist's circumstances, but it is modified by the declarations on the character of Yahweh which provides a reason why the psalmist ought to trust in Yahweh for deliverance.

The fact that the psalmist's own experiences continue to shape the motivation for Yahweh to act becomes clearer in verses 20-22. Once again, there is a description of the experience of the psalmist, with special reference to the experiences brought about by the enemies. This section is, in fact, quite similar in content to verses 8-10, though the opening יָדַעְתָּ of verse 20 stresses Yahweh's awareness of the psalmist's need, suggesting that once again it is a motivation for Yahweh to act that is being provided.

The psalmist's response to this violence is seen in the imprecatory prayer in verses 23-29, though its roots are found in the declaration of Yahweh's חֶסֶד and רַחֲמִים in verse 17.[82] There are a number of elements to the prayer, notably illness (verses 23-26) and the desire that the guilt of the enemies in making false accusations should be demonstrated (28-29). In fact, these are precisely the elements that the enemies have brought to the psalmist. The prayer, for all its anger, simply asks that the enemies receive from Yahweh exactly the same as they have inflicted. Since the enemies have made a false accusation, something that is to some extent linked to illness, the psalmist asks that they should suffer in the same way.

The prayer is thus an expression of the *lex talionis*, in that Yahweh is asked to place back upon the enemies the experiences that they had themselves generated for the psalmist. The climax of this sequence is that they should be blotted out (יִמָּחוּ) from the book of life (verse 29), something that demonstrates that they are not to be understood as being among the צַדִּיקִים. Such an experience would, of course, be identical to that of the psalmist was the charge of robbery to have been sustained.

In terms of our concerns, verse 30 is of particular significance:-

---

[81]On the combination טוֹב חסד, cf. Michael L. Barré, "The Formulaic Pair טוֹב (ו)חסד in the Psalter", *ZAW* 98 (1986), 100-105.

[82]Johnson, *Cultic Prophet in Israel's Psalmody*, 393.

> I am humble and in pain,
> may your salvation protect me.

What is important here is that the psalmist does not seek to justify personal action against the enemies, nor is an attempt made to have private revenge justified.[83] Rather, in spite of all that has been sought in the imprecation, the psalmist finally submits the whole case to Yahweh. Indeed, the poet is here personally submitted to the decision of Yahweh. What the psalmist desires is expressed in verses 23-29. But the choice to act finally belongs to Yahweh alone. The psalmist thus finally summons protection (יְשׁוּעָתְךָ), but leaves all other matters in Yahweh's hands to act. The psalmist has suffered torment and scorn, and there is an awareness of the fact that the enemies desire the psalmist's destruction. These factors have shaped the prayer, but there is no agenda for implementation demanded. Instead, they are submitted to Yahweh for decision.

That the hope of the psalmist in the midst of an experience of oppression is grounded in Yahweh alone becomes apparent from the vow of praise with which the psalm closes (verses 31-37). All references to violence have fallen away in this section as the experience of the psalmist becomes a paradigm for the experience of the community.[84] This is a natural extension of the prayer in verse 7 where the psalmist has asked that those who hope in Yahweh should not be shamed because of the poet. The psalm there placed the psalmist in the context of the community, so the shift to a communal summons to praise is by no means unexpected. What is celebrated, however, is the fact that Yahweh alone is worthy of worship because Yahweh alone can work redemption in a context of violence.

In summary, we can observe that Psalm 69 reflects a similar pattern of references to violence as we saw in Psalm 38. Again, the primary form of violence that is inflicted by the enemies is psychological in that it generates an intense dread because of the perceived goal of the enemies being the death of the psalmist. Mixed in with this is the factor of illness which is a physical manifestation of the judgment of Yahweh on the psalmist. In light of this, the psalmist's guilt was confessed. We also noted, however, that the actions of the enemies seem to contribute to the experience of illness. There is thus a complex of psychological and physical violence. This same combination is present in the psalmist's prayer for Yahweh to act against the enemies.

---

[83]As noted above, the structure of the psalm demands that the verb תְּשַׂגְּבֵנִי be understood as a jussive and not an imperfect. Cf. Tate, *Psalms 51-100*, 191 and van der Ploeg, *Psalmen I*, 413. On the protective dimension of the root שׂגב, cf. Johnson, *The Cultic Prophet in Israel's Psalmody*, 392.
[84]Cf. Kraus, *Psalms 60-150*, 64.

Response to Violence

In some senses the response to violence in this psalm is fairly simple. Facing a combined problem of illness and the assault of enemies in the form of a false accusation and the scorn that goes with it, the psalmist presents the case to Yahweh for adjudication. There is no attempt to justify any personal action in response. Further, what is sought in retribution is based exactly on what the enemies have brought to the psalmist, so the *lex talionis* is once again operative.

In spite of these factors, the psalm does introduce some new elements. In particular, the stress on the character of Yahweh, and especially his loyalty and compassion, suggests the reason why such trust is an appropriate response to violence. The perception of the psalmist is that the character of Yahweh is such that no injustice could be tolerated, and the actions of the enemies therefore constitute a violation of the moral universe. Unlike Psalm 7, and to a lesser extent Psalm 17, the emphasis here remains on Yahweh's goodness rather than his justice, though the two are obviously linked to each other. It is on this basis that Yahweh is summoned to act.

This summons takes place in the imprecatory prayer of verses 23-30. Anyone who notes the vigour of the language that is used will note that it poses certain difficulties. Although they need to be faced, the central point remains that nothing more is requested in retribution than what the enemies have inflicted on the psalmist. Further, it is something that is given for Yahweh to do as the one who is fit to act rather than being something that the psalmist personally seeks to enact. As with the imprecation in Psalm 109, it is finally submitted to Yahweh alone as an expression of covenant faithfulness.[85]

The inter-relationship between false accusation and sickness makes this psalm more difficult to analyse than Psalm 38, but the perspective that violence is something initiated only by the wicked and to which the righteous can only respond through an expression of trust in Yahweh is retained. Indeed, the emphasis on the character of Yahweh strengthens the grounds for the psalmist to express such trust. Although it is less explicit than in Psalm 38, the psalm continues the perspective that one is to accept the violence of Yahweh, expressed in illness, as just.

Through the inclusion of this psalm, the final editors thus once again instruct the faithful that the appropriate response to violence of any form is submission to Yahweh. The inclusion of the imprecatory prayer may suggest that such desires are to be presented to Yahweh to act, but the modification we noted in verse 30 also stresses that trust in Yahweh automatically implies submission to his final decision. It is, finally, the character of Yahweh that provides the basis for such trust, and this in turn leads to a summons to universal praise.

---

[85] Although we have not sought to demonstrate it in this study because of its communal nature, it is also arguable that the same is true of Psalm 137:7-9.

Conclusion

The presence of these two psalms in the Psalter continues to demonstrate the focus of the psalms of the individual in response to violence. Both psalms retain the perspective that the right of the response to violence is not something that belongs to the individual. Instead, it belongs to Yahweh alone. Of course, they express this perspective in slightly different ways. Psalm 38 does so by simply presenting the situation to Yahweh and asking that he be revealed as saviour. The salvation anticipated, however, includes the resolution of the problem of the violence initiated by the enemies. Psalm 69, by contrast, includes an extended imprecation against the enemies, but finally submits this imprecation to Yahweh as judge. They are, therefore, consistent in theology with the other psalms that we have examined.

These two psalms, however, provide an additional dimension that is not present in the other ones that we have examined. Consistently, of course, it has been implicitly assumed that only the violence of Yahweh can truly be just since it is his violence alone that is sought in retribution. These two psalms carry the logic of that position one step further. Both of them use the language of violence to describe the infliction of the illness from Yahweh, but neither of them reacts against this, even though it is seen as a present experience of violence that is suffered. Yahweh's mercy may be sought, but the assumption of both psalms is that when violence is received from Yahweh then it is, by definition, just. The confession of guilt in both psalms is clear evidence of this fact. The psalmists confess because they believe that their sin generated the need for a disciplinary action of violence from Yahweh. On the other hand, the violence of the enemies remains unjust, because the right of human violence is never conceded.

These two psalms thus provide a consistent model of prayer. Through them, the editors of the Psalter have created a pattern of instruction that guides the faithful on the appropriate types of prayer in the context of illness and violence. Yahweh's violence, perceived as generating illness must be accepted, but human violence at the same time can be resisted. The means of resistance is not, however, further human violence, but a submission of the situation to Yahweh so that he may act as judge and saviour.

CHAPTER 5

Conclusion

Summary of Results

The examination of the lament psalms of the individual that reflect a motif of violence has yielded evidence of a consistent pattern. The presence of such a pattern is suggestive of a policy with which the final editors of the Psalter worked, demonstrating a specific view on violence. It is not necessary that this policy be something of which the editors were conscious. But the presence of such a pattern is suggestive of a policy.

Our study of the psalms of false accusation, prayers for protection and psalms of sickness has indicated that although there were individual nuances to be seen within each group, these related to the type of context envisaged by that group. That is to say, the psalms within each group sought to model a response to violence that was appropriate to the nature of violence that was experienced within that type of setting. For example, the prayers of false accusation sought to model a response to a false accusation and the violence associated with that issue. They did not seek to model a response beyond that context, and neither would we expect that they should. As we have already outlined the elements specific to each group in the preceding chapters there is no need to repeat what was said there. However, there are some implications for Psalms research that arise from this pattern that we will note below.

Across the patterns that were established within each group, we have also noted a consistent pattern that covers all the psalms that were examined. This pattern reveals itself in four main areas – the consistent imminence of physical violence, the predominance of psychological violence, the rejection of the right of human retribution and the limitation on the violence that could be sought from God. We may group these areas together by suggesting that they seek to model a response to violence which is an adoption of a position of powerlessness, a posture of total trust in God, even though there is no attempt to indicate how this posture would work itself out in reality. What matters, though, is the inculcation of an attitude of dependence on God. We need to briefly demonstrate this pattern by noting how it is worked out across all the psalms examined.

The Imminence of Physical Violence

Although we noted that the language of physical violence is used, the consistent pattern is that such violence is imminent rather than actual. This confirms the observation made by Tate on violence as it occurs in the psalms of the individual.[1] Our exegesis has indicated that consistently it is the threat of physical violence that is present rather than its actuality.

The way in which such violence was imminent varied from group to group. Indeed, this is the aspect where the differences between each group were most clearly defined. Among the psalms of false accusation, physical violence was considered to be imminent because of the accusation itself. Although it was not clear in Psalms 7 and 17, both 109 and 139 presume that the charge against the psalmist was of a capital crime, the threat of which obviously makes physical violence imminent. Even where the evidence did not clearly point to a capital crime, it is apparent that the punishment that would be invoked would involve physical suffering. This situation was modified in the prayers for protection. Here, the situation was consistently one of enemies who were seeking a means of launching an attack on the psalmist. The pattern followed was consistent in that the focus was on the threat of physical violence, although the threat itself could have physical repercussions, as we noted in the case of Psalm 143. The psalms of sickness added a further dimension. In these psalms the psalmist expressed the belief that the current physical suffering (i.e., the illness) had been inflicted by Yahweh. There was, therefore, a current experience of physical violence, though it was perceived as just. However, a factor motivating the prayer in both of these psalms was the threat of further physical violence from enemies, and protection was sought from this threat. There is therefore evidence of a consistent pattern within these psalms where the major physical violence from the enemies is considered to be imminent, but not yet actual.

The Predominance of Psychological Violence as the Experience of the Psalmist

Arising from this first observation, we noted that the violence experienced by the psalmists was predominantly psychological. Although there are some references to social and physical violence in these psalms, they are widely scattered and did not constitute the principle form of violence in any of the psalms examined. We observed across all the groups examined that the threat of physical violence was perceived as being in itself a form of violence. This was evident from the fact that the language of violence was used in all these psalms even though, as noted above, the main physical violence was perceived as imminent and not yet actual. The distress caused by the threat of physical violence, and in particular when there is apparently some real likelihood of it

---

[1] Tate, *Psalms 51-100*, 61.

occurring, is thus in itself a form of violence. Since this manifested itself primarily in an experience of dread or fear, we described this as "psychological violence."

We cannot, however, limit the violence experienced by the psalmists to psychological violence alone. We noted in Psalm 55, for example, that the psalmist reflected both psychological and social violence. Similarly, there were points (such as Psalm 143) where psychological violence produced a present physical distress in the form of illness. And the psalms of sickness both indicated that the illness of the psalmist is as a result of the violence of Yahweh. Nevertheless, the dominant form of violence experienced was consistently psychological.

The Rejection of the Right of Human Retribution

Although all the psalms examined reflected a consistent position of violence that was currently suffered and in which retribution was sought, in no case did the psalmist seek approval for the enactment of personal retribution. In every case we noted that the retributive action that was desired against the enemies was sought from Yahweh alone. The only variation to this pattern was in those psalms where specific retribution was not sought, in particular Psalms 7, 27, 38 and 64. However, in the case of Psalms 7 and 64 we noted the presence of a wisdom world view that presumed that Yahweh would act against the wicked anyway. In the case of Psalm 38 we noted that although the psalmist does not specifically seek retribution, the pattern of the psalm works on the assumption that Yahweh disciplines the unrighteous. In effect, then, the presentation of the need to Yahweh functions in a manner equivalent to a request for retribution. Finally, Psalm 27 does not seek retribution, though there is a hint to be noted in the opening song of confidence. Verse 6 suggests that Yahweh exalts "the head of the righteous" above their enemies. If this is so, then there is no need to seek retribution because the world view of the psalm again assumes that Yahweh acts on behalf of the righteous against the wicked.

It is possible to go slightly further and note that all the psalms examined adopt a purely defensive posture with regard to the violence of the enemies. It is the consistent assumption of all these psalms that only the wicked enact violence against other humans. On the other hand, only the violence enacted by Yahweh can be truly righteous, a factor that was present in all the psalms, but was especially notable in the Psalms of Sickness. That is why the psalmists must trust in Yahweh and not seek to act on their own behalf. How Yahweh's violence is to be enacted is never made clear. But what these psalms seek to do is to encourage an attitude that rejects the right to human violence. It encourages a position of powerlessness among the faithful so that they may trust instead in the power of Yahweh.

The Limitation on the Retribution Sought

The final element that we noted as being consistently present within these psalms was the limitation on the retribution that was sought. Not only did these psalms refuse to concede the right of human retributive violence, but they also showed a consistent limitation on the violence that was sought. Obviously, the four psalms that did not specifically seek retribution are not directly relevant here, although it is certainly arguable that they implicitly demonstrate this limitation.

The limitation was expressed in two ways. By far the most common was that the prayer for retribution requested God to act against the enemy in a way that was equivalent to the way in which the enemy had acted against the psalmist. Such a prayer would seem to be controlled by the *lex talionis*. We noted this in all the prayers that either sought or assumed retribution apart from Psalm 109 and, to some extent, 139. Again, we should stress that these prayers never specify how this was to take place. Neither, of course, should we expect that they would. The implication, though, is that these psalms model a prayer that is built upon a conception of justice that is rooted in Israel's legal traditions. To pray as the righteous is by implication to pray with justice.

The alternative limitation on retributive violence is also shaped by a conception of justice that is rooted in Israel's legal traditions. In Psalms 109 and 139 we noted that the retribution that was sought seems to have been shaped by the law of false accusation, a law reflected by Deuteronomy 19:16-21. In these instances, the legal tradition specified that in the case of an accusation proving to be false then the accuser should suffer the penalty that would have been suffered had the accusation been proved. In effect, this is a specialised form of the *lex talionis* except that it deals with a level of potential violence rather than what was actually experienced. Again, however, the perspective is that the prayer for retribution that comes from the righteous is to be shaped by a consciousness of justice so that the violence sought in retribution is thereby limited. In the particular case of Psalm 109 we noted that the retributive violence sought was extreme. Even so, it was still shaped by this limitation, however slight its effect was in that instance.

Implications of Results for the Study of the Psalms

We need here to note some possible implications for the study of the psalms that arise from this research. Two issues that are particularly important are the use of form criticism as a guide to final function and evidence that points to definite editorial planning in the book of Psalms. In some senses, these two elements are related, but they can be described separately.

Form Criticism as a Guide to Function

From the time of Gunkel and on, form critical studies of the psalms have sought to determine the *Sitz im Leben* of the various psalms. Particularly under the influence of Mowinckel, this *Sitz im Leben* was typically sought in the cult. The research that has been undertaken within this paradigm has been particularly important in opening up our understanding of the various psalms and their role within Israel's worship, even if some of the results are necessarily speculative. On the basis of this method, various festivals and cultic rituals have been proposed, though none have gained universal assent. Even though this assent has not been gained, the method has raised important questions for us in the field of Psalms research.

The research undertaken here has attempted to use form criticism in a slightly different way. Although we are still concerned with the *Sitz im Leben*, we have attempted to study the various psalms as religious texts that were available to the compilers of the Psalter. In following this approach we have noted that form criticism, when used as a descriptive tool and not a prescriptive one, opens a window to the function that a given psalm fulfils within the book of Psalms. The presence of common features within a group of psalms is therefore not only significant in terms of the *Sitz im Leben*, but also for the instructional value assigned to the psalm by the final editors. The Psalms of False Accusation, for example, probably had a specific function within the cult of Israel, even if it is not really possible to recreate the exact form of the ritual today. But within the book of Psalms they now function to instruct the faithful in terms of the appropriate nature of prayer when faced by such circumstances. Given the burgeoning interest in the final form of the book of Psalms, this could well prove to be a useful methodological approach in discovering the purposes behind the formation of the book.

Evidence of Editorial Consistency in the Construction of the Book of Psalms

Our research has demonstrated a consistent response to violence within the Book of Psalms. The presence of such consistency is suggestive of the possibility that the final editors of the Psalter had specific theological purposes active in their selection of the various psalms that make up the book.

Obviously, the presence of such a pattern within one part of the book does not demonstrate beyond doubt that such purposes exist. Nor can we assert that the editors always had a conscious theological agenda that guided the process of selection. We simply do not have the evidence at this stage to prove such a claim. Equally, we can note that some of the research done on the formation of the book of Psalms is not conclusive, and some of the suggestions as to structuring purposes still need to be demonstrated.[2] What is suggested here is

---

[2]For example, the suggestion of Wilson, *Editing*, that there are royal psalms at the seams of the Psalter seems to lack conclusive proof, especially at the join between books 1 and

simply that the evidence gathered in this research makes the presence of such an agenda a very strong possibility. Such a possibility needs to be tested through further research on various themes within the Psalter. As a working hypothesis, though, it offers a strong probability of opening new vistas onto the book as a unified work.

Areas for Further Research

The above comments on the implications of the methodology followed here have already indicated some areas for further research. Those observations are of a more general nature in terms of Psalms research. We need now to comment on some areas for further research that arise directly from the current study. Two areas seem particularly important if the conclusions reached here are to be validated across all the whole of the Psalter. First, there is a need to examine the response to violence in the royal and communal psalms. Secondly, the continued application of such materialist concerns in reading the psalms may open up the possibility of describing the social context out of which the book of Psalms arose. The concerns of this study cannot, however, be limited solely to the study of Psalms. Apart from the theoretical issues mentioned above, there are also the practical concerns of communities facing various forms of violence. Some suggestions about the practical impact of this study must therefore be made.

The Role of Royal and Communal Psalms

Because of the need to keep the current project within manageable bounds, it was necessary to focus only on the response to violence within the psalms of the individual. In particular, we addressed the individual laments. Although there are references to violence in other types of psalms of the individual, such as individual thanksgivings[3] and songs of trust,[4] these psalms do not describe a response to violence as such. Rather, they seek to model an appropriate attitude to violence. In a sense, this means that although they are still psalms of the individual, they are starting to move to a communal function since the individual in these psalms seeks to some extent to instruct the community. Further research here is necessary if the paradigm of the psalms of the individual is to be fully established.

More importantly, further research is necessary in terms of the royal and communal psalms. Although it is probably true to say that in some sense a royal psalm is functionally a communal psalm, it is also true that the royal psalms

---

2. Cf. Gerald H. Wilson, "The Use of Royal Psalms at the 'Seams' of the Hebrew Psalter", *JSOT* 35 (1986), 8594, for the argument.
[3] For example, Psalm 92.
[4] For example, Psalm 11.

have a distinct role assigned to them by the book. In particular, further research needs to examine the response to violence that we find in these psalms so as to determine what light they shed on the responses that we noted in the psalms of the individual.

A particular methodological problem that needs to be addressed in this context is the question of how one determines what constitutes a royal psalm within the finished book of Psalms. Communal psalms are easier to identify as their original function more or less carries over into the book, even if the elements that were cultic are harder to trace. However, this is not so in the case of the royal psalms. Traditional form criticism has sought to determine this in terms of the *Sitz im Leben* of the psalm, and the results of this endeavour have been mixed. It is possible, however, that psalms that were originally royal have been assigned a different function by the editors. A method of determining which psalms have been assigned to the functional role of a royal psalm by the editors needs to be clarified.[5] Only then can the function of the king and the community be properly assessed in terms of the issue of violence.

Social Context of Editors of Psalter

Finally, the evidence of this research suggests that it is possible through the use of materialist issues to address the question of the social setting of the editors of the Psalter. If the evidence gathered here is substantiated in other parts of the book, then we would have important indicators that would enable us to situate the editors in life, especially with reference to their social setting. In particular, the evidence gathered here would suggest that the final editors are to be placed within a quietist group, perhaps similar to that which produced the book of Daniel.[6] This is, however, only a preliminary observation, and needs to be tested by further research. The point is that the raising of such materialist concerns may enable us to determine the context in which the book finally arose. Such awareness may then inform other aspects of Psalm studies as it would help address questions as to the shape and purpose of the book. Artur Weiser felt that the psalms are "pictures without a frame."[7] Research on the social context of the final editors may start to construct that frame. It is hoped that this current project has moved us in that direction.

---

[5]Hopefully, such a method would overcome the apparent confusion that seems to occur between identifying psalms that were originally royal and those that now function as royal psalms.

[6]Cf. John Goldingay, *Daniel*, Dallas: Word, 1989, 328f, for a brief sketch of the community that produced Daniel. Whether or not we could also associate the Psalter with the Hasidim is unclear, but if we were to date the finished book to that period (not improbable in view of the title to Psalm 30) it would seem likely that they would have at least been sympathetic to them.

[7]Weiser, *Psalms*, 9.

Practical Implications of this Research

As was indicated by the statement of the problem in chapter 1, concerns over the matter of violence do not arise solely out of a reflection on the text of Psalms. Instead, these concerns are something that arise from the life experience of the community. We also noted that although it is a sociological problem, theological answers to it are possible, and that this answer ought to come in part through an exegesis of the biblical material, something that we have sought to provide. In examining certain Psalms we have not, of course, provided an answer to the problem of violence itself. Rather, we have sought to demonstrate that integral to the instructional value of Psalms is the aim of inculcating an attitude of dependence upon Yahweh. This attitude in and of itself suggests a non-retaliatory stance. This is not an answer to the problem of violence as such, but it is an answer to the question of how one might react to violence.

The orientation of this examination of the Psalms remains largely theoretical. Further research is therefore required on the question of how this model of responding to violence can inform the practice of communities affected by it. Our statement of the problem indicates the line that this further research must take. It was suggested that theological reflection and sociological research can mutually inform one another. In this study we have tried to validate a sociological model of violence. The theological concerns of the Psalter can equally be tested within various social contexts, among both Jewish and Christian congregations. Such field testing of this model would need proper sociological controls, and the leaders of these communities would need to be instructed in the theological foundation for it. An awareness of it could, however, inform groups affected by violence of the possible forms of it that they might experience as well as indicating a possible response.

The South African context provides a particularly fitting context for such practical research on the possibilities of the model provided by Psalms for responding to violence. The post-apartheid era has not seen any substantial reduction in violence, although it may now take some different forms. A different type of response is clearly necessitated, and the model offered by the Psalms may therefore be appropriate.

Bibliography

Alden, R., *Psalms: Songs of Devotion*, Chicago: Moody, 1974.
Allen, L. C., "Faith on Trial: An Analysis of Psalm 139", *Vox Evangelica* 10 (1977), 5-23.
— *Psalms 101-150*, Waco: Word, 1983.
— "The value of Rhetorical Criticism in Psalm 69", *JBL* 105 (1986), 577-598.
Anderson, A. A., *Psalms 1-72*, Grand Rapids: Eerdmans, 1972.
— *Psalms 73 – 150*, Grand Rapids: Eerdmans, 1972
Anderson, G. W. "Enemies and Evildoers in the Psalms", *BJRL* 48 (1965), 16-29.
Anderson, R. D., "The Division and Order of the Psalms", *WTJ* 56 (1994), 219-241.
Barré, M. L., "The Formulaic Pair טוב (ו)חסד in the Psalter", *ZAW* 98 (1986), 100-105.
Bellinger, W. H., Jr., *Psalmody and Prophecy*, Sheffield: JSOT Press, 1984.
— *Psalms: Reading and Interpreting the Book of Praises*, Peabody: Hendrickson, 1990.
Beyerlin, W., *Die Rettung der Bedrängten in den Feindpsalmen der Einzelnen auf institutionelle Zusammenhänge untersucht*, Göttingen: Vandenhoeck & Ruprecht, 1970.
Birkeland, H., *Die Feinde des Individuums in der israelitischen Psalmenliteratur*, Oslo: Grøndahl and Sons, 1933.
— *The Evildoers in the Book of Psalms*, Oslo, Jacob Dybwad, 1955.
Booij, T. H., *Psalmen III*, Nijkerk: G. F. Callenbach, 1994.
Bratcher, R. G., "A Translator's Note on Psalm 7:4b", *TBT* 23 (1972), 241-242.
Brettler, M., "Images of Yahweh the Warrior in the Psalms", *Semeia* 61 (1993), 135-165.
Briggs, C. A. and E. G., *A Critical and Exegetical Commentary on the Book of Psalms*, 2 vols., Edinburgh: T & T Clark, 1906 and 1907.
Brown, M. L., *Israel's Divine Healer*, Grand Rapids: Zondervan, 1995.
Broyles, C. C., *The Conflict of Faith and Experience in the Psalms: A Form Critical and Theological Study*, Sheffield: JSOT Press, 1989.
Brueggemann, W., *The Message of the Psalms*, Minneapolis: Augsburg, 1984.
— "Bounded by Obedience and Praise: The Psalms as Canon," *JSOT* 50 (1991), 63-92.
Burger, J. A., "The Psalms", in J. J. Burden and W. S. Prinsloo (eds.), *Dialogue With God*, Cape Town: Tafelberg, 1987, 9-39.
Childs, B. S., *Introduction to the Old Testament as Scripture*, London: SCM Press, 1979.

Clines, D. J. A., *Job 1-20*, Dallas: Word, 1989.
Coetzee, J. H., *Die Spanning tussen God se "verborge wees" en Sy "ingrype om te red." 'n Eksegetiese Ondersoek na 'n Aantal Klaagpsalms*. unpublished DD thesis, University of Pretoria, 1986.
— "Lyding 'Om U Ontwil' in Psalms 44 en 69", *Skrif en Kerk* 9 (1988), 1-9.
— "Die Funksionering van Spanningselemente in 'n Aantal Klaagpsalms", *NGTT* 30 (1988), 6-20.
Collins, T., "The Physiology of Tears in the Old Testament: Part I", *CBQ* 33 (1971), 18-38.
— "The Physiology of Tears in the Old Testament: Part II", *CBQ* 33 (1971), 185-197.
Craigie, P. C., *Psalms 1-50*, Waco: Word, 1983.
— *The Book of Deuteronomy*, Grand Rapids: Eerdmans, 1976.
Creager, H. L., "Note on Psalm 109", *JNES* 6 (1947), 121-123.
Croft, S. J. L., *The Identity of the Individual in the Psalms*, Sheffield: JSOT Press, 1987.
Dahood, M., *Psalms I: 1-50*, Garden City: Doubleday, 1965.
— *Psalms II: 51-100*, Garden City: Doubleday, 1968.
— *Psalms III: 101-150*, Garden City: Doubleday, 1970.
— "'A Sea of Troubles': Notes on Psalms 55:3-4 and 140:10-11", *CBQ* 41 (1979), 604-607.
— "Philological Observations on Five Bib Texts", *Biblica* 63 (1982), 390-94.
Dannell, G. A., *Psalm 139*, Uppsala: Almqvist Wiksells Boktryckeri, 1951.
Delekat, L., *Asylie und Schutzorakel am Zionheiligtum: Eine Untersuchung zu den privaten Feindpsalmen*, Leiden: E. J. Brill, 1967.
Delitzsch, F., *Biblical Commentary on the Psalms*, Trans. J. Martin, Grand Rapids: Eerdmans, n.d.
Dorn, L., *The Beatific Vision in Certain Psalms: An Investigation of Mitchell Dahood's Hypothesis*, Unpublished ThD Thesis, Lutheran School of Theology, Chicago, 1980.
Driver, G. R., "Psalm LVI. 9 'Thou Tellest My Wanderings'", *JTS* 21 (1970), 402-403.
Durham, J. I., "Psalms", in C. J. Allen (ed.), *The Broadman Bible Commentary* vol. 4, Nashville: Broadman, 1971.
Eaton, J. H., *Psalms: Introduction and Commentary*, London: SCM Press, 1967.
— "Some Questions of Philology and Exegesis in the Psalms", *JTS* 19 (1968), 603-609.
— *Kingship and the Psalms*, London: SCM Press, 1976.
Eichrodt, W., *Theology of the Old Testament* (2 vols.), Trans. J. A. Baker, London: SCM Press, 1961, 1967.
Ellul, J., *Violence: Reflections from a Christian Perspective*, Trans. C. G. Kings, London: SCM Press, 1970.
Gaster, T. H., "Short Notes", *VT* 4 (1954), 73-79.

Gerstenberger, E. S., *Psalms Part 1: With an Introduction to Cultic Poetry*, Grand Rapids: Eerdmans, 1988.
Goldingay, J., *Daniel*, Dallas: Word, 1989.
Goulder, M. D., *The Psalms of the Sons of Korah*, Sheffield: JSOT Press, 1982.
— *The Prayers of David (Psalms 51-72)*, Sheffield: JSOT Press, 1990.
Guillaume, A., "A Note on Psalm CIX. 10", *JTS* 14 (1963), 92-93.
Gunkel, H., *The Psalms: A Form Critical Introduction*, Trans. T. M. Horner, Philadelphia: Fortress Press, 1967.
Haag, H., "חמס", in G. Johannes Botterweck and Helmer Ringgren (eds.), *Theological Dictionary of the Old Testament*, vol. IV, Trans. D. E. Green, Grand Rapids: Eerdmans, 1980, 478-487.
Harman, A. M., "The Continuity of the Covenant Curses in the Imprecations in the Psalter", *RTR* 54/2 (1995), 65-72.
Hartley, J. E., *The Book of Job*, Grand Rapids: Eerdmans, 1988.
Hayes, J. H., *An Introduction to Old Testament Study*, Nashville: Abingdon, 1979.
Holman, J., "Analysis of the Text of Ps 139", *BZ* 14 (1970), 37-71, 198-227.
— "The Structure of Psalm CXXXIX", *VT* 21 (1971), 298-310.
Hossfeld, F. L. and E. Zenger, *Die Psalmen I: Psalm 1-50*, Würzburg: Echter Verlag, 1993.
Hubbard, R. L., "Dynamistic and Legal Processes in Psalm 7", *ZAW* 94 (1982), 267-279.
Human, D. J., *Die Begrip 'Berit' in 'n Aantal Klaagpsalms: 'n Perspektief*, unpublished DD dissertation, University of Pretoria, 1993.
Janzen, J. G., "The Root *škl* and the Soul Bereaved in Psalm 35", *JSOT* 65 (1995), 55-69.
Johnson, A. R., *The Cultic Prophet and Israel's Psalmody*, Cardiff: University of Wales Press, 1979.
Kaiser, W. C. Jr., *The Messiah in the Old Testament*, Grand Rapids: Zondervan, 1995.
Kidner, D., *Psalms 1 - 72*, Leicester: IVP, 1973
— *Psalms 73 - 150*, Leicester: IVP, 1975.
Kim, E. K., *A Study of the Rapid Change of Mood in the Lament Psalms, With a Special Inquiry into the Impetus for its Expression*, unpublished PhD Thesis, Union Theological Seminary, 1984.
— "'Outcry': Its Context in Biblical Theology", *Interpretation* 42 (1988), 229-239.
Kirkpatrick, A. F., *The Book of Psalms*, Cambridge: Cambridge University Press, 1902.
Kissane, E. J., *The Book of Psalms* (2 vols.), Dublin: Browne & Nolan, 1954.
Kittel, R., *Die Psalmen übersetzt und erklärt*, Leipzig: Deichert-Scholl, 1922.
Knight, G. A. F., *A Christian Theology of the Old Testament*, revised edition, London: SCM Press, 1964.
— *The Psalms*, 2 vols., Edinburgh: St. Andrews Press, 1982, 1983.

Kraus, H-J., *Psalms 1-59*, Trans. H. C. Oswald, Minneapolis: Augsburg, 1988.
— *Psalms 60-150*, Trans. H. C. Oswald, Augsburg: Minneapolis, 1989.
— *The Theology of the Psalms*, Trans. K. Crim, Minneapolis: Fortress, 1992.
Kselman, J. S., "Psalm 3: A Structural and Literary Study", *CBQ* 49 (1987), 572-580.
Lattey, C., "A Note on Psalm lv 14 (13)", *ExpT* 64 (1953), 221-222.
Leupold, H. C., *Exposition of the Psalms*, Grand Rapids: Baker, 1969.
Leveen, J., "The Textual Problems of Psalm XVII", *VT* 11 (1961), 48-54.
— "The Textual Problems of Psalm VII", *VT* 16 (1966), 439-445.
— "Textual Problems in the Psalms", *VT* 21 (1971), 48-58.
Lindblom, J., "Bemerkungen zu den Psalmen I.", *ZAW* 59 (1942-43), 1-13.
Lindström, F., *Suffering and Sin: Interpretations of Illness in the Individual Complaint Psalms*, Stockholm: Almqvist & Wiskell, 1994.
Lohfink, N. (ed.), *Gewalt und Gewaltlosigkeit im Alten Testament*, Freiburg: Herder, 1983.
— "Gewalt als Thema alttestamentlicher Forschung", in N. Lohfink (ed.), *Gewalt und Gewaltlosigkeit*, 15-50.
Longman, T. III and D. G. Reid, *God is a Warrior*, Grand Rapids: Zondervan, 1995.
Loretz, O., *Die Psalmen II: Beitrag der Ugarit Texte zum Verständnis von Kolometrie und Textologie der Psalmen, Psalm 90-150*, Neukirchener Verlag: Neukirchen-Vluyn, 1979.
Macholz, C., "Bemerkungen zu Ps 7:4-6", *ZAW* 91 (1979), 127-129.
Mays, J. L., *Psalms*, Louisville: John Knox, 1994.
McCann, J. C. (ed.), *The Shape and Shaping of the Psalter*, Sheffield: Sheffield Academic Press, 1993.
— *A Theological Introduction to the Book of Psalms: The Psalms as Torah*, Nashville: Abingdon, 1993.
McCarthy, D. J., "An Installation Genre?", *JBL* 90 (1971), 31-41.
McConville, J. G., *Grace in the End: A Study in Deuteronomic Theology*, Carlisle: Paternoster, 1993.
McCullough, W. S. and W. R. Taylor, "Psalms", in G. A. Buttrick (ed.), *The Interpreter's Bible* vol. 4, Nashville: Abingdon, 1955.
McFall, L., *The Enigma of the Hebrew Verbal System*, Sheffield: Almond Press, 1982.
McIntosh, A. A., "A Consideration of Psalm vii. 12f.", *JTS* 33 (1982), 481-490.
McKay, J. W., "Psalms of Vigil", *ZAW* 91 (1979), 229-247.
Miller P. D., Jr., *Interpreting the Psalms*, Philadelphia: Fortress Press, 1986.
— *They Cried to the Lord: The Form and Theology of Biblical Prayer*, Minneapolis: Fortress Press, 1994.
Moore, R. K., *An Investigation of the Motif of Suffering in the Psalms of Lamentation*, unpublished ThD dissertation, New Orleans Baptist Theological Seminary, 1988.
Mowinckel, S., *The Psalms in Israel's Worship* (2 vols.), Oxford: Basil

Blackwell, 1962.
Niehaus, J. J. "The Use of *lûlē* in Psalm 27", *JBL* 98 (1979), 88-89.
— *God at Sinai: Covenant and Theophany in the Bible and Ancient Near East*, Grand Rapids: Zondervan, 1995.
Noordtzij, A., *De Psalmen*, 4th edition, Kampen: Kok, n.d.
Noort, E., *Geweld in het Oude Testament*, Delft: Zoetermeert, 1985.
Oesterley, W. O. E., *The Psalms* (2 vols.), London: SPCK, 1939.
Paul, S. M., "Psalm XXVII 10 and the Babylonian Theodicy", *VT* 32 (1982), 489-492.
Perowne, J. J. S., *Commentary on the Psalms*, Grand Rapids: Kregel, 1989.
Prinsloo, W. S., *Die Psalms Leef!*, Pretoria: NGKB, 1991.
— "Die Psalms as Samehangende Boek", *NGTT* 36 (1995), 459-469.
Raabe, P. R., *Psalm Structures: A Study of Psalms with Refrains*, Sheffield: JSOT Press, 1990.
Ridderbos, J., *De Psalmen*, Kampen: Kok (2 vols.),1955, 1958.
Ridderbos, N. H., *De Psalmen: Psalm 1-41*, Kampen: Kok.
— *Die Psalmen. Stilistiche Verfahren und Aufbau mit besonderer Berücksichtigung von Ps 1-41*, Berlin: Walter de Gruyter, 1972.
Rodd, C. S., *Psalms 1-72*, London: Epworth Press, 1963.
Rogerson, J. W. and J. W. McKay, *Psalms 1-50*, Cambridge: Cambridge University Press, 1977.
— *Psalms 51-100*, Cambridge: Cambridge University Press, 1977.
— *Psalms 101-150*, Cambridge: Cambridge University Press, 1977.
Rosenbaum, S. N., *The Concept "Antagonist" in Hebrew Psalm Poetry: A Semantic Field Study*, unpublished PhD Thesis, Brandeis University, 1974.
Sabourin, L., *The Psalms: Their Origin and Meaning*, New York: Alba House, 1974.
Sawyer, J. F. A., *Semantics in Biblical Research: New Methods of Defining Hebrew Words for Salvation*, London: SCM Press, 1972.
Schmidt, H., *Das Gebet der Angeklagten im Alten Testament*, Giessen: Alfred Töpelmann, 1928.
Schüngel-Straumann, H., "Zur Gattung und Theologie des 139. Psalms", *BZ* 17 (1973), 39-51.
Smith, M. S., "'Seeing God' in the Psalms: The Background to the Beatific Vision in the Hebrew Bible", *CBQ* 50 (1988), 171-183.
Snaith, N. H., *The Seven Psalms*, London: Epworth, 1964.
Snyman, S. D., "'Violence' in Amos 3,10 and 6,3", *ETL* 71 (1995), 30-47.
Tate, M. E., *Psalms 51 -100*, Dallas: Word, 1990.
Thomas, D., "A Further Note on Psalm 7:4", *TBT* 25 (1974), 247-248.
Thomas, D. W., "A Note on לִבִּי סְחַרְחַר in Psalm XXXVIII 11", *JTS* 40 (old series, 1939), 390-391.
— "Psalm XXXV. 15f", *JTS* 12 (1961), 50-51.
Tigay, J. H., "Psalm 7:5 and Ancient Near Eastern Treaties", *JBL* 89 (1970),

178-186.
Tournay, R. J., *Seeing and Hearing God with the Psalms*, Sheffield: JSOT Press, 1991.
Van der Ploeg, J. P. M., *Psalmen I*, Roermond: J. J. Romen & Zonen, 1973.
— *Psalmen II*, Roermond: J. J. Romen & Zonen, 1974.
Van der Toorn, K., "Ordeal Procedures in the Psalms and the Passover Meal", *VT* 38 (1988), 427-445.
Van Gemeren, W. A., "Psalms", in F. E. Gaebelein (ed.), *The Expositor's Bible Commentary*, vol. 5, Grand Rapids: Zondervan, 1991.
Van Uchelen, N. A., *Psalmen I*, Nijkerk: G. F. Callenbach, 1971.
— *Psalmen II*, Nijkerk: G. F. Callenbach, 1977.
Van Zyl, D. C., "Psalmhermeneuse en Psalmberyming", *NGTT* 29 (1985), 61-65.
Von Rad, G., *Wisdom in Israel*, Trans. J. D. Martin, Nashville: Abingdon, 1972.
— *Old Testament Theology*, (2 vols.), Trans. D. M. G. Stalker, London: SCM Press, 1975.
— *Holy War in Ancient Israel*, Trans. B. C. Ollenburger, Grand Rapids: Eerdmans, 1991.
Vorster, W. (ed.), *Views on Violence*, Pretoria: UNISA, 1985.
Wagner, S., "Zur Theologie des Psalms CXXXIX", *Congress Volume Göttingen 1977*, VT Supp. 29, Leiden: E. J. Brill, 1978, 357-376.
Weiser, A., *The Psalms*, Trans. H. Hartwell, London: SCM Press, 1962.
Westermann, C., *The Psalms: Structure, Content and Message*, Minneapolis: Augsburg, 1980.
— *The Living Psalms*, Trans. J. R. Porter, Edinburgh: T & T Clark, 1989.
Whitelaw, D. P., "Christian Responses to Violence: A Historical Survey", in W. Vorster (ed.), *Views on Violence*, 21-40.
Wilson, G. H., *The Editing of the Hebrew Psalter*, Chico: Scholars Press, 1985.
— "The Use of Royal Psalms at the 'Seams' of the Hebrew Psalter", *JSOT* 35 (1986), 85-94.
— "The Shape of the Book of Psalms", *Interpretation* 46:2 (1992), 129-142.
Wright, D. P., "Ritual Analogy in Psalm 109", *JBL* 113 (1994), 385-404.
Young, E. J., *Psalm 139: A Study in the Omniscience of God*, Edinburgh: Banner of Truth, 1965.
Zimmerli, W., *Man and His Hope in the Old Testament*, Trans. G. W. Bowen, London: SCM Press, 1971.

Author Index

Alden, R. 28
Allen, L. C. 37, 38, 45, 46, 47, 104, 129, 130, 131
Anderson, A. A. 11, 26, 29, 34, 60, 61, 77, 83, 88, 92, 102, 107, 130, 134
Anderson, R. D. 2
Anderson, G. W. 10, 52
Barré, M. L. 135
Bellinger, W. H., Jr. 12, 18, 21, 26, 80, 95, 96, 99, 100
Beyerlin, W. 17, 21, 29, 52, 64, 80, 89, 96, 103
Birkeland, H. 9, 51, 52, 54, 78, 95, 102, 113, 116, 117, 125, 126, 128
Booij, T. H. 37, 39
Bratcher, R. G. 24
Brettler, M. 60
Briggs, C. A. and E. G. 20, 22, 25, 37, 38, 77, 95, 115, 118, 125, 130, 131
Brown, M. L. 113
Broyles, C. C. 70, 75, 122, 128
Brueggemann, W. 2, 40, 42, 64, 66, 69, 74, 106, 110
Burger, J. A. 3
Childs, B. S. 8
Clines, D. J. A. 83
Coetzee, J. H. 61, 63, 65, 104, 127, 129, 130, 131, 134
Collins, T. 123
Craigie, P. C. 7, 13, 25, 28, 31, 32, 34, 54, 55, 61, 63, 70, 74, 119, 121, 122
Creager, H. L. 37, 38
Athanasius 53.
Croft, S. J. L. 7, 8, 9, 12, 13, 14, 20, 28, 29, 36, 43, 52, 54, 70, 78, 79, 88, 95, 102, 115, 116, 117
Dahood, M. 23, 25, 29, 32, 34, 35, 36, 37, 40, 45, 72, 74, 78, 82, 83, 85, 88, 91, 98, 107, 119, 121, 122, 126
Dannell, G. A. 43, 44, 46
Delekat, L. 17, 21, 36, 52, 64, 70, 80, 95, 128

Delitzsch, F. 127
Dorn, L. 64
Driver, G. R. 92
Durham, J. I. 44, 101, 103, 123
Eaton, J. H. 7, 12, 20, 28, 33, 36, 37, 54, 55, 62, 63, 69, 77, 78, 88, 95, 102, 126
Eichrodt, W. 102, 124
Ellul, J. 1, 6
Gaster, T. H. 73
Gerstenberger, E. S. 71, 82, 88
Goldingay, J.145
Goulder, M. D. 8, 78, 83, 89, 127, 130, 131
Guillaume, A. 41
Gunkel, H. 2, 6, 81, 113
Haag, H. 5
Harman, A. M. 73
Hartley, J. E. 83
Hayes, J. H. 7
Holman, J. 46
Hossfeld, F. L. and E. Zenger. 24, 31, 57, 71, 120
Hubbard, R. L. 24
Human, D. J. 77, 78, 82
Janzen, J. G. 71
Johnson, A. R. 28, 33, 102, 106, 126, 135, 136
Kidner, D. 32, 55, 58, 127, 130
Kim, E. K. 55, 59, 71
Kirkpatrick, A. F. 38, 79, 99, 127
Kissane, E. J. 38, 39, 57, 60, 74, 77, 81, 83, 105
Kittel, R. 61, 102
Knight, G. A. F. 39, 94, 121
Kraus, H-J. 13, 14, 20, 24, 26, 29, 31, 32, 37, 43, 44, 52, 57, 64, 75, 77, 82, 83, 84, 90, 93, 95, 98, 99, 107, 118, 122, 128, 134, 136
Kselman, J. S. 56
Lattey, C.
Leupold, H. C. 122, 127
Leveen, J. 24, 25, 26, 28, 34

Lindblom, J. 28
Lindström, F. 29, 57, 62, 105, 113, 115, 121, 128, 130, 131
Lohfink, N. 1, 2
Longman, T. III and D. G. Reid 20
Loretz, O. 103, 104
Macholz, C. 24
Mays, J. L. 93
McCann, J. C. 2, 38
McConville, J. G. 31
McCullough, W. S. and W. R. Taylor 43, 45, 97, 99
McFall, L. 86
McIntosh, A. A. 25, 26
McKay, J. W. 108
Miller P. D., Jr. 6, 51, 63, 69, 79, 93
Moore, R. K. 115
Mowinckel, S. 2, 7, 12, 13, 21, 36, 51, 79, 94, 113, 114, 125
Niehaus, J. J. 121
Noort, E. 1,
Oesterley, W. O. E. 17, 33, 48, 59, 62, 71, 105, 133
Perowne, J. J. S. 127
Prinsloo, W. S. 2, 55, 56, 57, 59
Raabe, P. R. 89, 90
Ridderbos, J. 58, 127
Ridderbos, N. H. 20, 61, 120
Rodd, C. S. 22
Rogerson, J. W. and J. W. McKay 41, 70, 100, 106, 119, 127

Rosenbaum, S. N. 9
Sabourin, L. 13, 21, 37, 88
Sawyer, J. F. A. 9
Schmidt, H. 17, 127
Schüngel-Straumann, H. 43
Smith, M. S. 35
Snaith, N. H. 107, 115
Snyman, S. D. 1
Tate, M. E. 10, 78, 82, 83, 84, 88, 91, 92, 97, 99, 100, 132, 134, 136, 140
Thomas, D. 24
Thomas, D. W. 74
Tigay, J. H. 24
Tournay, R. J. 12, 55, 62, 65
Van der Ploeg, J. P. M. 34, 57, 61, 106, 136
Van der Toorn, K. 17
Van Gemeren, W. A. 25, 31, 32, 33, 59, 65, 66, 84, 119, 120
Van Uchelen, N. A. 57, 62, 82, 119
Van Zyl, D. C. 72
Von Rad, G. 2, 29, 44, 55
Vorster, W. 4
Wagner, S. 44
Weiser, A. 7, 37, 54, 95, 99, 145
Westermann, C. 44
Whitelaw, D. P. 4
Wilson, G. H. 2, 8, 143, 144
Wright, D. P. 41
Young, E. J. 46
Zimmerli, W. 67

Paternoster Biblical Monographs

(All titles uniform with this volume)
Dates in bold are of projected publication

Joseph Abraham
Eve: Accused or Acquitted?
A Reconsideration of Feminist Readings of the Creation Narrative Texts in Genesis 1–3
Two contrary views dominate contemporary feminist biblical scholarship. One finds in the Bible an unequivocal equality between the sexes from the very creation of humanity, whilst the other sees the biblical text as irredeemably patriarchal and androcentric. Dr Abraham enters into dialogue with both camps as well as introducing his own method of approach. An invaluable tool for any one who is interested in this contemporary debate.

2002 / 0-85364-971-5 / xxiv + 272pp

Octavian D. Baban
Mimesis and Luke's on the Road Encounters in Luke-Acts
Luke's Theology of the Way and its Literary Representation
The book argues on theological and literary (mimetic) grounds that Luke's on-the-road encounters, especially those belonging to the post-Easter period, are part of his complex theology of the Way. Jesus' teaching and that of the apostles is presented by Luke as a challenging answer to the Hellenistic reader's thirst for adventure, good literature, and existential paradigms.

2005 */ 1-84227-253-5 / approx. 374pp*

Paul Barker
The Triumph of Grace in Deuteronomy
This book is a textual and theological analysis of the interaction between the sin and faithlessness of Israel and the grace of Yahweh in response, looking especially at Deuteronomy chapters 1–3, 8–10 and 29–30. The author argues that the grace of Yahweh is determinative for the ongoing relationship between Yahweh and Israel and that Deuteronomy anticipates and fully expects Israel to be faithless.

2004 / 1-84227-226-8 / xxii + 270pp

Jonathan F. Bayes
The Weakness of the Law
God's Law and the Christian in New Testament Perspective
A study of the four New Testament books which refer to the law as weak (Acts, Romans, Galatians, Hebrews) leads to a defence of the third use in the Reformed debate about the law in the life of the believer.

2000 / 0-85364-957-X / xii + 244pp

July 2005

Mark Bonnington
The Antioch Episode of Galatians 2:11-14 in Historical and Cultural Context

The Galatians 2 'incident' in Antioch over table-fellowship suggests significant disagreement between the leading apostles. This book analyses the background to the disagreement by locating the incident within the dynamics of social interaction between Jews and Gentiles. It proposes a new way of understanding the relationship between the individuals and issues involved.

2005 / 1-84227-050-8 / approx. 350pp

David Bostock
A Portrayal of Trust
The Theme of Faith in the Hezekiah Narratives

This study provides detailed and sensitive readings of the Hezekiah narratives (2 Kings 18–20 and Isaiah 36–39) from a theological perspective. It concentrates on the theme of faith, using narrative criticism as its methodology. Attention is paid especially to setting, plot, point of view and characterization within the narratives. A largely positive portrayal of Hezekiah emerges that underlines the importance and relevance of scripture.

2005 / 1-84227-314-0 / approx. 300pp

Mark Bredin
Jesus, Revolutionary of Peace
A Non-violent Christology in the Book of Revelation

This book aims to demonstrate that the figure of Jesus in the Book of Revelation can best be understood as an active non-violent revolutionary.

2003 / 1-84227-153-9 / xviii + 262pp

Robinson Butarbutar
Paul and Conflict Resolution
An Exegetical Study of Paul's Apostolic Paradigm in 1 Corinthians 9

The author sees the apostolic paradigm in 1 Corinthians 9 as part of Paul's unified arguments in 1 Corinthians 8–10 in which he seeks to mediate in the dispute over the issue of food offered to idols. The book also sees its relevance for dispute-resolution today, taking the conflict within the author's church as an example.

2006 / 1-84227-315-9 / approx. 280pp

Daniel J-S Chae
Paul as Apostle to the Gentiles
His Apostolic Self-awareness and its Influence on the Soteriological Argument in Romans
Opposing 'the post-Holocaust interpretation of Romans', Daniel Chae competently demonstrates that Paul argues for the equality of Jew and Gentile in Romans. Chae's fresh exegetical interpretation is academically outstanding and spiritually encouraging.
1997 / 0-85364-829-8 / xiv + 378pp

Luke L. Cheung
The Genre, Composition and Hermeneutics of the Epistle of James
The present work examines the employment of the wisdom genre with a certain compositional structure and the interpretation of the law through the Jesus tradition of the double love command by the author of the Epistle of James to serve his purpose in promoting perfection and warning against doubleness among the eschatologically renewed people of God in the Diaspora.
2003 / 1-84227-062-1 / xvi + 372pp

Youngmo Cho
Spirit and Kingdom in the Writings of Luke and Paul
The relationship between Spirit and Kingdom is a relatively unexplored area in Lukan and Pauline studies. This book offers a fresh perspective of two biblical writers on the subject. It explores the difference between Luke's and Paul's understanding of the Spirit by examining the specific question of the relationship of the concept of the Spirit to the concept of the Kingdom of God in each writer.
2005 / 1-84227-316-7 / approx. 270pp

Andrew C. Clark
Parallel Lives
The Relation of Paul to the Apostles in the Lucan Perspective
This study of the Peter-Paul parallels in Acts argues that their purpose was to emphasize the themes of continuity in salvation history and the unity of the Jewish and Gentile missions. New light is shed on Luke's literary techniques, partly through a comparison with Plutarch.
2001 / 1-84227-035-4 / xviii + 386pp

Andrew D. Clarke
Secular and Christian Leadership in Corinth
A Socio-Historical and Exegetical Study of 1 Corinthians 1–6
This volume is an investigation into the leadership structures and dynamics of first-century Roman Corinth. These are compared with the practice of leadership in the Corinthian Christian community which are reflected in 1 Corinthians 1–6, and contrasted with Paul's own principles of Christian leadership.
2005 / 1-84227-229-2 / 200pp

Stephen Finamore
God, Order and Chaos
René Girard and the Apocalypse
Readers are often disturbed by the images of destruction in the book of Revelation and unsure why they are unleashed after the exaltation of Jesus. This book examines past approaches to these texts and uses René Girard's theories to revive some old ideas and propose some new ones.
2005 / 1-84227-197-0 / approx. 344pp

David G. Firth
Surrendering Retribution in the Psalms
Responses to Violence in the Individual Complaints
In *Surrendering Retribution in the Psalms*, David Firth examines the ways in which the book of Psalms inculcates a model response to violence through the repetition of standard patterns of prayer. Rather than seeking justification for retributive violence, Psalms encourages not only a surrender of the right of retribution to Yahweh, but also sets limits on the retribution that can be sought in imprecations. Arising initially from the author's experience in South Africa, the possibilities of this model to a particular context of violence is then briefly explored.
2005 / 1-84227-337-X / xviii + 154pp

Scott J. Hafemann
Suffering and Ministry in the Spirit
Paul's Defence of His Ministry in II Corinthians 2:14–3:3
Shedding new light on the way Paul defended his apostleship, the author offers a careful, detailed study of 2 Corinthians 2:14–3:3 linked with other key passages throughout 1 and 2 Corinthians. Demonstrating the unity and coherence of Paul's argument in this passage, the author shows that Paul's suffering served as the vehicle for revealing God's power and glory through the Spirit.
2000 / 0-85364-967-7 / xiv + 262pp

Scott J. Hafemann
Paul, Moses and the History of Israel
The Letter/Spirit Contrast and the Argument from Scripture in 2 Corinthians 3
An exegetical study of the call of Moses, the second giving of the Law (Exodus 32–34), the new covenant, and the prophetic understanding of the history of Israel in 2 Corinthians 3. Hafemann's work demonstrates Paul's contextual use of the Old Testament and the essential unity between the Law and the Gospel within the context of the distinctive ministries of Moses and Paul.
2005 / 1-84227-317-5 / xii + 498pp

Douglas S. McComiskey
Lukan Theology in the Light of the Gospel's Literary Structure
Luke's Gospel was purposefully written with theology embedded in its patterned literary structure. A critical analysis of this cyclical structure provides new windows into Luke's interpretation of the individual pericopes comprising the Gospel and illuminates several of his theological interests.
2004 / 1-84227-148-2 / xviii + 388pp

Stephen Motyer
Your Father the Devil?
A New Approach to John and 'The Jews'
Who are 'the Jews' in John's Gospel? Defending John against the charge of antisemitism, Motyer argues that, far from demonising the Jews, the Gospel seeks to present Jesus as 'Good News for Jews' in a late first century setting.
1997 / 0-85364-832-8 / xiv + 260pp

Esther Ng
Reconstructing Christian Origins?
The Feminist Theology of Elizabeth Schüssler Fiorenza: An Evaluation
In a detailed evaluation, the author challenges Elizabeth Schüssler Fiorenza's reconstruction of early Christian origins and her underlying presuppositions. The author also presents her own views on women's roles both then and now.
2002 / 1-84227-055-9 / xxiv + 468pp

Robin Parry
Old Testament Story and Christian Ethics
The Rape of Dinah as a Case Study

What is the role of story in ethics and, more particularly, what is the role of Old Testament story in Christian ethics? This book, drawing on the work of contemporary philosophers, argues that narrative is crucial in the ethical shaping of people and, drawing on the work of contemporary Old Testament scholars, that story plays a key role in Old Testament ethics. Parry then argues that when situated in canonical context Old Testament stories can be reappropriated by Christian readers in their own ethical formation. The shocking story of the rape of Dinah and the massacre of the Shechemites provides a fascinating case study for exploring the parameters within which Christian ethical appropriations of Old Testament stories can live.

2004 / 1-84227-210-1 / xx + 350pp

Ian Paul
Power to See the World Anew
The Value of Paul Ricoeur's Hermeneutic of Metaphor in Interpreting the Symbolism of Revelation 12 and 13

This book is a study of the hermeneutics of metaphor of Paul Ricoeur, one of the most important writers on hermeneutics and metaphor of the last century. It sets out the key points of his theory, important criticisms of his work, and how his approach, modified in the light of these criticisms, offers a methodological framework for reading apocalyptic texts.

2006 / 1-84227-056-7 / approx. 350pp

Robert L. Plummer
Paul's Understanding of the Church's Mission
Did the Apostle Paul Expect the Early Christian Communities to Evangelize?

This book engages in a careful study of Paul's letters to determine if the apostle expected the communities to which he wrote to engage in missionary activity. It helpfully summarizes the discussion on this debated issue, judiciously handling contested texts, and provides a way forward in addressing this critical question. While admitting that Paul rarely explicitly commands the communities he founded to evangelize, Plummer amasses significant incidental data to provide a convincing case that Paul did indeed expect his churches to engage in mission activity. Throughout the study, Plummer progressively builds a theological basis for the church's mission that is both distinctively Pauline and compelling.

2006 / 1-84227-333-7 / approx. 324pp

David Powys
'Hell': A Hard Look at a Hard Question
The Fate of the Unrighteous in New Testament Thought
This comprehensive treatment seeks to unlock the original meaning of terms and phrases long thought to support the traditional doctrine of hell. It concludes that there is an alternative—one which is more biblical, and which can positively revive the rationale for Christian mission.
1997 / 0-85364-831-X / xxii + 478pp

Sorin Sabou
Between Horror and Hope
Paul's Metaphorical Language of Death in Romans 6.1-11
This book argues that Paul's metaphorical language of death in Romans 6.1-11 conveys two aspects: horror and hope. The 'horror' aspect is conveyed by the 'crucifixion' language, and the 'hope' aspect by 'burial' language. The life of the Christian believer is understood, as relationship with sin is concerned ('death to sin'), between these two realities: horror and hope.
2005 / 1-84227-322-1 / approx. 224pp

Rosalind Selby
The Comical Doctrine
The Epistemology of New Testament Hermeneutics
This book argues that the gospel breaks through postmodernity's critique of truth and the referential possibilities of textuality with its gift of grace. With a rigorous, philosophical challenge to modernist and postmodernist assumptions, Selby offers an alternative epistemology to all who would still read with faith *and* with academic credibility.
2005 / 1-84227-212-8 / approx. 350pp

Kiwoong Son
Zion Symbolism in Hebrews
Hebrews 12.18-24 as a Hermeneutical Key to the Epistle
This book challenges the general tendency of understanding the Epistle to the Hebrews against a Hellenistic background and suggests that the Epistle should be understood in the light of the Jewish apocalyptic tradition. The author especially argues for the importance of the theological symbolism of Sinai and Zion (Heb. 12:18-24) as it provides the Epistle's theological background as well as the rhetorical basis of the superiority motif of Jesus throughout the Epistle.
2005 / 1-84227-368-X / approx. 280pp

Kevin Walton
Thou Traveller Unknown
The Presence and Absence of God in the Jacob Narrative
The author offers a fresh reading of the story of Jacob in the book of Genesis through the paradox of divine presence and absence. The work also seeks to make a contribution to Pentateuchal studies by bringing together a close reading of the final text with historical critical insights, doing justice to the text's historical depth, final form and canonical status.
2003 / 1-84227-059-1 / xvi + 238pp

George M. Wieland
The Significance of Salvation
A Study of Salvation Language in the Pastoral Epistles
The language and ideas of salvation pervade the three Pastoral Epistles. This study offers a close examination of their soteriological statements. In all three letters the idea of salvation is found to play a vital paraenetic role, but each also exhibits distinctive soteriological emphases. The results challenge common assumptions about the Pastoral Epistles as a corpus.
2005 */ 1-84227-257-8 / approx. 324pp*

Alistair Wilson
When Will These Things Happen?
A Study of Jesus as Judge in Matthew 21–25
This study seeks to allow Matthew's carefully constructed presentation of Jesus to be given full weight in the modern evaluation of Jesus' eschatology. Careful analysis of the text of Matthew 21–25 reveals Jesus to be standing firmly in the Jewish prophetic and wisdom traditions as he proclaims and enacts imminent judgement on the Jewish authorities then boldly claims the central role in the final and universal judgement.
2004 / 1-84227-146-6 / xxii + 272pp

Lindsay Wilson
Joseph Wise and Otherwise
The Intersection of Covenant and Wisdom in Genesis 37–50
This book offers a careful literary reading of Genesis 37–50 that argues that the Joseph story contains both strong covenant themes and many wisdom-like elements. The connections between the two helps to explore how covenant and wisdom might intersect in an integrated biblical theology.
2004 / 1-84227-140-7 / xvi + 340pp

Stephen I. Wright
The Voice of Jesus
Studies in the Interpretation of Six Gospel Parables
This literary study considers how the 'voice' of Jesus has been heard in different periods of parable interpretation, and how the categories of figure and trope may help us towards a sensitive reading of the parables today.
2000 / 0-85364-975-8 / xiv + 280pp

Paternoster
9 Holdom Avenue,
Bletchley,
Milton Keynes MK1 1QR,
United Kingdom
Web: www.authenticmedia.co.uk/paternoster

Paternoster Theological Monographs

(All titles uniform with this volume)
Dates in bold are of projected publication

Emil Bartos
Deification in Eastern Orthodox Theology
An Evaluation and Critique of the Theology of Dumitru Staniloae

Bartos studies a fundamental yet neglected aspect of Orthodox theology: deification. By examining the doctrines of anthropology, christology, soteriology and ecclesiology as they relate to deification, he provides an important contribution to contemporary dialogue between Eastern and Western theologians.

1999 / 0-85364-956-1 / xii + 370pp

Graham Buxton
The Trinity, Creation and Pastoral Ministry
Imaging the Perichoretic God

In this book the author proposes a three-way conversation between theology, science and pastoral ministry. His approach draws on a Trinitarian understanding of God as a relational being of love, whose life 'spills over' into all created reality, human and non-human. By locating human meaning and purpose within God's 'creation-community' this book offers the possibility of a transforming engagement between those in pastoral ministry and the scientific community.

2005 / 1-84227-369-8 / approx. 380 pp

Iain D. Campbell
Fixing the Indemnity
The Life and Work of George Adam Smith

When Old Testament scholar George Adam Smith (1856–1942) delivered the Lyman Beecher lectures at Yale University in 1899, he confidently declared that 'modern criticism has won its war against traditional theories. It only remains to fix the amount of the indemnity.' In this biography, Iain D. Campbell assesses Smith's critical approach to the Old Testament and evaluates its consequences, showing that Smith's life and work still raises questions about the relationship between biblical scholarship and evangelical faith.

2004 / 1-84227-228-4 / xx + 256pp

Tim Chester
Mission and the Coming of God
Eschatology, the Trinity and Mission in the Theology of Jürgen Moltmann
This book explores the theology and missiology of the influential contemporary theologian, Jürgen Moltmann. It highlights the important contribution Moltmann has made while offering a critique of his thought from an evangelical perspective. In so doing, it touches on pertinent issues for evangelical missiology. The conclusion takes Calvin as a starting point, proposing 'an eschatology of the cross' which offers a critique of the over-realised eschatologies in liberation theology and certain forms of evangelicalism.
2006 / 1-84227-320-5 / approx. 224pp

Sylvia Wilkey Collinson
Making Disciples
The Significance of Jesus' Educational Strategy for Today's Church
This study examines the biblical practice of discipling, formulates a definition, and makes comparisons with modern models of education. A recommendation is made for greater attention to its practice today.
2004 / 1-84227-116-4 / xiv + 278pp

Darrell Cosden
A Theology of Work
Work and the New Creation
Through dialogue with Moltmann, Pope John Paul II and others, this book develops a genitive 'theology of work', presenting a theological definition of work and a model for a theological ethics of work that shows work's nature, value and meaning now and eschatologically. Work is shown to be a transformative activity consisting of three dynamically inter-related dimensions: the instrumental, relational and ontological.
2005 / 1-84227-332-9 / xvi + 208pp

Stephen M. Dunning
The Crisis and the Quest
A Kierkegaardian Reading of Charles Williams
Employing Kierkegaardian categories and analysis, this study investigates both the central crisis in Charles Williams's authorship between hermetism and Christianity (Kierkegaard's Religions A and B), and the quest to resolve this crisis, a quest that ultimately presses the bounds of orthodoxy.
2000 / 0-85364-985-5 / xxiv + 254pp

Keith Ferdinando
The Triumph of Christ in African Perspective
A Study of Demonology and Redemption in the African Context
The book explores the implications of the gospel for traditional African fears of occult aggression. It analyses such traditional approaches to suffering and biblical responses to fears of demonic evil, concluding with an evaluation of African beliefs from the perspective of the gospel.
1999 / 0-85364-830-1 / xviii + 450pp

Andrew Goddard
Living the Word, Resisting the World
The Life and Thought of Jacques Ellul
This work offers a definitive study of both the life and thought of the French Reformed thinker Jacques Ellul (1912-1994). It will prove an indispensable resource for those interested in this influential theologian and sociologist and for Christian ethics and political thought generally.
2002 / 1-84227-053-2 / xxiv + 378pp

David Hilborn
The Words of our Lips
Language-Use in Free Church Worship
Studies of liturgical language have tended to focus on the written canons of Roman Catholic and Anglican communities. By contrast, David Hilborn analyses the more extemporary approach of English Nonconformity. Drawing on recent developments in linguistic pragmatics, he explores similarities and differences between 'fixed' and 'free' worship, and argues for the interdependence of each.
2006 / 0-85364-977-4 / approx. 350pp

Roger Hitching
The Church and Deaf People
A Study of Identity, Communication and Relationships with Special Reference to the Ecclesiology of Jürgen Moltmann
In *The Church and Deaf People* Roger Hitching sensitively examines the history and present experience of deaf people and finds similarities between aspects of sign language and Moltmann's theological method that 'open up' new ways of understanding theological concepts.
2003 / 1-84227-222-5 / xxii + 236pp

John G. Kelly
One God, One People
The Differentiated Unity of the People of God in the Theology of Jürgen Moltmann
The author expounds and critiques Moltmann's doctrine of God and highlights the systematic connections between it and Moltmann's influential discussion of Israel. He then proposes a fresh approach to Jewish–Christian relations building on Moltmann's work using insights from Habermas and Rawls.
2005 / 0-85346-969-3 / approx. 350pp

Mark F.W. Lovatt
Confronting the Will-to-Power
A Reconsideration of the Theology of Reinhold Niebuhr
Confronting the Will-to-Power is an analysis of the theology of Reinhold Niebuhr, arguing that his work is an attempt to identify, and provide a practical theological answer to, the existence and nature of human evil.
2001 / 1-84227-054-0 / xviii + 216pp

Neil B. MacDonald
Karl Barth and the Strange New World within the Bible
Barth, Wittgenstein, and the Metadilemmas of the Enlightenment
Barth's discovery of the strange new world within the Bible is examined in the context of Kant, Hume, Overbeck, and, most importantly, Wittgenstein. MacDonald covers some fundamental issues in theology today: epistemology, the final form of the text and biblical truth-claims.
2000 / 0-85364-970-7 / xxvi + 374pp

Keith A. Mascord
Alvin Plantinga and Christian Apologetics
This book draws together the contributions of the philosopher Alvin Plantinga to the major contemporary challenges to Christian belief, highlighting in particular his ground-breaking work in epistemology and the problem of evil. Plantinga's theory that both theistic and Christian belief is warrantedly basic is explored and critiqued, and an assessment offered as to the significance of his work for apologetic theory and practice.
2005 / 1-84227-256-X / approx. 304pp

Gillian McCulloch
The Deconstruction of Dualism in Theology
With Reference to Ecofeminist Theology and New Age Spirituality
This book challenges eco-theological anti-dualism in Christian theology, arguing that dualism has a twofold function in Christian religious discourse. Firstly, it enables us to express the discontinuities and divisions that are part of the process of reality. Secondly, dualistic language allows us to express the mysteries of divine transcendence/immanence and the survival of the soul without collapsing into monism and materialism, both of which are problematic for Christian epistemology.
2002 / 1-84227-044-3 / xii + 282pp

Leslie McCurdy
Attributes and Atonement
The Holy Love of God in the Theology of P.T. Forsyth
Attributes and Atonement is an intriguing full-length study of P.T. Forsyth's doctrine of the cross as it relates particularly to God's holy love. It includes an unparalleled bibliography of both primary and secondary material relating to Forsyth.
1999 / 0-85364-833-6 / xiv + 328pp

Nozomu Miyahira
Towards a Theology of the Concord of God
A Japanese Perspective on the Trinity
This book introduces a new Japanese theology and a unique Trinitarian formula based on the Japanese intellectual climate: three betweennesses and one concord. It also presents a new interpretation of the Trinity, a co-subordinationism, which is in line with orthodox Trinitarianism; each single person of the Trinity is eternally and equally subordinate (or serviceable) to the other persons, so that they retain the mutual dynamic equality.
2000 / 0-85364-863-8 / xiv + 256pp

Eddy José Muskus
The Origins and Early Development of Liberation Theology in Latin America
With Particular Reference to Gustavo Gutiérrez
This work challenges the fundamental premise of Liberation Theology, 'opting for the poor', and its claim that Christ is found in them. It also argues that Liberation Theology emerged as a direct result of the failure of the Roman Catholic Church in Latin America.
2002 / 0-85364-974-X / xiv + 296pp

Jim Purves
The Triune God and the Charismatic Movement
A Critical Appraisal from a Scottish Perspective
All emotion and no theology? Or a fundamental challenge to reappraise and realign our trinitarian theology in the light of Christian experience? This study of charismatic renewal as it found expression within Scotland at the end of the twentieth century evaluates the use of Patristic, Reformed and contemporary models of the Trinity in explaining the workings of the Holy Spirit.
2004 / 1-84227-321-3 / xxiv + 246pp

Anna Robbins
Methods in the Madness
Diversity in Twentieth-Century Christian Social Ethics
The author compares the ethical methods of Walter Rauschenbusch, Reinhold Niebuhr and others. She argues that unless Christians are clear about the ways that theology and philosophy are expressed practically they may lose the ability to discuss social ethics across contexts, let alone reach effective agreements.
2004 / 1-84227-211-X / xx + 294pp

Ed Rybarczyk
Beyond Salvation
Eastern Orthodoxy and Classical Pentecostalism on Becoming Like Christ
At first glance eastern Orthodoxy and classical Pentecostalism seem quite distinct. This ground-breaking study shows they share much in common, especially as it concerns the experiential elements of following Christ. Both traditions assert that authentic Christianity transcends the wooden categories of modernism.
2004 / 1-84227-144-X / xii + 356pp

Signe Sandsmark
Is World View Neutral Education Possible and Desirable?
A Christian Response to Liberal Arguments
(Published jointly with The Stapleford Centre)
This book discusses reasons for belief in world view neutrality, and argues that 'neutral' education will have a hidden, but strong world view influence. It discusses the place for Christian education in the common school.
2000 / 0-85364-973-1 / xiv + 182pp

Hazel Sherman
Reading Zechariah
The Allegorical Tradition of Biblical Interpretation through the Commentary of Didymus the Blind and Theodore of Mopsuestia
A close reading of the commentary on Zechariah by Didymus the Blind alongside that of Theodore of Mopsuestia suggests that popular categorising of Antiochene and Alexandrian biblical exegesis as 'historical' or 'allegorical' is inadequate and misleading.
2005 / 1-84227-213-6 / approx. 280pp

Andrew Sloane
On Being a Christian in the Academy
Nicholas Wolterstorff and the Practice of Christian Scholarship
An exposition and critical appraisal of Nicholas Wolterstorff's epistemology in the light of the philosophy of science, and an application of his thought to the practice of Christian scholarship.
2003 / 1-84227-058-3 / xvi + 274pp

Damon W.K. So
Jesus' Revelation of His Father
A Narrative-Conceptual Study of the Trinity with Special Reference to Karl Barth
This book explores the trinitarian dynamics in the context of Jesus' revelation of his Father in his earthly ministry with references to key passages in Matthew's Gospel. It develops from the exegeses of these passages a non-linear concept of revelation which links Jesus' communion with his Father to his revelatory words and actions through a nuanced understanding of the Holy Spirit, with references to K. Barth, G.W.H. Lampe, J.D.G. Dunn and E. Irving.
2005 / 1-84227-323-X / approx. 380pp

Daniel Strange
The Possibility of Salvation Among the Unevangelised
An Analysis of Inclusivism in Recent Evangelical Theology
For evangelical theologians the 'fate of the unevangelised' impinges upon fundamental tenets of evangelical identity. The position known as 'inclusivism', defined by the belief that the unevangelised can be ontologically saved by Christ whilst being epistemologically unaware of him, has been defended most vigorously by the Canadian evangelical Clark H. Pinnock. Through a detailed analysis and critique of Pinnock's work, this book examines a cluster of issues surrounding the unevangelised and its implications for christology, soteriology and the doctrine of revelation.
2002 / 1-84227-047-8 / xviii + 362pp

Scott Swain
God According to the Gospel
Biblical Narrative and the Identity of God in the Theology of Robert W. Jenson
Robert W. Jenson is one of the leading voices in contemporary Trinitarian theology. His boldest contribution in this area concerns his use of biblical narrative both to ground and explicate the Christian doctrine of God. *God According to the Gospel* critically examines Jenson's proposal and suggests an alternative way of reading the biblical portrayal of the triune God.
2006 / 1-84227-258-6 / approx. 180pp

Justyn Terry
The Justifying Judgement of God
A Reassessment of the Place of Judgement in the Saving Work of Christ
The argument of this book is that judgement, understood as the whole process of bringing justice, is the primary metaphor of atonement, with others, such as victory, redemption and sacrifice, subordinate to it. Judgement also provides the proper context for understanding penal substitution and the call to repentance, baptism, eucharist and holiness.
2005 / 1-84227-370-1 / approx. 274 pp

Graham Tomlin
The Power of the Cross
Theology and the Death of Christ in Paul, Luther and Pascal
This book explores the theology of the cross in St Paul, Luther and Pascal. It offers new perspectives on the theology of each, and some implications for the nature of power, apologetics, theology and church life in a postmodern context.
1999 / 0-85364-984-7 / xiv + 344pp

Adonis Vidu
Postliberal Theological Method
A Critical Study
The postliberal theology of Hans Frei, George Lindbeck, Ronald Thiemann, John Milbank and others is one of the more influential contemporary options. This book focuses on several aspects pertaining to its theological method, specifically its understanding of background, hermeneutics, epistemic justification, ontology, the nature of doctrine and, finally, Christological method.
2005 / 1-84227-395-7 / approx. 324pp

Graham J. Watts
Revelation and the Spirit
A Comparative Study of the Relationship between the Doctrine of Revelation and Pneumatology in the Theology of Eberhard Jüngel and of Wolfhart Pannenberg

The relationship between revelation and pneumatology is relatively unexplored. This approach offers a fresh angle on two important twentieth century theologians and raises pneumatological questions which are theologically crucial and relevant to mission in a postmodern culture.

2005 / 1-84227-104-0 / xxii + 232pp

Nigel G. Wright
Disavowing Constantine
Mission, Church and the Social Order in the Theologies of John Howard Yoder and Jürgen Moltmann

This book is a timely restatement of a radical theology of church and state in the Anabaptist and Baptist tradition. Dr Wright constructs his argument in dialogue and debate with Yoder and Moltmann, major contributors to a free church perspective.

2000 / 0-85364-978-2 / xvi + 252pp

Paternoster
9 Holdom Avenue,
Bletchley,
Milton Keynes MK1 1QR,
United Kingdom
Web: www.authenticmedia.co.uk/paternoster

July 2005

www.ingramcontent.com/pod-product-compliance
Lightning Source LLC
Chambersburg PA
CBHW071448150426
43191CB00008B/1276